CONTEMPORARY SOCIAL PROBLEMS

CONTEMPORARY SOCIAL PROBLEMS

Selected Readings in Sociology and the Law

By

WARREN FREEDMAN

and

CARY STEWART SKLAREN

CHARLES C THOMAS • PUBLISHER
Springfield • Illinois • U.S.A.

Published and Distributed Throughout the World by
CHARLES C THOMAS • PUBLISHER
BANNERSTONE HOUSE
301-327 East Lawrence Avenue, Springfield, Illinois, U.S.A.
NATCHEZ PLANTATION HOUSE
735 North Atlantic Boulevard, Fort Lauderdale, Florida, U.S.A.

ISBN 0-398-02285-2
Library of Congress Catalog Card Number: 78-180812

Printed in the United States of America
I-1

PREFACE

THERE IS A CLASSIC story about a visitor from South America who was attending a dinner party in New York City. Talking about himself he said, "I have a sympathetic wife but unfortunately we have no children. My wife, she is UNBEARABLE." Noting the puzzled glances of his listeners he tried to explain: "My wife, she is INCONCEIVABLE." Realizing from the audience reaction that he was muddying the situation even more, he made one final and hopeful effort by saying, "I mean, my wife, she is IMPREGNABLE." Your authors also have this problem of communication, for *Contemporary Social Problems* was and still is the result of our own selective process as to the thirteen current social issues of the day. Perhaps we should have dealt with other topics such as the trade unionism and strikes, suburban zoning requirements, rights of the accused in a criminal trial, or the problems of poverty, welfare, and, in depth, ecology.

But if war, youth, and security-happiness are the keystones of our present-day American society, it is submitted that we have run the gamut well. Under "war" we have delineated the United Nations Genocide Convention, the constitutional issue of declaration of war, the women's liberation movement and fight for economic equality, and the deterrence of airplane hijacking. Under "youth" we discussed the revolt on the college campuses, marihuana, and the neighborhood school. And under "security-happiness" we have analyzed the problem of chronic alcoholism as a disability, the proposed "prayer amendment," extremist organizations in the United States, anti-Semitism and the Christian community, licensing of radio and television stations (particularly as to program content) and noise pollution. The aforesaid grouping by subject matter is primarily for instructional purposes, so that the reader can participate more readily in discussions about war, youth, and security-happiness.

The Appendix contains the United States Constitution and

the Bill of Rights for reference purposes and Title VII of the Civil Rights Act of 1964. The Alcohol Abuse Act, the Convention For the Suppression of Unlawful Seizure of Aircraft, and the United Nations Genocide Convention, are also reproduced for further study within, or at the end of, the applicable chapters.

The Index was prepared by the authors themselves in an effort to highlight those key words and key phrases which would be most meaningful for the reader.

Footnotes are minimal, and citations of court decisions are given solely for the purpose of enabling the reader to read the entire court opinion, which is readily available at law libraries.

Appreciation is herewith expressed to our two excellent typists, Misses Evelyn Sakai and Carol Connolly.

WARREN FREEDMAN
CARY STEWART SKLAREN

CONTENTS

CONTEMPORARY
SOCIAL
PROBLEMS

Chapter 1

THE CAMPUS REVOLT TODAY: A LESSON IN FREE SPEECH

"The conclusion is inescapable that the Report neither serves nor was intended to serve any purpose, but . . . to inhibit further speech on college campuses by those listed individuals and others whose political persuasion is not in accord with that of members of the committee."

IN LATE OCTOBER, 1970, the United States District Court in Washington, D.C., issued a permanent injunction barring publication and distribution of an official government report by the House Internal Security Committee that listed 65 persons who in the past appeared as speakers on college campuses. Judge Gerhard Gesell, aware of the sensitivity of a judicial decision adversely affecting the legislative branch of government, emphasized the prime consideration in today's "revolt" on the college campuses, to wit: free speech must be protected, even in the face of continuing campus unrest. However, the Court stressed the fact that the injunction in no way prevented publication of the report nor of the "blacklist," through private or commercial channels, offensive as was the intent of the "list." Judge Gesell drew the line only against the use of the Government printing press and Federal funds to turn into propaganda literature a document which did none of the things a Congressional investigation is authorized to do!

What exactly was the avowed purpose of the House Internal Security Committee (formerly the House Committee on Unamerican Activities)? It was to show that "the radical rhetoricians of the New Left, promoting violence and encouraging the destruction of our system of government" are receiving fees for their "inflammatory" speeches on college campuses, thus evidencing "how and where revolutionary movements . . . obtain financing." But the House Committee failed to prove any connection between the fees paid to the speakers and the fiscal affairs of allegedly dangerous organizations and their actions. Apart from describing the speakers collectively as "Pied Pipers of Pernicious Propaganda," the House Committee suggested no instance where the speeches had presented "any clear or immediate danger." The House Committee, in effect, wanted to appeal "to college administrators, alumni and parents," but NOT to members of Congress pursuant to any possible legislation! Indeed the purpose of the report was, according to the Court, "to inhibit further speech on college campuses by those listed individuals and others whose political persuasion is not in accord with that of members of the Committee." This intent, the Court continued, "exceeds the legislative function of Congress, and where publication will inhibit free speech and assembly, publication and distribution in official form at Government expense may be enjoined." While this lower federal court decision is but one cog in the wheel, it nevertheless represented a rebuttal to the governmental posture of repression and uniformity designed to still the campus revolt. (But in December, 1970, Congress expressly authorized publication of the "list," thereby nullifying the court decision.) Free speech should never be sacrificed at the altar of expediency.

In February, 1969, the United States Supreme Court in *Tinker*[1] *v. Des Moines Independent School District,* faced the issue of campus unrest when it considered the validity of an Iowa high school's ban on black armbands by students protesting the Vietnam war. John Tinker was 15 years old and his sister, Mary Beth, was 13 years old; both decided to wear black armbands during the Christmas season, although two days previous their schools had announced a policy that any student wearing a black armband to classes would be asked to remove it, and if he refused, he would be suspended from school. Both John and Mary wore the armbands and were suspended. A suit was thereupon brought to restrain the schools from so disciplining

[1]393 U.S. 503, 1969.

the children. The federal district court dismissed the case upon the ground that the school order was reasonable in order to prevent disturbance of school discipline. But the United States Supreme Court disagreed, holding that "the wearing of armbands in the circumstances of this case was entirely divorced from or potentially disruptive conduct by those participating in it. It was closely akin to 'pure speech' which, we have repeatedly held, is entitled to comprehensive protection under the First Amendment." Mr. Justice Fortas, speaking for the Court, gave the following opinion:

> First Amendment rights, applied in light of the special characteristics of the school environment, are available to teachers and students. It can hardly be argued that either students or teachers shed their constitutional rights to freedom of speech or expression at the schoolhouse gate. This has been the unmistakable holding of this Court for almost 50 years. . . . The school officials banned and sought to punish petitioners for a silent, passive, expression of opinion, unaccompanied by any disorder or disturbance on the part of petitioners. There is here no evidence whatever of petitioners' interference, actual or nascent, with the school's work or of collision with the rights of other students to be secure and to be let alone.

The Court pointed out that

> Undifferentiated fear or apprehension of disturbance is not enough to overcome the right to freedom of expression. Any departure from absolute regimentation may cause trouble. Any variation from the majority's opinion may inspire fear. Any word spoken, in class, in the lunchroom or on the campus, that deviates from the views of another person, may start an argument or cause a disturbance. But our Constitution says we must take this risk . . . and our history says that it is this sort of hazardous freedom—this kind of openness—that is the basis of our national strength and of the independence and vigor of Americans who grow up and live in this relatively permissive, often disputatious, society.

Indeed, the Court was introspective in declaring:

> The action of the school authorities appears to have been based upon an urgent wish to avoid the controversy which might result from the expression, even by the silent symbol of armbands, of opposition to this Nation's part in the conflagration in Vietnam. It is revealing, in this respect, that the meeting at which the school principals decided to issue the contested regulation was called in

response to a student's statement to the journalism teacher in one of the schools that he wanted to write an article on Vietnam and have it published in the school paper. (This student was dissuaded.)

The highest United States Court answered critics of "permissiveness" and of the campus revolt in general in the eloquent words:

> Students in school as well as out of school are "persons" under our Constitution. They are possessed of fundamental rights which the State must respect, just as they themselves must respect their obligations to the State. In our system, students may not be regarded as closed-circuit recipients of only that which the State chooses to communicate. They may not be confined to the expression of those sentiments that are officially approved. In the absence of a specific showing of constitutionally valid reasons to regulate their speech, students are entitled to freedom of expression of their views. . . . A student's rights therefore, do not embrace merely the classroom hours. When he is in the cafeteria or on the playing field or on the campus during the authorized hours, he may express his opinions, even on controversial subjects like the conflict in Vietnam, if he does so without materially and substantially interfering with appropriate discipline in the operation of the school and without colliding with the rights of others.

And then the United States Supreme Court concluded:

> Under our Constitution, free speech is not a right that is given only to be so circumscribed that it exists in principle but not in fact. Freedom of expression would not truly exist if the right could be exercised only in an area that a benevolent government has provided as a safe haven for crackpots. The Constitution says that Congress (and the States) may not abridge the right to free speech. This provision means what it says. We properly read it to permit reasonable regulation of speech-connected activities in carefully restricted circumstances. But we do not confine the permissible exercise of First Amendment rights to a telephone booth or the four corners of a pamphlet, or to supervised and ordained discussion in a school classroom.

Thus, the decision in the *Tinker* case stands squarely for unbridled free speech on the high school and college campus.

Campus revolt, in essence, requires a choice between the competing values of freedom and order. Some universities have admittedly been paralyzed by chaos in the name of academic freedom. Armed men in uniform have been brought upon the campus to preserve order. Students *and* college officials frequently have resorted to the courts to resolve the impasse. But the courts have not always reacted with equal fervor to preserve freedom on the campuses of both public and private colleges and universities. *Public* educational facilities are sometimes deemed creatures of the state government, and hence protection of constitutional rights is the duty of the state. On the other hand, courts are reluctant to intervene on *private* campuses, although immense sums of public assistance to private colleges and universities should delineate the actions of these universities as "state actions" and therefore make the campus revolt there subject to the same constitutional restraints. (The Fourteenth Amendment prohibits interference *by the State* with the constitutionally guaranteed freedoms.)[2] In *Grossner v. Trustees of Columbia University,*[2a] the major participants in the now-famous April, 1968, riots at Columbia University sued in a federal court to enjoin the disciplinary procedures that Columbia had instituted against them. The students premised the jurisdiction of the federal courts on 42 U.S.C. § 1983, which statute created a cause of action against "[e]very person who, under color of any statute, ordinance, regulation, custom, or usage of any State . . . subjects . . . any citizen of the United States . . . to the deprivation of any rights, privileges, or immunities secured by the Constitution." Such a suit can be maintained only if the deprivation of constitutional rights is the result of "state action" or action taken by state officials acting under color of state law. The students therefore alleged that the disciplinary procedures undertaken by Columbia University constituted "state action" that deprived them of their constitutional rights of free speech, of assembly, and of their right to petition for a redress of grievances. The federal court dismissed the suit for lack of jurisdiction upon three separate grounds. First, it found that 80 per

[2]Section 1 of the Fourteenth Amendment provides in part: "No state shall make or enforce any law which shall abridge the privileges or immunities of citizens of the United States; nor shall any state deprive any person of life, liberty, or property, without due process of law; nor deny any person within its jurisdiction the equal protection of the laws."

[2a]287 F. Supp. 535, USDC NY, 1968.

cent of the public funds received by Columbia came from the federal and not the state government and that the jurisdiction upon which the students relied had to be premised on a finding of state and not federal action. Second, and more fundamental, the Court refused to find that the receipt of government aid, in itself, was enough to make the recipient an agency or instrumentality of government. Finally, the Court held that the plaintiff's complaint suffered from a basic failure, to wit: it was devoid of even the implication that the state itself was somehow involved in the disciplinary procedures under constitutional attack. The Court read the applicable judicial precedents as dictating the necessity of showing that the state must actually participate in the action that violates the plaintiff's constitutional rights. Since the plaintiffs had not even suggested that the State of New York was involved in the allegedly unconstitutional disciplinary proceedings, the complaint itself had to fail. Thus, the Court refused to step into a private quarrel between students and the administration of a private university.

Injunctive relief against campus disorders bordering upon deprivations of free speech should be frowned upon because the remedy is so potent that a court may encounter difficulty in enforcing its decree. In *Dickey v. Alabama State Board of Education,*[8] the federal court in Alabama in 1967 reinstated a student who had been forbidden by the university authorities to return to college following his summer vacation because he had written an editorial in the student paper supporting a stand in favor of academic freedom taken by the president of the University of Alabama. Relying on the First Amendment (as applied to the states through the Fourteenth Amendment), the Court declared: "A state cannot force a college student to forfeit his constitutionality protected right of freedom of expression as a condition to his attending a state-supported institution." Accordingly, the University of Alabama was enjoined from depriving the student of his college education, and the University accepted the decision in good faith. But if the University had balked at the court's decision, the court would have been compelled to take

[8] 273 F. Supp. 613, USDC Ala., 1967.

over the operation of the University in order to insure that its judicial decree was carried out. The summary nature of the court injunction makes it a judicial weapon that must be used wisely. However, the use of injunctions to halt student demonstrations on the campus is becoming more freqeunt, and therefore a balancing of interests and an examination of the facts in each case is required. A demonstration will generally involve both protected and unprotected activity; diverse groups may simultaneously be acting lawfully and unlawfully, and therefore a court must carefully mold its decree to fit the facts in order to insure that protected activity is not sacrificed in the desire to reach the unprotected conduct. The court must preserve opportunities for peaceful expression, yet prohibit the willful destruction of property. When more than one group of demonstrators is involved, the court may have to tailor its order to fit each group. In balancing the interests of the demonstrators against the interests of the university, the court must also consider the need for university administrators to regulate the places and times students are allowed to use campus facilities: "The establishment of an educational program requires the formulation of rules and regulations necessary for the maintenance of an orderly program of classroom learning."[4] If a demonstration does not impair the use of campus buildings or facilities by the nondemonstrating portion of the university community, university officials probably cannot constitutionally prohibit it. But the Constitution would not prevent university officials from making "a prompt and severe disciplinary response to violence and rioting and other constitutionally unprotected conduct."[5] In November, 1969, the Massachusetts Institute of Technology obtained a temporary injunction restraining the November Action Coalition, a loose organization of approximately 30 antiwar groups, from violence or the threat of violence during a protest against defense research. Reluctant to suppress legitimate expression, M.I.T. nevertheless felt compelled to protect "the fundamental rights of this institution." Ac-

[4]Burnside v. Byars, 363 F 2d 744, CCA5, 1966.
[5]Soglin v. Kauffman, 295 F. Supp. 978, USDC Wisc., 1968.

cording to the *New York Times* (Nov. 4, 1969, p. 1) the president of M.I.T. summed up the problem in these words:

> Of all the institutions in our society, the university is most nearly defenseless. It has to be. The university exists so that there may be somewhere a place for the courageous and direct confrontation of ideas. The free flow of ideas cannot take place in an atmosphere of physical confrontation; an open mind cannot long exist in the face of force or threat. It does not matter where force may come from—from the legislature, from the police, from the alumni, from outsiders, or indeed, from the administrators. Once force crosses the threshold, the university is diminished. It is clear to me that . . . we cannot ourselves and with only our own resources deal with force or the threat of force. We are vulnerable; we were created vulnerable; and we will remain so as long as we are free.

Freedom of speech on the college campus today frequently involves new and unique infringements. Hidden television cameras, tape recorders, and similar surreptitious devices can be misused, for example, to stifle free speech by discrediting a teacher or a fellow student. Accordingly, students who wish to use tape recorders for the purpose of recording class lectures and/or discussions should do so only with the explicit knowledge and consent of the teacher and participants, and then only for that purpose. Similarly, school officials should not subvert the educational usages of such devices so as to eavesdrop upon student conversation. Faculty and student committees should establish guidelines for the use of electronic recording devices and for the disposition of the recordings. Freedom of speech entails free speech in the classroom so that a student's views on politics or social policy or what have you are not communicated outside of the college community so as to prejudice that student's opportunity subsequently to earn a living. Only information as to a student's competence and fitness for a particular position are relevant. As a safeguard against the danger of placing the student in an unfavorabale light with government agencies or employers of any category, teachers should preface any employment questionnaire with a brief *pro forma* statement that the academic policy to which they subscribe makes it inadvisable to answer certain types of questions about any or all students. Once this academic policy becomes widespread, presumptive inferences about individual students will no longer be made by employers. On the academic side, students should be free, without restraint by either the college administration or the student government, to organize and join campus clubs or associations for educational, political, social, religious, or cultural purposes. The fact of affiliation with any extramural association should not, in itself, be a bar to employment, but disclosure of such affiliation may be required. If the organization's funds, in whole or in part, are derived from a political organization, this information should be made public. The school administration should not discriminate against a student because of membership in any campus organization. Students should be free through organized action on campus to register their political views of their disapprobation of university policies but within peaceful limits. The use of force on a college campus—whether by students, the campus police, or outside police called in by the administration—is always to be regretted. Outside police should not be summoned to a campus to deal with internal problems unless all other procedures have clearly failed, and then preferably on the basis of rules made in advance with the participation, consultation, and concurrence of representatives of students and faculty who have been selected in a truly representative fashion. Campus papers subsidized by student fees should impartially cover news of special student interest but should also be free to express their own editorial opinions and serve as a forum for opposing views on controversial issues, as do public newspapers. Campus newspapers may also be expected to deal in news columns and editorials with the political and social issues that are relevant to the concerns of the students as citizens of the larger community. Neither the faculty, administration, boards of trustees nor legislatures should be immune from criticism. In no case should the independent decision of the editors be overruled by pressures from alumni, boards of trustees, state legislatures, the college administration, or the student government. Student initiation of competing campus publications should be encouraged.

Freedom of expression by students involves personal freedom, so that students should be free to organize their personal lives and determine their private behavior free from institutional interference. In the past, many colleges, with the approval of parents and the acquiescence of students, have played the role of surrogate parents. But this function is now being strongly challenged. An increasing number of institutions today recognize that students, as part of the maturing process, must be permitted to assume responsibility for their private lives—even if, in some instances, their philosophy or conduct is at variance with traditional standards. The college community should not regard itself as the arbiter of personal behavior or morals, as long as the conduct does not interfere with the rights of others. Regulation is appropriate only if necessary to protect the health and safety of members of the academic community or the fulfillment of the basic academic process. Any such rules should be adopted by elected representative student committees or by committees on which these students have a majority voice. Dress and grooming are modes of personal expression and taste which should be left to the individual student, except for such occasions as are designed by the students themselves. If a student is pregnant, she should be free to decide, in consultation with her own physician or with college health authorities, when to take leave of her studies. A student's locker should not be opened nor his room searched without his consent, except in conformity with the spirit of the Fourth Amendment which requires that a warrant first be obtained on a showing of probable cause, supported by oath or affirmation, and particularly describing the things to be seized. An exception may be made in cases involving a grave danger to the health or safety of other members of the campus community.

A survey of selected recent court decisions involving this right of "personal freedom" on the college campus is in order.

Virginia Polytechnic Institute was enjoined from denying readmission to a student (tentatively accepted for the fall quarter) because he participated in a peaceful demonstration. The Court ruled that V.P.I. was powerless to restrict a student's freedom to express peaceful dissent on campus.[6]

---

[6]Saunders v. Virginia Polytechnic Institute, 38 Law Week 2292, CCA4, 1969.

Central Missouri State College, on the other hand, was permitted to suspend students who violated its rules by participating in "unruly" or "unlawful" mass demonstrations adjacent to and overflowing onto the campus. Judge Harry Blackmun (now on the United States Supreme Court) declared that a college has the inherent authority to maintain order and discipline students, and it may reasonably require of its students that their behavior comport with "ordinary and accepted social customs."[7]

Madison College in Virginia brought disciplinary proceedings against several students who violated its regulations by participating in an unregistered "vigil" outside the college president's office in order to protest the college's decision not to retain various teachers. Two meetings were held, admittedly in compliance with college rules; the meetings were intended to air broad issues of campus government. After these meetings, a group of the participants decided to move on to a college hall and to assemble there later in the evening, although prior arrangements for its use had not been made. It was the group's intention to remain overnight in the hall in order to dramatize their concern and then to meet the next morning with the president of the college whose offices were in the same building. At 12:35 A.M. the next morning, the dean of the college entered the hall and warned the group that they were conducting a demonstration contrary to regulations and would be subject to sanctions provided in the regulations unless they left. At 1:15 A.M., the dean again entered the building and took photographs and the names of those students present. The dean announced that a violation of regulations had occurred. Everyone listened courteously, and a few minutes later the entire group left. That morning, the group sought permission, over 48 hours in advance, to conduct a "vigil" in the same hall. Permission was refused since this function would constitute a "demonstration" inside a building, impermissible under the regulations. Two days later, more than 48 hours after this registration attempt had failed, the group of students again assembled

---

[7]Esteban v. Central Missouri State College, 38 Law Week 2152, CCA8, 1969.

in the college hall. As before, some of the students sat on the floor, but the hallways were not blocked. The group was fairly quiet and peaceful. The dean again arrived and announced that an unauthorized demonstration was being held, and stated that students present would be subject to disciplinary action including suspension. He gave them 15 minutes to leave. The group remained in the lobby of the hall; no property damage was done, and order was maintained. The police arrived some time later and arrested about 30 of the students in the hall. The students made no resistance, and in fact even swept the hall before leaving. Disciplinary proceedings against several of the students were initiated and a number of students were punished. The federal district court in West Virginia on October 2, 1970, after reviewing these facts, declared:

> The faults of the Madison College rules are manifold. Demonstrations by means of mass gatherings, marches, and rallies are entitled to the protection of the First Amendment. . . . To be sure, they are subject to more extensive regulation than those forms of expression which come less into conflict with others' legitimate interests. . . . But insofar as the State seeks to regulate such activities, it must not act in such a sweeping manner as needlessly stifles expression nor vest the power to censor in its officials. . . . The Madison rules fall afoul of both these constitutional requirements. Rules subjecting the exercise of First Amendment activities to prior approval are inherently suspect. They are invalid if they permit those empowered to enforce them to deny permission upon criteria unrelated to proper regulation of the use of public places. However, reasonable and equally enforced regulation of the time, place, manner and duration of forms of expression less pure than speech alone is permissible. . . . The First Amendment protects spontaneous as well as planned activities. There is no indication that safety and police precautions can only be prepared on two days' notice. In addition, the rule against indoor demonstrations of any kind is overboard. No showing has been made that every building on campus houses such facilities that the presence of even a limited number of persons would be disruptive of those facilities.

District Judge Merhige further pointed out:

> The students further contend that the disbanding order rule included in the penalty section of the regulations is unconstitutional

> in that it empowers a college official to impose sanctions based upon his sole judgment that a failure to register what he considers to be a 'demonstration' renders a given activity illegal. The legitimacy of such a rule turns largely on the question of what issues will be considered open in subsequent judicial hearings. If the only issue subject to review is whether the students in fact complied with the order to disband, the regulation acts as an unconstitutional prior restraint, since the official's determination that the activity has wandered into unprotected areas is insulated from review. However, if the hearing includes a determination of whether there were grounds for issuing the order, then the disbanding rule is valid. According to the only evidence before the court as to the manner in which disciplinary hearings are conducted, the sole issue in dispute is *compliance vel non* with the order to disband. So enforced, the rule enables any named official to impose an instant cutoff on protected activities; it is consequently invalid.

The Court thereupon concluded:

> This is not to say that indoor or outdoor activities are not regulatable by narrow rules which address themselves to factors unrelated to the content of the reviews expressed and protect the legitimate interests of members of the college community in operating and making use of the educational facilities that the citizens of Virginia have furnished. . . . These are substantial, valid interests which defendants have the unquestioned right and the duty to defend. However, the protective framework they erect must be one which does not by its very existence infringe upon students' right to engage in First Amendment activities unhampered by fears of penalty under outstanding regulations.[8]

East Tennessee State University, on the other hand, suspended certain students (after a hearing) on charges of distributing on the campus "material of a false, seditious and inflammatory nature." One pamphlet compared the apathy of local students to other American students who seized buildings and raised havoc, and urged local students to "stand up and fight." The pamphlet also referred to the university administration with an obscenity and called them "despots"; it suggested that women students might next be required to wear chastity belts, although the United States Supreme Court had declared that students could "damn well wear what they want

[8]Sword v. Fox, 39 Law Week 2225, USDC W. Va., 1970.

and say what they please." The second pamphlet referred to the school administration as a "problem child," and advocated that students should now reprimand "our misguided child" and educate him. The federal district court found that the students' constitutional right had *not* been violated by their suspension because the inflammatory nature and disruptive characteristics of these two pieces of literature appeared on its face. Furthermore, the Court found the literature was abrasive and calculated to arouse resentment on the part of the university administration and the students. The language in the first pamphlet calling attention to the seizing of buildings and raising havoc was deemed by the federal district court to be an open exhortation to the students to engage in disorderly and destructive activity. Calling the university administration "despots" and referring to it with an obscenity was calculated to subject the administration to ridicule and contempt, and hence to damage the reputation of the university. "The reference to 'chastity belts' for girls is a crude, vulgar remark offensive to women students and beyond the diginity of most college students to make." The Court declared that the students' reliance on the U.S. Supreme Court for the proposition that students have the right to wear what they want and say what they please is misplaced. There is no constitutional right to misbehave on the college campus, according to the Court. The reference in the second pamphlet to the university administration as a "problem child" apparently indicated that these students want to educate their teachers rather than go to college to acquire an education themselves. The lower court decision in favor of East Tennessee State University was affirmed by the 6th United States Court of Appeals which opined that

> It would be difficult to maintain discipline on the campus of an institution of higher learning if conduct of this type were tolerated. We would doubt that parents would send their college-age children to such an institution if they knew that the philosophy as contained in the literature was taught or sanctioned there. We cannot imagine that a student could have confidence in the teachers in a university such as the literature portrays.

Judge Weick of the higher federal court pointed out that the United States Supreme Court decision in the *Tinker* case, above, did not help the students in this case because "[the Tinker] children did not urge a riot, nor were they disrespectful to the teachers." Furthermore:

> It is not required that the college authorities delay action against the inciters until after the riot has started and buildings have been taken over and damaged. The college authorities had the right to nip such action in the bud and prevent it in its inception . . . . It was not necessary to have specific regulation providing for disciplinary action for the circulation of false and inflammatory literature. The university had inherent authority to maintain order and to discipline students.

The dissenting opinion by Judge Celebrezze argued that there was no "clear and present danger" here to warrant suppression of free speech:

> The fact that 25 students visited the dean and wanted him to get rid of the agitators is not significant evidence of a clear and present danger. The dean could have suggested peaceful ways for the students to voice their opinions. . . . . The United States Supreme Court has rejected the notion that an unlawful effect can be inferred from the face of a document which contains false and inflammatory language. Indeed, the Court has insisted upon a specific evidentiary showing of the prohibited effect before permitting proscription of speech. . . . . Even assuming that this were not so, the breadth of discretion given to campus officials is constitutionally impermissible.[9]

On the high school campus, there have been similar court decisions, and two recent decisions are of interest:

A 16-year-old 11th grade student in a Michigan high school was sent home for having several copies of a publication entitled, "White Panther Statement" and when readmitted was told that any student found with obscene literature in his possession in the future would be suspended from school. Subsequently, the student was suspended when a tabloid printed newspaper called *Argus* was found in his possession. The federal district court pointed out initially that the type of regulation involved here was not in the area of "speech or action that intrudes upon the work of the school or the rights of other stu-

---

[9]Norton v. East Tennessee State University, 38 Law Week 2717, CCA5, 1969.

dents," as delineated by the United States Supreme Court in *Tinker* v. *Des Moines Independent Community School District*, above. At the hearing, there was introduced into evidence J. D. Salinger's *The Catcher in the Rye*, and the April, 1969, issue of *Harper's* magazine, with reference to an article entitled "Temptations of a Boston Atheist," by Nat Hentoff. The student's attorney pointed out that the issue of *Harper's* could be found in the school library, and further stated:

> And in connection with it, I would like to call the board's attention to page 82 of it, in which the word—and I have underlined it as [the school principal] did with the *Argus* so that you could see it—the work 'f-u-c-k' is used, and on page 84, that word with an '——e-r' at the end and 'mother' in front of it is also used in the article by Nat Hentoff, a writer who has written many books. And, apparently, I would also like to point out to the board and point out for your attention the book *The Catcher in the Rye*, which has been testified to that the boy in this case, David, was required to read in the tenth grade and was read in other classes and is being read, according to his information now, in the ninth grade, and in a book that he said was, when he was in English, he was taught to distinguish between the word and content and to use the content. I would say the word 'f-u-c-k' is used once on page 201, twice on page 202, three times on page 204."

In the student's attorney's cross-examination of the high school principal, the following ensued:

> *Q*. Now, what was it that was objectionable about *Argus*?
>
> *A*. Well, . . . you have looked this over as carefully as I have and you know the words as well as I, and you were hesitant to mention them in court and I am hesitant to mention them in court and I am hesitant to mention them here, even though they are not supposed to be obscene.
>
> *Q*. Is that what you find objectionable about *Argus*?
>
> *A*. Yes, sir.
>
> *Q*. That is, the words that are in there?
>
> *A*. Yes, sir.

The Court observed that the exhibit, *The Catcher in the Rye*, was required reading or offered as optional reading in this high school for ninth and tenth graders. It was therefore an enigma in the light of the stand taken by the principal at the board hearing. The same enigma existed with relation to the presence of the *Harper's* magazine in the school library. The Court declared:

> [The student] has been expelled from school for having possesion of the *Argus* publication, on the ground that it contains certain four-letter words. . . . Plaintiff's expulsion is not based on the general content of the *Argus*, or its literary quality or lack of literary quality, or its philosophic bent, or the type of publication it is, but is based solely on its containing certain four-letter words. . . . We are compelled to reject the position of the defendants in this case because it is preposterous on its face. It is contrary to any sense of fairness or consistency—a student, placed in the situation in which this school has placed this student, is required to make a judgment that we, as a court, would find difficult to make. The plaintiff herein was expelled for possession of a copy of the *Argus* publication. This is an entirely different type of material from the "White Panther" statements referred to in the "directive." It is a 24-page tabloid-type publication containing serious articles written grammatically, which, according to the testimony of University of Michigan English professor (a witness in this court at the first hearing held in this court on the motion for preliminary injunction), has literary quality and perception, even though it contains certain four-letter words. For possession of this one magazine on one occassion—for this and no more—plaintiff was expelled. The expulsion was based on his "violation" of the "directive." We make the observation that even though plaintiff testified he realized he might be considered in violation of the "directive," the drastic action of expulsion for such single incident, carrying as it does a lifetime stigma, is hardly punishment fitting the crime.

The Court thereupon concluded that the suspension of the high school student was "so inherently unfair as to be arbitrary and unreasonable, constituting denial of due process, thus compelling us to conclude that the plaintiff's expulsion may not stand."[10]

In a Minnesota high school, the student appeared at the opening of school with shoulder-length hair and was not permitted to remain in school on the basis of a school rule stating that "the boys should have neat, conventional male hair cuts." Having been refused further entrance until his hair was shortened, the student sought to have the school enjoined from refusing to allow him to enroll. The federal district court ob-

---

[10]Vought v. Van Buren Public Schools, 38 Law Week 2034, USDC, Mich., 1969.

served that as far back as his sophomore year, when plaintiff was not wearing long hair, he was the butt of physical attack or attacks by one or more bigger boys. Indeed,

> Any word spoken in class, in the lunchroom or on the campus that deviates from the views of another person may start an argument or cause a disturbance. But our Constitution says we must take this risk . . . and our history says that it is this sort of hazardous freedom—this kind of openness—that is the basis of our national strength and of the independence and vigor of Americans who grow up and live in this relatively permissive, often disputatious society. . . . Certainly where there is no finding and no showing that the exercise of the forbidden right would "materially and substantially interfere with the requirements of appropriate discipline in the operation of the school," the prohibition cannot be sustained. In the instant case, there has been no convincing showing by defendant that shoulder-length hair will "materially and substantially interfere with the requirement of appropriate discipline in the operation of the school."

Furthermore, according to the Court, no safety hazard was presented, since the student could wear protective gear or even tie his hair in shop or laboratory. Accordingly, the Court concluded:

> The restriction here is one of appearance, not based on health or morals. Query whether the length of a boy's hair is distractive today as would be girls scantily clad for instance so as to justify regulation. The rule here has effect beyond school, so were a school to prohibit a boy attending school with no shirt and bare to the waist, if he desires to go bare waisted in life at home or beyond the school he may take off the shirt as he leaves the school grounds. Such is not the case with hair. . . . Regulation of conduct by school authorities must bear a reasonable basis to the ordinary conduct of the school curriculum or to carrying out the responsibility of the school."[11]

The President's Commission on Campus Unrest reported on November 6, 1970, that only 8 per cent of the 805 incidents covered by the survey of two thirds of the nation's colleges were defined as serious—involving personal injury or property damage. The survey also found that administrators, faculty, and students each gave a long list of reasons for campus unrest. The

---

[11]Westley v. Rossi, 38 Law Week 2257, USDC, Minn., 1969.

three reasons cited most often by each group were (a) the war in Indochina, (b) the lack of internal campus communication, and (c) the perceived unresponsiveness of the Federal Government to domestic problems. In essence, these "reasons" are matured convictions of adults, not of children, and few courts and university officials recognize that today's students are adults. Students are considerably more mature than previous generations were at their age, and this is true both physically and intellectually. Society has fed them on a better diet, has dosed them with vitamin pills and infants, has given them excellent medical protection from the ravages of disease and illness. Society has, in fact, done all the things that any botanist does to plants or any livestock breeder does to animals to bring them to early maturity, and then society denies that such early maturity occurs. This maturity of the student population is evident in such facts as the earlier ages at which they reach full growth, the larger physical size they attain, and in such an obvious fact as the age at onset of the menstrual period in young women, which has moved since 1900 from age 16 down to age 14. Students today are also more mature intellectually, for just as society has given them excellent physical care, society has given them better schooling than previous generations had. Today's students have been put through the finest school system any civilization has ever provided for the young. Students come to college with a much more sophisticated set of intellectual tools than previous generations. What students today may be lacking in experience (and admittedly they do not know everything) is more than compensated for by the fact that they have had a *wider* set of experiences than previous generations.

Indeed, every educational board, every university administration, and every faculty, in recognition of these markings of student maturity, should make an honest and thoroughgoing effort to provide for students a legitimate and real place in the affairs of educational institution—not by the tokenism of nonvoting membership on university committees but by full and effective participation as one of the three segments, i.e. faculty, students, and administration, that determine the course of the educational enterprise. After all, it is the lives of the students that the university is dealing with, and to accomplish these changes, all segments must work together to improve the quality of education. Universities must encourage and support innovation, creativity, and flexibility. Administration, faculty, and students must work at developing new approaches and new techniques. While preserving what is good in the present system, the bad must be ferreted out and ways found to improve it. How can the student-teacher relationship be improved? How can student involvement be assured to the satisfaction of all? Is there a need for more flexible scheduling of instructional programs? Are grades necessary or harmful? Are students able to work as well or better by abolishing classes and having instructors available only for consultation when students get into trouble with the learning process? How can knowledge be integrated better so that the student's total learning experience is more meaningful? Above all, how can there be introduced into education a significant component of concern for human values and for the human treatment of men and their world? Today's society must recognize that some student activists have been moved by conscience to use extraordinary means in the belief that ordinary means have failed to build a just and equal society and secure peace! The burden of changing and adapting social institutions and policies to demonstrate that America has the capacity and will to redress the evils of the social order falls upon the shoulders of the young. And the college campus is where these values take fruition in an atmosphere chock full of displays of free speech. In the final analysis, America must be prepared to recognize that free speech on the college campus is an integral part of the democratic tradition.

QUESTIONS FOR REVIEW

1. Is there indeed a campus "revolt," or is it merely campus "violence" which we are delineating so as to justify and perhaps even applaud the American tradition of revolting against tyranny?
2. Why is "free speech" the most salient aspect of the campus revolt today?

3. What is the intrinsic guideline for any congressional investigating committee?
4. How would the distribution of a "blacklist" of radical speakers on campus interfere with "free speech?"
5. Explain why the wearing of black armbands is "closely akin to 'pure speech'."
6. Is order and discipline on the college campus the *summum bonum*? Is free expression of ideas and unbridled conduct the modus operandi on the campus today? How is the conflict between these two extremes harmonized?
7. What place does and should the Vietnam war play on the college campus today?
8. Does the Fourteenth Amendment prohibit the states from abridging the right to free speech? Explain.
9. Why are courts legally reluctant to enjoin disorders on the campus? Is the judicial remedy appropriate to quell riots?
10. What is meant by the term "balancing the interests" with respect to the role of the courts in curbing the campus revolt?
11. Do you agree or disagree with the "philosophy" of the President of M.I.T., quoted in this chapter? Why?
12. List surreptitious devices (other than tape recorders and hidden television cameras) which infringe upon free speech. When is a questionnaire a violation of free speech?
13. Can you define a proper role for campus police in terms of promoting free speech, or is the mere presence of campus police the antithesis of free speech?
14. Explain how freedom of expression is but a facet of the student's personal freedom.
15. Do you agree with the court that the rules and regulations on student conduct in the Madison College case were infringements upon free speech? How potent was the court's argument about "fears of penalty"?
16. Contrast the actions of the East Tennessee State University officials with the actions of the Madison College officials.

Explain the differing court rulings with special emphasis upon the meaning of "clear and present danger."

17. How do the "high school" cases differ from the "college campus" cases delineated in this chapter? Is the age of the student a crucial factor?

Chapter 2

"WOMEN'S LIB": THE STRUGGLE FOR ECONOMIC EQUALITY

WE ARE TODAY FACED with a great civil war involving not brother against brother, but sister against brother, with its resounding battle cry that all men *and women* are created equal.

What the fighters for feminism are seeking, however, is not political equality, (they already have that) but economic equality and the full implementation of Section 703(a) of Title VII of the Civil Rights Act of 1964. This statute declares that employers engaged in commerce, employment agencies servicing such employers, and labor organizations engaged in such industries, will be charged with committing an unfair employment practice if they:

> (1) . . . fail or refuse to hire or to discharge any individual, or otherwise to discriminate against any individual with respect to his compensation, terms, conditions, or privileges of employment, because of such individual's race, color, religion, sex, or national origin; or (2) to limit, segregate, or classify his employees in any way which would deprive or tend to deprive any individual of employment opportunities or otherwise adversely affect his status as an employee, because of such individual's race, color, religion, sex, or national origin."

In essence, the law states that an employer may not discriminate against a woman with respect to hiring or firing, wages, fringe benefits, or working conditions, and may not categorize a woman worker so as to deny her job opportunities merely because of her sex. Yet throughout American history, employers have been unashamedly doing all of these now-prohibited acts and discriminating against women, although the "fair" sex has been crying "foul" for centuries.

The struggle against job discrimination for women had its

beginnings more than 300 years ago when the first adventurous souls voyaged to the New World, and today's skirmishes cannot be disconnected from the society and laws that our American forebears created. The very statutes that contemporary advocates of women's liberation seek to expunge as discriminatory are those that were born amidst the romantic paternalism and protectionism that has pervaded the very spirit as well as the very essence of those early laws. Man was meant to protect woman and his traditional role as provider and protector supposedly clothed him in such a way that he should know how best to surround women with laws that would enable them to avoid the harsher realities of the world.

The soldiers of feminism—1970's style—seek no protection and ask for no quarter. They desire a complete and absolute egalitarianism in all aspects of economic life, from the exploitation of the earth's crust to the exploration of space. They give fair warning to the "executive suites" of industry, the union hiring halls of skilled labor, and the lofty Brahmins of the professions that nothing is sacred in their desire for financial equality.

To discover the reasons behind the slow, often frustrating progress of American womanhood towards economic equality, it is essential to examine the heritage of the "English Common Law" which crossed the Atlantic with the first settlers from the British Isles. According to *Black's Law Dictionary* (4th ed.), "English Common Law"

> Comprises the body of those principles and rules of action relating to the government and security of persons and property, which derive their authority solely from the usages and customs of immemorial antiquity or from the *judgments and decrees of the courts,* recognizing, affirming, and enforcing such usages and customs; and, in this sense, particularly the ancient unwritten law of England. (Emphasis added.)

However, inasmuch as most American colonial lawyers were far from completely knowledgeable in the labyrinthine ways of English Common Law, they sought advice in the tomes of that most famous of legal scholars and commentators, Sir William Blackstone. In his *Commentaries on the Laws of England,* a digest of legal dissertations, precedent-setting decisions, and general wisdom, first published in 1765, Blackstone took a rather lowly view of women in general and wives in particular. Since his word was nearly unquestioned dogma to American lawyers, they followed his unenlightened and misogynal lead: *"The husband and wife are one, and that one is the husband."*

Although most females beyond the age of puberty were married, (legally called *femme couvert* rather than *femme sole*) and were thus united-in-interest with their husbands, few American jurists at first exercised any creative thought beyond Blackstone's teachings of the woman's slave-like status. Thus, this attitude and posture with respect to American females became self-perpetuating. Ever since, in the woman's battle for equality under the law, either the male had to be dragged under the law with her or she had to rise up and join him on the balances of the scales of blind Justice.

In the early days, women could not vote (other than in New Jersey for a short period in the 1790's), hold public office, or serve on juries (except when a pregnant woman committed a capital crime—and then only to decide if she should be executed before or after she gave birth). For the unusual "reckless" female who independently sought employment outside of her husband's, father's, or brother's home, the scope of employment was rigidly limited, especially in the professions. Furthermore, a *femme couvert* could neither hold, sell, devise by will, or make a gift of property, nor enter into independent contracts. A married woman was, in Blackstonian terms, "civilly dead," because her husband was the "one" legally possessed of all rights and responsibilities.

During the Colonial and Revolutionary War eras, and before the changes wrought by the importation of the factory system from England, the home was the economic center of society. On the farm, the husband tilled the fields and the wife engaged in domestic duties, preparing the fruits of her spouse's labor for market. In the towns and cities, wives of the middle and upper classes earned "pin-money" by the sale of their handicraft and dutifully turned over the money to their husbands as required by law. (It was not until the mid-19th century that a wife was entitled to retain her own wages). Some townswomen were employed as cooks or servants, but it was rare and extraordinary for a woman to work in other than a domestic capacity in an American household. However, with the coming of the Industrial Revolution, the working woman moved out of the kitchen and into the factory. At first, native-born American women became power loom and spinning jenny operators predominantly in the Northeast, and their male employers and foremen tended to treat them with respect and consideration. Although wages were low, (often only 25 per cent of that received by men working in the same capacity) hours for women were long, but working conditions were tolerable and, in a term of the age, "moral."

In the mid-19th century, the so-called "potato famine" hit Ireland, and between 1840 and 1860 nearly a million and a half Irish men and women, mostly unskilled and semiliterate peasant farmers, migrated to the United States. Labor, and especially female labor, was in overabundant supply, and as a consequence, wages were lowered and working hours and conditions became intolerable. Throughout the remainder of the nineteenth century and into the first decade of the twentieth, new immigrants from Europe flooded into the thriving United States to assume places in American industry. As poorly as the male immigrants were treated, the female's lot was infinitely worse. If she worked in a factory, there was unguarded machinery, poisonous fumes and vapors, and other industrial hazards; even if she maintained her health, she stood little chance of ever changing her employment. If she worked at home rolling cigars or sewing, for example, she had to contend with the severity of the slums where she lived. But wherever the immigrant woman was employed, she was mercilessly exploited by her employers, the barons of industry. Outside of the factory (or employment as a "domestic"), the educated woman stood a little better chance of economic success, but she still had to cope with often insurmountable obstacles. The only jobs open were in teaching and in the later part of the nineteenth century, in nursing but in almost every case at a lower wage level than a man in the identical position. And in the professions, although wages were better, the woman's climb was appreciably harder. One of the earliest female pioneers in the professions was Doctor Elizabeth Blackwell, who, after repeated refusals of admission to numerous medical schools, was finally allowed to matriculate at the Medical College at Geneva, New York, but only following a favorable vote by its male student body. She subsequently in 1849 became the first female physician qualified to practice medicine in the United States. (In 1971, still very few females have followed her lead; only 3 per cent of all doctors today are women.) But Dr. Blackwell's "fellow" professionals in the field of law had an even harder time than she had.

A few years after the War Between the States, Mrs. Myra Bradwell, a resident of Chicago, filed a necessary petition with two justices of the Supreme Court of Illinois in her effort to become licensed as an Illinois practicing attorney and counselor at law. The Court refused her petition, claiming that "as a married woman [she] would be bound neither by her express contracts nor by those implied contracts which it is the policy of the law to create between attorney and client." Mrs. Bradwell nevertheless pressed her suit and filed a written rebuttal argument. The Court thereupon delivered an opinion stating that it was not within the contemplation of the Illinois Legislature to admit women to practice law, basing its opinion upon the fact that Illinois had adopted the Common Law of England:

> It is to be also remembered that female attorneys at law were unknown in England, and a proposition that a woman should enter the courts of Westiminster Hall in that capacity, or as a barrister, would have created hardly less astonishment than one that she should ascend the bench of bishops, or be elected to a seat in the House of Commons. . . .
>
> That God designed the sexes to occupy different spheres of action, and that it belonged to men to make, apply, and execute the laws, was regarded as an almost axiomatic truth.

The highest court in the land, the Supreme Court of the United States, the following year, in *Bradwell* v. *The State*,[1] agreed with the highest court of Illinois and denied her contention that

[1]83 U.S. 130, 1872.

Illinois had violated the Equal Protection Clause of the Fourteenth Amendment. In a concurring opinion, using words which still boil the blood of women's liberationists, Mr. Justice Bradley said:

> The claim that, under the Fourteenth Amendment of the Constitution, which declares that no State shall make or enforce any law which shall abridge the privileges and immunities of citizens of the United States, the statute law of Illinois, or the common law prevailing in that State, can no longer be set up as a barrier against the right of females to pursue any lawful employment for a livelihood (the practice of law included), assumes that it is one of the privileges and immunities of women as citizens to engage in any and every profession, occupation, or employment in civil life.
>
> It certainly cannot be affirmed, as an historical fact, that this has ever been established as one of the fundamental privileges and immunities of the sex. On the contrary, the civil law, as well as nature herself, has always recognized a wide difference in the respective spheres and destinies of man and woman. Man is, or should be, woman's protector and defender. The natural and proper timidity and delicacy which belongs to the female sex evidently unfits it for many of the occupations of civil life. The constitution of the family organization, which is founded in the divine ordinance, as well as in the nature of things, indicates the domestic sphere as that which properly belongs to the domain and functions of womanhood. The harmony, not to say identity, of interests and views which belong, or should belong, to the family institution is repugnant to the idea of a woman adopting a distinct and independent career from that of her husband. So firmly fixed was this sentiment in the founders of the common law that it became a maxim of that system of jurisprudence that a woman had no legal existence separate from her husband, who was regarded as her head and representative in the social state; and, notwithstanding some recent modifications of this civil status, many of the special rules of law flowing from and dependent upon this cardinal principle still exist in full force in most States.

Furthermore, the Court also noted:

> The paramount destiny and mission of woman are to fulfil the noble and benign offices of wife and mother. This is the law of the Creator. And the rules of civil society must be adapted to the general constitution of things and cannot be based upon exceptional cases. . . . I am not prepared to say that it is one of her fundamental rights and privileges to be admitted into every office and position,

> including those which require highly special qualifications and demanding special responsibilities. In the nature of things it is not every citizen of every age, sex and condition that is qualified for every calling and position. It is the prerogative of the legislator to prescribe regulations founded on nature, reason, and experience for the due admission of qualified persons to professions and callings demanding special skill and confidence. This fairly belongs to the police power of the State; and, in my opinion, in view of the peculiar characteristics, destiny, and mission of woman, it is within the province of the legislature to ordain what offices, positions, and callings shall be filled and discharged by men, and shall receive the benefit of those energies and responsibilities, and that decision and firmness which are presumed to predominate in the sterner sex.

Some 22 years later, in the case of Ex parte *Lockwood,*[2] the United States Supreme Court again refused to entertain the problem by declaring that it is within the province of the State of Virginia to grant or deny a woman admission to the bar. Mr. Chief Justice Fuller noted:

> It was for the Supreme Court of Appeals to construe the statute of Virginia in question, and to determine whether the word 'person' as therein used is confined to males, and whether women are admitted to practice law in that commonwealth.

(In 1971, still very few females have followed Mrs. Lockwood's lead; only 3 per cent of all attorneys today are women.)

During the first 20 years of the twentieth century, a woman began to be considered a "person," although she was not given the right to vote until the enactment of the Nineteenth Amendment in 1920. In the economic sphere, however, much was being done to alleviate the sweatshop conditions in which she worked in the factories all over America. Restrictive legislation was passed, recognizing the difference between a man's and a woman's physical capacity to work, i.e. weight limits were established and night-time jobs for women prohibited, and the number of hours per day or week that a woman could work was similarly circumscribed. Other laws prohibited her from "unladylike" employment, such as wrestling or bartending. In 1919, two states even passed "drastic" laws requiring *equal* pay for women. Nevertheless, soon after the introduction of such

---

[2]154 U.S. 116, 1893.

protective laws, American industry challenged their validity in the courts on the basis that a state could not interfere with an adult person's right to enter into contracts. (By this time the contractual prohibition against *femme couverts* had disappeared.) However, the courts frequently considered such legislation dealing with working conditions or hours of employment with respect to women to be a valid exercise of the state's police power. For example, in *Muller v. Oregon,*[3] Oregon passed a law whereby it was a misdemeanor to employ a woman "in any mechanical factory or laundry" more than ten hours in any one day. The United States Supreme Court upheld the constitutionality of this statute and noted that although such a law might be invalid as to a man or generally, without sexual designation (as was so held in *Lochner v. New York*[4]), the Court observed that it was *not* so as to a woman, because "this assumes that the difference between the sexes does not justify a different rule respecting a restriction of hours of labor." The attorney for the State of Oregon was Louis D. Brandeis, later to sit upon the United States Supreme Court. He presented to the Court a copious collection of sociological, scientific, and medical statistics (called "a Brandeis brief") which justified this sort of restrictive legislation. Mr. Justice Brewer, writing the opinion for a unanimous court, agreed:

> That woman's physical structure and the performance of maternal functions place her at a disadvantage in the struggle for subsistence is obvious. This is especially true when the burdens of motherhood are upon her. Even when they are not, by abundant testimony of the medical fraternity continuance for a long time on her feet at work, repeating this from day to day, tends to injurious effects upon the body, and as healthy mothers are essential to vigorous offspring, the physical well-being of woman becomes an object of public interest and care in order to preserve the strength and vigor of the race.
>
> Still again, history discloses the fact that woman has always been dependent upon man. He established his control at the outset by superior physical strength, and this control in various forms,

---

[3]208 U.S. 421, 1908.
[4]198 U.S. 45, 1905.

with diminishing intensity, has continued to the present. As minors, though not to the same extent, she has been looked upon in the courts as needing especial care that her rights may be preserved. Education was long denied her, and while now the doors of the schoolroom are opened and her opportunities for acquiring knowledge are great, yet even with that and the consequent increase of capacity for business affairs it is still true that in the struggle for subsistence she is not an equal competitor with her brother. Though limitations upon personal and contractual rights may be removed by legislation, there is that in her disposition and habits of life which will operate against a full assertion of those rights. She will still be where some legislation to protect her seems necessary to secure a real equality of right. Doubtless there are individual exceptions, and there are many respects in which she has an advantage over him; but looking at it from the viewpoint of the effort to maintain an independent position in life, she is not upon an equality. Differentiated by these matters from the other sex, she is properly placed in a class by herself, and legislation designed for her protection may be sustained, even when like legislation is not necessary for men, and could not be sustained. It is impossible to close one's eyes to the fact that she still looks to her brother and depends upon him. Even though all restrictions on political, personal, and contractual rights were taken away, and she stood, so far as statutes are concerned, upon an absolutely equal plane with him, it would still be true that she is so constituted that she will rest upon and look to him for protection; that her physical structure and a proper discharge of her maternal functions— having in view not merely her own health, but the well-being of the race—justify legislation to protect her from the greed as well as the passion of man. The limitations which this statute places upon her contractual powers, upon her right to agree with her employer as to the time she shall labor, are not imposed solely for her benefit, but also largely for the benefit of all. Many words cannot make this plainer. The two sexes differ in structure of body, in the functions to be performed by each, in the amount of physical strength, in the capacity for long continued labor, particularly when done standing, the influence of vigorous health upon the future well-being of the race, the self-reliance which enables one to assert full rights, and in the capacity to maintain the struggle for subsistence. This difference justifies a difference in legislation and upholds that which is designed to compensate for some of the burdens which rest upon her.

Fifteen years later, the United States Supreme Court again had the opportunity to review legislation dealing with women's employment in the case of *Adkins v. Children's Hospital of the District of Columbia.*[5] On this occasion, a Washington, D.C., hospital was trying to resist paying a minimum wage to a female worker in accordance with a recently passed congressional law.[6] Mr. Justice Sutherland, writing for a majority of the Court, struck down the statute:

> But the ancient inequality of the sexes, otherwise than physical, . . . has continued "with diminishing intensity." In view of the great—not to say revolutionary—changes which have taken place since that utterance, in the contractual, political, and civil status of women, culminating in the Nineteenth Amendment, it is not unreasonable to say that these differences have now come almost, if not quite, to the vanishing point. In this aspect of the matter, while the physical differences must be recognized in appropriate cases and legislation fixing hours or conditions of work may propel to be then into account, we cannot accept the doctrine that women of mature age, *sui juris*, require or may be subjected to restrictions upon their liberty of contract which could not lawfully be imposed in the case of men under similar circumstances. To do so would be to ignore all the implications to be drawn from the present day trend of legislation, as well as that of common thought and usage, by which woman is accorded emancipation from the old doctrine that she must be given special protection or be subjected to special restraint in her contractual and civil relationships.

Strangely, Justice Sutherland's words in 1923 effectively sum up the position of the militant feminists of the 1970's towards this very same type of legislation—while the feminists of the Flapper Era were appalled by the "reactionary" approach of our nation's highest court!

But women were not to be outdone, because in 1937, the United States Supreme Court overruled the *Adkins* decision and gave its blessings to minimum-wage legislation passed by the State of Washington. In *West Coast Hotel Co. v. Parrish,*[7]

> What can be closer to the public interest than the health of women and their protection from unscrupulous and overreaching

---

[5]261 U.S. 525, 1923.

[6]Congress has the exclusive responsibility for legislation dealing with the District of Columbia.

[7]300 U.S. 379, 1937.

Chief Justice Charles Evans Hughes wrote the decision for the 5 to 4 divided bench:

> employers? And if the protection of women is a legitimate end of the exercise of state power, how can it be said that the requirement of the payment of a minimum wage fairly fixed in order to meet the very necessities of existence is not an admissible means to that end? The Legislature of the state was clearly entitled to consider the situation of women in employment, the fact that they are in the class receiving the least pay, that their bargaining power is relatively weak, and that they are the ready victims of those who would take advantage of their necessitous circumstances. The Legislature was entitled to adopt measures to reduce the evils of the "sweating system," the exploiting of workers at wages so low as to be insufficient to meet the bare cost of living, thus making their very helplessness the occasion of a most injurious competition.

More recently, in 1948, the United States Supreme Court dealt with protecting hapless females from the wiles of alcohol, or rather from dispensing its wiles to others, by prohibiting a woman from working in an "unladylike" profession, to wit, bartending. In *Goesaert v. Cleary*,[8] Mr. Justice Frankfurter wrote the majority opinion which upheld a Michigan statute forbidding women who were neither the wife nor the daughter of the proprietor from being employed as bartenders.

> Michigan could, beyond question, forbid all women from working behind a bar. This is so despite the vast changes in the social and legal position of women. The fact that women may now have achieved the virtues that men have long claimed as their prerogatives and now indulge in vices that men have long practiced, does not preclude the States from drawing a sharp line between the sexes, certainly in such matters as the regulation of the liquor traffic. . .

In 1964, during the House debate on Title VII of the Civil Rights Law of 1964, Representative Martha Griffiths of Michigan described the *Goesaert* decision in these words: "The most vulgar and insulting of decisions handed down in this century by the Supreme Court, notable for its lack of legal learning as well as its arrogant prejudice." It would appear therefore that

---

[8] 335 U.S. 64, 1948.

women in 1964 were on their way toward some form of equality with men.

Although state legislatures were protecting women from exploitation with respect to hours, working conditions, and "unladylike" jobs, little was done towards effectuating equality of pay for women. More often than not, a man employed in exactly the same capacity as a woman received more money for his daily labor. Beginning after World War I, in 1919, the states of Montana and Michigan passed "toothless" equal pay laws which employers either avoided by simply not hiring women or completely ignored. The woman in need of the job had little choice and took a lower salary than her male counterpart so as to be employed. Even during the Depression years when many of the New Deal reform acts specified that women were to receive equal pay for equal work, the laws were widely flouted or not enforced. Yet for the women seeking employment, it was far better to have a job at any salary than to starve or go on welfare. During World War II, when "Rosie the Riveter" became a national symbol, women had little problem with equal pay for equal work, as they had no male competitors and no men to whom to be equal. Notwithstanding, between 1943 and 1944, beginning first with the legislatures of Washington and then the legislatures of California, Connecticut, Illinois, Massachusetts, New Hampshire, New York, Pennsylvania, Rhode Island and Alaska, equal pay laws for women were enacted. After V-J Day in 1945, however, more than 300,000 women were laid off from the "male-type" jobs they had held while our Armed Forces fought overseas. Those women who were not fired once again began to receive less pay than their male counterparts, even in the above states with equal pay laws. In 1946 and again in 1949, California Congresswoman Helen Gahagan Douglas attempted to have the House of Representatives pass a Federal Equal Pay Act, but to no avail. It was not until the administration of President John Fitzgerald Kennedy that Congress, after particularly strong urging by the President and the President's Commission on the Status of Women, passed the Equal Pay Act of 1963 as an amendment to the Fair Labor Standards Act of 1938. This Act, in part, states:

> (d) (1) No employer having employees subject to any provisions of this section shall discriminate, within any establishment in which such employees are employed, between employees on the basis of sex by paying wages to employees in such establishment at a rate less than the rate at which he pays wages to employees of the opposite sex in such establishment for equal work on jobs the performance of which requires equal skill, effort, and responsibility, and which are performed under similar working conditions, except where such payment is made pursuant to (i) a seniority system; (ii) a merit system; (iii) a system which measures earnings by quantity or quality of production; or (iv) a differential based on any other factor other than sex; *Provided,* That an employer who is paying a wage rate differential in violation of this subsection shall not, in order to comply with the provisions of this subsection, reduce the wage rate of any employee."

Thus an employer could not in any single "establishment" where he employed workers pay women employees less than men employees, so long as the workers performed the same job. Further, although an employer could justify wage differentials on factors other than the sex of the employee, he could not reduce the wages of men so as to avoid violating the law. The Equal Pay Act, however, did not cover all or even the majority of female workers, as it was restricted to those limited situations covered by the Fair Labor Standards Act. Furthermore, there were a number of loopholes through which noncomplying employers could escape the Act's impact. One such loophole was the so-called "establishment" clause which allows a single employer to pay one salary to employees working at one location and another salary to those working elsewhere. In the words of the Department of Labor guidelines:

> It is clear from the language of the Act that in each distinct physical place of business where the employees of an employer work (including but not limited to, the employer's own establishments), the obligation of the employer to comply with the equal pay requirements must be determined separately with reference to those of his employees who are employed in that particular establishment.

This meant that if an employer owned two factories, not only could he pay the workers in one factory less than the workers in the other, but he could totally segregate the men and women performing the same task by having them work in separate factories and thus avoid complying with the Act and pay women less than men.

With the passage of Title VII of the Civil Rights Act of 1964, this loophole has been, for all practical purposes, plugged. A woman working in a different establishment from a man for the same employer may now sue to receive the same salary for the same type of work if the purpose of the separate establishment was to discriminate because of sex.

Employers frequently resort to circumventing the Act by invoking the clause, "equal work on jobs the performance of which requires equal skill, effort, and responsibility, and which are performed under similar working conditions." In such a situation, the employer claims that he pays men more than women because they perform in a very slightly different way. The Courts, however, carefully scrutinize the facts of each case presented, and frequently find discrimination existing when the alleged difference between the "skill, effort and responsibility" is insignificant or insubstantial. For example, in *Schultz v. Wheaton Glass Co.*,[9] the employer paid male package selectors 10 per cent more than female because the males occasionally act as "snap-up boys" in doing lifting and crating tasks. Wheaton Glass claimed this element of flexibility justified the differential pay, although those men assigned to permanent "snap-up" duties received only one per cent more in pay than package selectors. The Court agreed with the Equal Employment Opportunity Commission and found that the wage differential herein was discriminatory:

> Differences in job classifications were in general expected to be beyond the coverage of the Equal Pay Act. This was because in the case of genuine job classifications, the differences in work necessarily would be substantial and the differences in compensation therefore would be based on the differences in work which justified them. Congress never intended, however, that an artificially created job classification which did not substantially differ from the genuine one could provide an escape for an employer from the operation of the Equal Pay Act. This would be too wide a door through which the content of the Act would disappear.

---

[9] 421 F2d 259, CCA3, 1970.

> This view is strengthened by the subsequent adoption of Title VII of the Civil Rights Act of 1964 which prohibits discrimination because of sex in the classification of employees as well as in their employment and compensation. Although the Civil Rights Act is much broader than the Equal Pay Act, its provisions regarding discrimination based on sex are *in pari materia* with the Equal Pay Act. . . . Since both statutes serve the same fundamental purpose against discrimination based on sex, the Equal Pay Act may not be construed in a manner which by virtue of §703(h) would undermine the Civil Rights Act.

Thus, the Court said that where "genuine" differences exist between different job categories, an employer is justified in paying different wages to men and women. However, where the different job category is "artificial" and is merely created by the employer to circumvent the Equal Pay Act so as to pay women less than men, women employees could recover the difference in wages from the employer in a court of law.

The greatest breakthrough in the struggle to bring about economic equality for women, however, arose not as a result of lengthy Congressional hearings or detailed study, but almost spontaneously as a result of the passage of the momentous Civil Rights Act of 1964. In Title VII (a part of which is quoted at the beginning of this chapter), sexual discrimination in employment is outlawed, and an Equal Employment Opportunity Commission established to investigate transgressing employers. It extended the coverage, by implication, of the Equal Pay Act of 1963 (which became effective on June 11, 1964, three weeks before President Lyndon B. Johnson signed the Civil Rights Act on July 2, 1964) and put teeth into an area of the law that had long been noted for its good intentions but lack of enforcement power. As originally introduced, however, Title VII of the Civil Rights Act of 1964 (reproduced in Appendix I) contained no provisions dealing with sexual discrimination. The addition of the word "sex" came from an amendment by Representative Howard W. Smith, then the 81-year-old Chairman of the Rules Committee. As noted in a *New York Herald Tribune* editorial of February 10, 1964: "The goal of the clause is worthy. It came, however, as an unplanned by-product of a confused debate, in which the implications could not be studied with the care they deserved. The issue was raised for mischevious reasons, and it may well have unhappy effects." According to Caroline Bird in her book *Born Female*,[10] Congressman Smith's amendment was a "joke," calculated to bring about the defeat of the entire Civil Rights Act. "He dropped his sex amendment into the hopper just at the moment when it could exasperate his opponents the most, then leaned back, with octogenarian patience, to hear the clerk read out the pages and lines of the bill where the word 'sex' was to be inserted." But it was no joke to the nearly 30 million women and their employers who were covered by the Act. The Equal Employment Opportunities Commission (EEOC), created by Title VII of the Civil Rights Act of 1964 and originally expected to deal almost primarily with discrimination against Negroes and other minority groups, received more than one third of its complaints the first year from Representative Smith's "minority sex." For the overall period July 2, 1965, the effective date of Title VII of the Civil Rights Act of 1964, to June 30, 1969, of the more than 24,000 complaints assigned for investigation, 6,700, or 22 per cent, were based upon sexual discrimination. And during 1970, complaints by women increased 91 per cent from the previous year. The obvious importance of this is that sexual discrimination is still with us notwithstanding the Act.

The EEOC, in dealing with such complaints, has limited power; all it may do is receive and investigate complaints and informally attempt to settle them between employer and employee. Further, it may not act at all if a state Equal Employment Bureau or civil rights agency with enforcement powers has also received the complaint. In addition, the EEOC may not institute lawsuits to support its rulings. This last prohibition is not as much of a problem as it at first might seem, because Title VII of the Civil Rights Act of 1964 authorizes a successful litigant to recover reasonable attorney's fees if it is shown that the employer practices sexual or any other type of pro-

---

[10]Chapter One, "Ladies Day in the House," New York, David McKay, 1968.

hibited discrimination.[11] (Reasonable attorney's fees may, if a case is appealed, amount to many thousands of dollars.)

Two issues raised by Title VII of the Civil Rights Act of 1964 that have been most often litigated are (a) the "exception" to barring sexual or other discrimination in employment—a "bona fide occupational qualification," and (b) the conflict between the federal mandate under Title VII of the Civil Rights Act of 1964 and state labor legislation. Simply stated, this means that employers have, in fact, attempted to discriminate against women because of their sex if the employer can appear to justify the discrimination because only a man is qualified to do the particular job or some state law makes it "impossible" for him to hire a woman. Inasmuch as both problems have not yet been ultimately resolved by judicial interpretation, it is necessary to examine what the courts have decided as well as guidelines issued by the EEOC.

State labor legislation with respect to the employment of women falls into two categories: (a) maximum hour and weight limits and other protective legislation and (b) minimum wage and other benefit laws. The most important of these categories is "protective legislation" for which the EEOC has promulgated the following unequivocal current guidelines:

> Many States have enacted laws or promulgated administrative regulations with respect to the employment of females. Among these laws are those which prohibit or limit the employment of females, e.g. the employment of females in certain occupations, in jobs requiring the lifting or carrying of weights exceeding certain prescribed limits, during certain hours of the night, or for more than a specified number of hours per day or week.
>
> (2) The Commission believes that such State laws and regulations, although originally promulgated for the purpose of protecting females, have ceased to be relevant to our technology or to the expanding role of the female worker in our economy. The Commission

---

[11]The 92nd Congress in 1970 attempted to pass a bill giving the EEOC authority to issue cease-and-desist orders against discriminating employers or labor unions and to have the order reviewed by a Federal Court of Appeals, but after approval by the Senate, the bill was blocked from reaching the floor of the House by Representative William M. Colmer of Mississippi, the Chairman of the Rules Committee.

> has found that such laws and regulations do not take into account the capacities, preferences, and abilities of individual females and tend to discriminate rather than protect. Accordingly, the Commission has concluded that such laws and regulations conflict with Title VII of the Civil Rights Act of 1964 and will not be considered a defense to an otherwise established unlawful employment practice or as a basis for the application of the bona fide occupational qualification exception. (Dated August 19, 1969.)

These guidelines say that the EEOC believes state laws originally passed for the protection of female workers are no longer valid because of the present position of women in America's contemporary economy. Furthermore, these laws tend to cause discrimination against women because employers use them as reasons not to hire women, and therefore, these laws are void because they violate the Civil Rights Act of 1964.

It should be noted that the EEOC in the beginning was hesitant and unwilling to take such affirmative action. Its earliest Guidelines of December, 1965, stated that if an employee alleges she is discriminated against because of state protective legislation, all that an employer need show in defense is good faith reliance upon a state law to avoid committing an unfair employment practice. An employer could not, however, discriminate, even in good faith, because of wage and other benefit legislation. Nine months later, in September 1966, the EEOC made a decided turnabout and refused to make determinations on the merits in those cases where administrative exceptions to state labor laws were available to employers. The most recent Guidelines, as stated above, were promulgated on February 21, 1968 and last amended on August 19, 1969.

With respect to "bona fide occupational qualification" (hereafter "bfoq"), Title VII of the Civil Rights Act of 1964 states, in part:

> (e) Notwithstanding any other provision of this title, (1) it shall not be an unlawful employment practice for an employer to hire and employ employees . . . on the basis of his religion, sex, or national origin in those certain instances where religion, sex, or national origin is a bonafide occupational qualification reasonably necessary to the normal operation of that particular business or enterprise.

Interpreting the intent of the above statute, both the EEOC and the courts have "narrowly construed" the bfoq exception in reliance upon the statements of the senator who managed the bill in the United States Senate. This exception bfoq is inherent in the Sexual Discrimination Guidelines, which were issued by the EEOC originally on November 22, 1965, and later amended; EEOC policy was enunciated as follows:

> The Commission believes that the bonafide occupational qualification exception as to sex should be interpreted narrowly. Labels—"men's jobs" and "women's jobs"—tend to deny employment opportunities unnecessarily to one sex or the other.
>
> (1) The Commission will find that the following situations do not warrant the application of the bona fide occupational qualification exception:
>
> (i) The refusal to hire a woman because of her sex, based on assumptions of the comparative employment characteristics of women in general. For example, the assumption that the turnover rate among women is higher than among men.
>
> (ii) The refusal to hire an individual based on stereotyped characterizations of the sexes. Such stereotypes include, for example, that men are less capable of assembling intricate equipment; that women are less capable of aggressive salesmanship. The principle of non-discrimination requires that individuals be considered on the basis of individual capacities and not on the basis of any characteristics generally attributed to the group.
>
> (iii) The refusal to hire an individual because of the preferences of co-workers, the employer, clients or customers except as covered specifically in subparagraph (2) of this paragraph.
>
> (iv) The fact that the employer may have to provide separate facilities for a person of the opposite sex will not justify discrimination under the bona fide occupational qualification exception unless the expense would be clearly unreasonable.
>
> (2) Where it is necessary for the purpose of authenticity or genuineness, the Commission will consider sex to be a bona fide occupational qualification, e.g. an actor or actress.

Thus, the EEOC is saying that a true job qualification or bfoq that would enable an employer to hire a man rather than a woman does not exist because of comparative employment characteristics such as young married women leaving a job to have a baby, stereotypes such as that women are the "weaker sex" and not as strong as a man, the sexual preference of other workers, or the necessity of providing separate facilities such as washrooms. Among the myriad of EEOC rulings with respect to the bfoq, it has been determined that an employer cannot refuse to hire a woman as a travelling sales person because women are not aggressive enough; nor can an employer refuse to hire a woman as a clerk in factory tool crib because she would have to climb ladders, and climbing is precarious. It has also been held that a female x-ray technician cannot be denied employment simply because some women are incapable of performing the tasks required, so long as the individual involved is able to perform the said task. Furthermore, a company cannot discriminate on account of sex against individuals employed as wrappers and weighers of meat or against a truck-driver—courier guard simply because the employer is fearful of losing customers who might be dissatisfied with the performance or appearance of a woman. On the other hand, the EEOC has held that theatrical performers, washroom and locker room attendants, and even newsboys are bfoqs and therefore the employer can discriminate between men and women.

The most celebrated judicial decision in this area is *Weeks v. Southern Bell Telephone and Telegraph Co.*[12] Mrs. Lorena Weeks, an employee of Southern Bell for 19 years, sought consideration from Southern Bell for her promotion to the position of switchman at an increased salary from 78 dollars to 125 dollars per week. The job description for a switchman stated:

> Engaged in the maintenance and operation of dial central office equipment, test, power, frame, switch, and other telephone equipment, including and locating and correcting of faults; making adjustments, additions, repairs, and replacements; performing routine operation tests, etc., and working with test-desk, field, and other forces connected with central office work. Also operates and maintains including adjusting and making repairs to or replacement of, air conditioning equipment, and performing other work as assigned in accordince with local circumstances and the current needs of the business.

Southern Bell, in defending the suit, contended it had denied Mrs. Weeks the promotion because it had decided not to

---

[12]408 F2d 228, CCA5, 1967.

assign the job to any woman. Following an unsuccessful conciliation attempt between the parties, Mrs. Weeks filed suit in Federal District Court which ruled that the job of a switchman was a bfoq and therefore her employer had *not* discriminated against her. The Fifth Circuit Court of Appeals *disagreed* and reversed the decision which was in Southern Bell's favor. According to the Court:

> We think it is clear that the burden of proof must be on Southern Bell to demonstrate that this position fits within the "bona fide occupational qualification" exception. The legislative history indicates that this exception was intended to be narrowly construed. This is also the construction put on the exception by the Equal Employment Opportunity Commission. Finally, when dealing with a humanitarian remedial statute which serves an important public purpose, it has been the practice to cast the burden of proving an exception to the general policy of the statute upon the person claiming it . . .
>
> The more important question that must be decided here, however, is the extent of the showing required to satisfy that burden. In the court below, Southern Bell contended that a bona fide occupational qualification was created whenever reasonable state protective legislation prevented women from occupying certain positions.

Southern Bell had relied upon a Georgia statute (later amended), delineating the maximum weight that women may lift. The Court noted:

> Mrs. Weeks does not dispute on appeal that the position of switchman occasionally requires lifting of weights in excess of 30 pounds. She has consistently contended that the Georgia limit is unreasonably low and that the Georgia Commissioner of Labor's Rule 59 does not have the intent or effect of protecting women from hazard. She also contends that the rule is arbitrary in violation of the equal protection clause of the Fourteenth Amendment and that it is contrary to Title VII and thus in violation of the supremacy clause, article 6, clause 2 of the Constitution.

Accordingly, Mrs. Weeks won her case because the weight limit statute, relied upon by Southern Bell, unreasonably assumed that women were incapable of performing a certain task, whereas in fact it depends upon the individual involved.

Another important bfoq case is *Bowe v. Colgate-Palmolive Co.*[13] At the employer's plant in Jeffersonville, Indiana, because of the uncertainty of week-to-week jobs, a special seniority system had been used, based upon job preference, which determined assignments for the following week. Two separate lists for men and for women were maintained, but women could not elect jobs which required lifting more than 35 pounds of weight. Obviously the women objected, claiming they were being discriminated against because of their sex. In defending the claim, Colgate-Palmolive alleged that an Indiana law specifically limited the weight that a woman could lift, and that they were merely avoiding violation of this state statue. The lower federal court agreed, but the appellate court did not agree because, as Circuit Judge Kerner expressed it, the lower court "succumbed to the erroneous argument that state laws setting weight-lifting restrictions on women were not affected by Title VII." Judge Kerner ruled that the federal legislation controlled here the applicable state law. After quoting the EEOC Guidelines, he noted:

> If anything is certain in this controversial area, it is that there is no general agreement as to what is a maximum permissible weight which can be safely lifted by women in the course of their employment. The states which have limits vary considerably. Most of the state limits were enacted many years ago and most, if not all, would be considered clearly unreasonable in light of the average physical development, strength and stamina of most modern American women who participate in the industrial work force. Almost all state limits are below the 33 to 44.1 pounds recommended by an investigatory committee of the International Labor Organization (I.L.O.) in March, 1964.
>
> . . . We agree with the Secretary of Labor insofar as he stated that it is best to consider individual qualifications and conditions, such as the physical capability and physiological makeup of an individual, climatic conditions, and the manner in which the weight is to be lifted.

However, rather than finding an unfair employment practice and ordering the opening of all jobs to women at the Colgate-Palmolive plant, the Court took a more pragmatic approach:

---

[13]416 F2d 711, CCA5, 1969.

> There is a significant difference in job requirements which must be considered just as carefully as the physiological capabilities of individual employees. Thus there are probably very few plant workers (male or female) who could not lift a 38-pound case with a handle and move it 10 feet once during a shift. If, however, the case had to be moved further, or more frequently, or lifted to a shoulder-height shelf, the degree of exertion is increased and the number of those capable of performing it is diminished.
>
> Accordingly, we hold that Colgate may, if it so desires, retain its 35-pound weight-lifting limit as a general guideline for all of its employees, male and female. However, it must notify all of its workers that each of them who desires to do so will be afforded a reasonable opportunity to demonstrate his or her ability to perform strenuous jobs on a regular basis. Each employee who is able to so demonstrate must be permitted to bid on and fill any position to which his or her seniority may entitle him or her. On remand, the court shall study the problem together with the parties and devise and adopt a system which will afford this opportunity to each employee desiring it.

In the area of *maximum hours,* perhaps the leading decision is *Rosenfeld v. Southern Pacific Co.,*[14] where a female employee who had worked for the railroad since 1944 sought promotion to the position of agent-telegrapher. She had seniority for the job, but a male worker was given the post because, according to the Southern Pacific, employment of a woman as an agent-telegrapher would violate the California Labor Code with regard to the maximum hours per day and per week that females were permitted to work. The federal court refused to accept this argument.

> The California hours and weights legislation does not create or constitute a bona fide occupational qualification . . . discrimination against women on account of sex . . . [and] violates the provisions of the Civil Rights Act of 1964. Accordingly, such legislation is contrary to the Supremacy Clause (Article VI, Clause 2) of the United States Constitution and therefore is void and of no force or effect.

The Court thus held that the Civil Rights Act of 1964 preempts all state legislation in the area of female employment. Judge Ferguson in closing, averred: "The effect of the California hours

---

[14]293 F. Supp. 1219, USDC Cal., 1968.

and weights legislation is to subject women to discrimination and such legislation establishes standards which are 'unreasonably low' within the meaning of the Equal Employment Opportunity Commission's 'Guidelines On Discrimination Because of Sex.'"[15]

Most recently, in 1970, in *Caterpillar Tractor Co. v. Grubiec,*[16] the employer contended that he could not promote a female employee or assign them an equal number of overtime hours as men because the Illinois Female Employment Act restricted a woman's hours to 48 per week and 8 hours per day, except for one day a week that she might work 9 hours. The federal court reminded the employer that the Illinois State Act is not a bfoq because it conflicts with Title VII of the Civil Rights Act of 1964 and is void as to the female employees because of the "supremacy" of the Federal law.

Although the area of female employee benefits has not received as much attention from the courts as state protective legislation, this paucity is perhaps more significant of the fact that there is little legislation rather than fewer problems.

One representative case was decided in California in 1968 in *Rivera v. Division of Industrial Welfare*[17] where the Court unfortunately lumped benefit legislation together with protective statutes. There, a female agricultural worker alleged that the agricultural organization which generally employed her refused to hire women for a specific job since males could be hired at a lower salary because the California Minimum Wage Law was higher for women than for men. The Court, in refusing to find sexual discrimination because of this benefit law, notwithstanding the EEOC Guidelines, unenlighteningly stated: "State regulation of wages, hours and working conditions, particularly affecting women and minors, has been such a widely and long established feature of American life that this argument comes

---

[15]On June 5, 1971, the *New York Times* reported that the 9th Circuit Court of Appeals in a 2-1 decision affirmed this ruling of Judge Ferguson's invalidating all California protective legislation with respect to women as being in violation of the Civil Rights Act of 1964.

[16]39 Law Week 2152, USDC Ill., 1970.

[17]265 C. App. 2d 576, 71 Cal. Rptr. 739, 3rd Dist.

as a distinct surprise. Doubtless it would arouse equal surprise in the halls of the federal Congress." It should be noted that in an identical situation, the EEOC issued an opinion letter calling such failure to hire females because a state minimum wage was higher for women than men an unfair employment practice.[18]

Another example of a benefit law constituting sexual discrimination is the requirement of separate facilities for women, such as lockers or washrooms. In 1969, the only Coast-Guard–certified female ship's purser was unable to obtain employment with the Merchant Marine and complained to the EEOC claiming sexual discrimination. The ship owners, in defense, claimed that since legislation and Coast Guard rules required separate shower and toilet facilities for women, and inasmuch as many ships did not have them, they had not practiced sexual discrimination. The Commission disagreed, stating that a purser is a ship's officer and an officer is generally entitled to a private room and bath in any event and that the ship owners' reliance upon the "benefit" law requiring separate facilities was a subterfuge and an unfair employment practice.

Title VII of the Civil Rights Act of 1964 received its first judicial scrutiny by the United States Supreme Court in respect to an allegation of sexual discrimination on January 25, 1971, when the Court handed down its decision in *Phillips v. Martin-Marietta Corp.*[19] Although the Court merely remanded the case back to the trial court "for fuller development of the record" and thus did not definitively decide any of the issues previously discussed, it is an early indication of the United States Supreme Court's approach to the bona fide occupational qualification exception. In 1966, Mrs. Ida Phillips, a mother with preschool age children, sought employment as an assembly trainee with Martin-Marietta. The corporation, however, informed Mrs. Phillips that they had a policy of not accepting job applications from women with preschool children. Mrs. Phillips then filed suit in

---

[18]The EEOC did not rule, however, whether or not the higher wage for women was in fact sexual discrimination against men!

[19]39 Law Week 4160, 1971.

Federal District Court alleging violation of Title VII of the Civil Rights Act of 1964 because of sexual discrimination. Martin-Marietta moved for summary judgment[20] and the trial court dismissed Mrs. Phillips' action. Among other information the lower court considered in making this decision was the fact that between 75 and 80 percent of all individuals hired as assembly trainees were women. It also noted that Martin-Marietta did not refuse to accept job applications from men who had preschool-age children. On appeal the Fifth Circuit Court of Appeals affirmed the Federal District Court but the United States Supreme Court disagreed. In a *per curiam* opinion, it vacated the granting of summary judgment by noting:

> Section 703(a) of the Civil Rights Act of 1964 requires that persons of like qualifications be given employment opportunities irrespective of their sex. The Court of Appeals therefore erred in reading this section as permitting one hiring policy for women and another for men—each having preschool-age children. The existence of such conflicting family obligations, if demonstrably more relevant to job performance for a woman than for a man, could arguably be a basis for distinction under §703(e) of the Act. But that is a matter of evidence tending to show that the condition in question "is a bona fide occupational qualification reasonably necessary to the normal operation of that particular business or enterprise." The record, however, is not adequate for resolution of these important issues . . . . Summary judgment was therefore improper and we remand for fuller development of the record and for further consideration.

Thus the Court was saying that it could not decide the issues on the facts presented because the determination of whether or not having preschool children is an obligation, the existence of which would create a bfoq, requires a careful evaluation of all the surrounding facts and circumstances.

In a concurring opinion, Justice Thurgood Marshall disagreed with the majority view that sufficient facts could possibly demonstrate that not having preschool-age children would be a bfoq for a woman and not for a man. The Justice remarked:

---

[20]A motion made early in an action where one party seeks to avoid a trial by having a judge decide if there are sufficient issues to be decided by a jury.

> I fear that in this case, where the issue is not squarely before us, the Court has fallen into the trap of assuming that the Act permits ancient canards about the proper role of women to be a basis for discrimination. Congress, however, sought just the opposite result.

Marshall then goes on to discuss many of the cases mentioned previously in this chapter, as well as the complete EEOC Guidelines respecting the "bfoq." He went to to state:

> That exception has been construed by the Equal Employment Opportunity Commission, whose regulations are entitled to 'great deference,' . . . to be applicable only to job situations that require specific physical characteristics necessarily possessed by only one sex. Thus the exception would apply where necessary 'for the purposes of authenticity or genuineness' in the employment of actors or actresses, fashion models, and the like. If the exception is to be limited as Congress intended, the Commission has given it the only possible construction.
>
> When performance characteristics of an individual are involved, even when parental roles are concerned, employment opportunity may be limited only by employment criteria that are neutral as to the sex of the applicant.

In essence, Justice Marshall believes that no matter what facts can be brought out, a bfoq cannot be created because a bfoq can only exist, with certain exceptions, when it can be applied *equally* to both sexes. In this case, he feels that a bfoq can only exist if it applies to both men and women who have preschool-age children.

The struggle for equal employment opportunities for women, however, is only first gathering steam. In the years to come, the foundation established by the Women's Liberationists of the 1960's and early 1970's through the Equal Pay Act of 1963 and the Civil Rights Act of 1964, and the jurisdictional as well as administrative interpretations of these acts, will unquestionably succeed in enabling the female to achieve a more equal partnership with the male in the heated competition of the economic sphere.

QUESTIONS FOR REVIEW

1. Discuss the history of employment of women in the United States.

2. What was the legal basis for the lowly position of women in the United States in the late Eighteenth and early Nineteenth centuries?
3. How did the *Bradley* case reaffirm the bar to women in the legal profession?
4. What reasoning did the United States Supreme Court employ in affirming maximum hour laws in the *Miller* case?
5. How does the United States Supreme Court's opinion in the *Adkins* case summarize the view of the feminists of the 1970's, and why was it considered reprehensible to the feminists of the 1920's?
6. Discuss the history of the equal pay laws for women until the Act of 1963.
7. What are the essential terms of the Equal Pay Act of 1963?
8. How did the "establishment" loophole undermine the impact of the Act of 1963 and how did the courts deal with this loophole?
9. What were the circumstances of the addition of the "sex" discrimination provision to Title VII of the Civil Rights Act of 1964?
10. What is the Equal Employment Opportunity Commission and what are its duties and powers?
11. What is the nature of state protective employment legislation for women and what are the EEOC guidelines with respect thereto?
12. What is a "bona fide occupational qualification" and what are the EEOC guidelines with respect thereto?
13. Give examples of what is and what is not considered a bfoq.
14. Why was Mrs. Weeks originally denied equal employment opportunity, and what reasoning did the court use in finding sexual discrimination?
15. What approach did the court in the *Bowe* case take with respect to sexual discrimination?
16. Why may a law providing for the maximum hours a week a woman may work be discriminatory, and what view have the courts taken with respect to such law?

Chapter 3

RADIO AND TELEVISION: GOVERNMENTAL REGULATION OF MEDIA PROGRAMMING

TODAY, RADIO AND television are practically indispensable, unavoidable, and indelible parts of American life. Yet, whatever the listener's or viewer's tastes are with respect to programming, he is permitted no control (except very indirectly) over the radio and television shows which are presented for his listening and viewing pleasure. Programming is controlled by the broadcasting and telecasting industries with only limited "outside" guidance from other sources, such as from commercial sponsors, industry-wide standards, or politically oriented pressure groups. However, the principal source of "outside" guidance in respect to the programming that a station airs derives from federal regulation under the Communications Act of 1934 and the rules and regulations of the Federal Communications Commission (FCC).

This Act, which is a broad, all-encompassing body of laws and has essentially remained unchanged since its enactment, stated in Section 301 the following purpose:

> . . . to maintain the control of the United States over all the the channels of interstate and foreign radio transmission; and to provide for the use of such channels, but not the ownership thereof, by persons for limited periods of time, under licenses granted by Federal authority, and no such license shall be construed to create any right, beyond the terms, conditions, and periods of the license.

Thus the Federal Government was entitled to exercise the exclusive right of regulation and control over the electronic media and to grant licenses to stations for limited periods of time for the transmission of programming. The Act also provided for the establishment of the Federal Communications Commission to "police" the airways and, among other things, to "prescribe the nature of the service to be rendered by each class of licensed stations and each station within any class." The Federal Communications Commission must, in addition, "Make such rules and regulations and prescribe such restrictions and conditions, not inconsistent with law, as may be necessary to carry out the provisions of this Chapter." The only *caveat* or guideline which the Act placed upon the FCC was that it must operate, just as all station licenses must operate, as the "public convenience, interest, or necessity shall require."

Shortly before the passage of this Act in 1931, a federal court found that radio station KFKB in Milford, Kansas, had violated the "public interest" guidelines in the Act of 1927 (which were the same as those in the 1934 Act) and accordingly lost its license to operate. This decision, *KFKB Broadcasting Ass'n. v. Federal Radio Commission,*[1] also marked the first time that a court had approved the authority of the then fledgling Federal Radio Commission (predecessor to the Federal Communications Commission) to revoke a station's license because of the station's failure in its programming to meet the lofty standards of the "public interest" guidelines. A typical program that had been broadcast over KFKB, prior to 1931, sounded like the following:

> Here's one from Tillie. She says she had an operation, had some trouble ten years ago. I think the operation was unnecessary, and it isn't very good sense to have an ovary removed with the expectation of motherhood resulting therefrom. My advice to you is to use Women's Tonic No. 50, 67, and 61. This combination will do for you what you desire, if any combination will, after three months' persistent use.

Dr. J. R. Brinkley, a physician in this small Kansas town, and the owner (as well as leading personality) of radio station KFKB, had sought to entertain his radio audience with these words. The Federal Radio Commission refused renewal of his station's license because it believed that the "operation . . . is conducted only in the personal interest of Dr. John R. Brink-

---

[1]47F2d 671, CCADC, 1931.

ley." The Federal Radio Commission based its decision upon Dr. Brinkley's own three half-hour daily programs, the "medical question box," whose format was quite simple. While on-the-air, Dr. Brinkley read letters from suffering listeners, describing the nature and symptoms of their ailments, and then went on to prescribe by number medicines which would allegedly cure the "patient's" ills. Another example of his medical dissertations sounded like this: "Sunflower State, from Dresden, Kansas. Probably he has gallstones. No, I don't mean that, I mean kidney stones. My advice to you is to put him on Prescription No. 80 and 50 for men, also 64. I think that he will be a whole lot better. Also drink a lot of water." These numbered prescriptions, however, were only available from druggists who were members of the Brinkley Pharmaceutical Association which had been established by the "radio doctor." The BPA member paid a fee to the radio station, KFKB, ostensibly for advertising purposes, for each prescription it filled for members of the public. In affirming the Federal Radio Commission's decision denying renewal, the Federal Circuit Court of Appeals[2] agreed that KFKB did not serve "the public interest, convenience and necessity." Furthermore, the court held that the Federal Radio Commission in fact had the discretionary authority to deny license renewals.

> Congress has imposed upon the Commission the administrative function of determining whether or not a station license should be renewed, and the Commission in the present case has in the exercise of judgment and discretion ruled against the applicant. We are asked upon the record and evidence before the Commission to substitute our judgment and discretion for that of the Commission. While section 16 of the Radio Act of 1927 . . . authorized an appeal to this court, we do not think it was the intent of Congress that we should disturb the action of the Commission in a case like the present.

In its defense, radio station KFKB attempted to assert that the Federal Radio Commission exceeded its authority by "censoring" a broadcaster's programming in violation of the Radio Act of 1927, but the Court found otherwise:

---

[2]47 F2d 671, CCADC, 1931.

> This contention [of censorship] is without merit. There has been no attempt on the part of the commission to subject any part of appellant's broadcasting matter to scrutiny prior to its release. In considering the question whether the public interest, convenience, or necessity will be served by a renewal of appellant's license, the Commission has merely exercised its undoubted right to take note of appellant's past conduct, which is not censorship.

The Federal Government did not always have the power to regulate the licensing of radio broadcasting. It received full discretionary authority by statute only after the airways had become "a tangled mass of indistinguishable babble." The first piece of legislation, the Wireless Ship Act of 1910, required all United States flagships and foreign steamers using American ports to have radio communications. Shortly thereafter, the Radio Act of 1912 was passed; this statute was rather ineffective and designed to control the then unknown electronic medium by empowering the United States Secretary of Commerce to license the few transmitting stations, other than those stations involved in governmental, military, or police functions, which the Secretary also regulated. But in 1920, a commercial radio station, KDKA in Pittsburgh, Pennsylvania, broadcast the results of the Harding-Cox presidential election. For the first time, many people began to realize the educational, economic, informational, and persuasional potential of radio. Notwithstanding, only 30 stations had been licensed by the United States Secretary of Commerce as of January 1, 1922. Within the next fifteen months, however, more than 550 radio stations were broadcasting, and the airways soon became an area of chaos. Radio stations chose whatever wave lengths they desired, even though the United States Secretary of Commerce had only licensed them for a single frequency. They broadcast at whatever hours and at whatever power they wished. Clearly, federal action was necessary, and Secretary of Commerce Herbert Hoover sought to use what he considered his discretionary authority to alleviate the problem when he refused to renew the licenses of transgressors. Some stations would not abide by this ruling and took the case to court. In the landmark decisions of *Hoover v. Intercity Radio*

Co.[3] and *U.S. v. Zenith Radio Corp.*,[4] the courts found that the United States Commerce Secretary's only authority was to issue licenses for a specific "frequency" in the first instance, and his discretion was limited to the "frequency" which he chose. Future President Hoover then asked the advice of the acting Attorney General, William J. Donovan, who stated in an Official Opinion Letter that the Radio Act of 1912 (under which authority Hoover was acting) required a radio station to obtain a license, and failure to do so was an offense. But the Secretary of Commerce had no discretion other than to determine normal wavelength; he could not fix times of broadcasting nor the power at which the station operated. Attorney General Donovan further suggested that legislation be passed to ameliorate the deteriorating situation which might put a damper on the uncontrolled growth of radio stations.

Congress then passed the Radio Act of 1927, creating a Federal Radio Commission to bring order to the airways by eliminating not only those stations that the radio spectrum could not accommodate but also by minimizing electronic interference. Although the Act contained no precise guidelines as to how the Federal Radio Commission should select those stations to be licensed, the legislative history reflects certain misgivings and fears that the Congressmen entertained. For example, there was a fear that there would be a concentration of electrically powerful transmitters in the East and in urban areas which would all but eliminate signals from local and rural stations throughout the country. For this reason, the Act had a provision that licensees must be geographically situated on the basis of a "fair, efficient and equitable distribution" (vague standards to be sure). Congress was also concerned with the growth of monopolies among radio broadcasters and therefore included limitations with respect to common ownership of stations. (This was later amended to allow formation of networks.) Congress did not, however, express any opinion as to the type of programming that a licensee

---

[3]286 Fed. 1003, CCADC, 1923.

[4]12 F2d 614, DCND Ill., 1926.

had to offer, although there were some suggestions as to religious, educational, or news formats. Congress simply and succinctly summed up the programming aspect by stating that a station had to maintain an attitude of "public interest, convenience and necessity." It is this language of this guideline phrase which federal regulatory agencies have used to control the licensing of radio, and later, television, stations.

One illustration of a situation in which the Federal Radio Commission believed that a radio station had failed to live up to the "public interest" was *Trinity Methodist Church, South v. Federal Radio Commission.*[5] (The same Court had rendered the decision in the *KFKB* case, above.) Here the Court approved the denial of the renewal of the station's license because the programming of station KGEE had been used by its "silent" owner, Reverend Doctor Shuler, as a means of expressing his admittedly bigoted and perverse views. Rev. Dr. Shuler had broadcast various programs, often in a sensational manner, reviling the trial courts of the State of California and the Roman Catholic Church, *inter alia.* The Court affirmed the power of the Federal Radio Commission to deny the radio license to this station which aired defamatory and knowingly untrue information.

> The evidence abundantly sustains the conclusion of the Commission that the continuance of the broadcasting programs of appellant is not in the public interest. . . . Appellant, not satisfied with attacking the judges of the courts in cases then pending before them attacked the bar association for its activities in recommending judges, charging it with ulterior and sinister purposes. With no more justification, he charged particular judges with sundry immoral acts. He made defamatory statements against the board of health. He charged that the labor temple in Los Angeles was a bootlegging and gambling joint. In none of these matters, when called on to explain or justify his statements, was he able to do more than declare that the statements expressed his own sentiments. On one occasion he announced over the radio that he had certain damaging information against a prominent unnamed man which, unless a contribution (presumably to the church) of a hundred dollars was forthcoming, he would disclose. As a result, he received contributions from several persons. He freely spoke of "pimps" and prostitutes. He alluded slightly to the Jews as a

---

[5]62 F2d 850, CCADC, 1932.

> a race, and made frequent and bitter attacks on the Roman Catholic religion and its relations to government. However inspired by Dr. Shuler may have been by what he regarded as patriotic zeal, however sincere in denouncing conditions he did not approve, it is manifest, we think, that it is not narrowing the ordinary conception of 'public interest' in declaring his broadcasts—without facts to sustain or to justify them—not within that term, and since that is the test the Commission is required to apply, we think it was its duty in considering the application for renewal to take notice of appellant's conduct in his previous use of the permit, and in the circumstances, the refusal, we think, was neither arbitrary nor capricious.

The Federal Court believed that it was the duty of the Federal Radio Commission to apply the "public convenience, interest, and necessity" guidelines to *all* programming, prior to granting renewal of a station's license, and that the broadcasting of defamatory, scurrilous, and baseless information was unquestionably not within the meaning of the "guideline," regardless of the avowed good intentions of the station's management.

Two years after the decision in the *Trinity* case, Congress, in order to synthesize the law of electronic broadcasting, passed the seminal Communications Act of 1934. Although essentially similar to the Radio Act of 1927, from which many sections and phrases, including "public convenience, interest, and necessity," were taken *in toto,* this Act is today the basic law in the field of broadcasting and telecasting, and the fount from which the authority of the Federal Communications Commission to regulate the radio-television industry springs. The Act's principal precepts include the following:

1. Exclusive regulatory control is given to the Federal Government (unlike many other, sweeping regulatory laws such as the Food, Drug, and Cosmetic Act, Federal Trade Commission Act, and the Internal Revenue Act), and the states may not, in any way, promulgate laws affecting radio and television. This exclusivity principle was reaffirmed in *Allen B. Dumont Labs. v. Carroll*[6] when the Federal Circuit Court of Appeals struck down a Pennsylvania state law requiring television films

---

[6]184 F2d 153, CCA3, 1950.

to be submitted to a state censor prior to release. The Court stated: "The language employed [in the Act] is so all-inclusive as to leave no doubt but that it was the intention of Congress to occupy the television broadcasting field in its entirety."

2. "Grandfather" rights, such as a "right" to continue broadcasting on a given "frequency," are outlawed, in that no preferences to licenses who were broadcasting at the time of the law's enactment in 1934 are given. (This was an abrupt departure from most of the regulatory statutes enacted during this period which favored the older companies who had operated under the older statutes). Section 304 states: "No station license shall be granted by the Commission until the applicant therefor shall have signed a waiver of any claim to the use of any particular frequency or of the ether as against the regulatory power of the United States because of the previous use of the same, whether by license or otherwise."

3. The Federal Communications Commission created by the Act is given a broad spectrum of powers and duties with respect to broadcasting and telecasting, including station classification, prescription of the nature of service to be given, assignment of frequencies, station locations and zones of transmission, regulation of equipment and prevention of interference, network regulation, license revocation, and the right to issue rules and regulations to carry out the Act. The details are set forth in Section 303 which states, in part:

> Except as otherwise provided in this chapter, the Commission from time to time, as public convenience, interest, or necessity requires, shall–
>
> (a) Classify radio stations;
>
> (b) Prescribe the nature of the service to be rendered by each class of licensed stations and each station within any class;
>
> (c) Assign bands of frequencies to the various classes of stations, and assign frequencies for each individual station and determine the power which each station shall use and the time during which it may operate;
>
> (d) Determine the location of classes of stations or individual stations;
>
> (e) Regulate the kind of apparatus to be used with respect to its external effects and the purity and sharpness of the emissions from each station and from the apparatus therein;

(f) Make such regulations not inconsistent with law as it may deem necessary to prevent interference between stations and to carry out the provisions of this chapter: *Provided, however,* That changes in the frequencies, authorized power, or in the times of operation of any station, shall not be made without the consent of the station licensee unless, after a public hearing, the Commission shall determine that such changes will promote public convenience or interest or will serve public necessity, or the provisions of this chapter will be more fully complied with;

(g) Study new uses for radio, provide for experimental uses of frequencies, and generally encourage the larger and more effective use of radio in the public interest;

(h) Have authority to establish areas or zones to be served by any station;

(i) Have authority to make special regulations applicable to radio stations engaged in chain broadcasting;

(j) Have authority to make general rules and regulations requiring stations to keep such records of programs, transmissions of energy, communications, or signals as it may deem desirable; . . .

(l) (1) Have authority to prescribe the qualifications of station operators . . .

(m) (1) Have authority to suspend the license of any operator upon proof sufficient to satisfy the Commission that the licensee—

(A) has violated any provision of any Act, treaty, or convention binding on the United States, which the Commission is authorized to administer, or any regulation made by the Commission under any such Act, treaty, or convention; or . . .

(D) has transmitted superfluous radio communications or signals or communications containing profane or obscene words, language, or meaning, or has knowingly transmitted—

(1) false or deceptive signals or communications, or . . .

(E) has willfully or maliciously interfered with any other radio communications or signals; . . .

(n) Have authority to inspect all radio installations associated with stations required to be licensed by any Act . . .

(o) Have authority to designate call letters of all stations;

(p) Have authority to cause to be published such call letters and such other announcements and data as in the judgment of the Commission may be required for the efficient operation of radio stations subject to the jurisdiction of the United States and for the proper enforcement of this chapter; . . .

(r) Make such rules and regulations and prescribe such restrictions and conditions, not inconsistent with law, as may be necessary to carry out the provisions of this chapter, or any international radio or wire communications treaty or convention, or regulations annexed thereto, including any treaty or convention insofar as it relates to the use of radio, to which the United States is or may hereafter become a party;

(s) Have authority to require that apparatus designed to receive television pictures broadcast simultaneously with sound be capable of adequately receiving all frequencies allocated by the Commission to television broadcasting when such apparatus is shipped in interstate commerce; or is imported from any foreign country into the United States, for sale or resale to the public.

Three years is designated as the duration of station licenses, and such stations must be equitably distributed throughout the nation. The prescription of qualifications for such license issuance is set forth in section 307 (a-d) and section 308 (b), which, in part, state:

§307.

(a) The Commission, if public convenience, interest, or necessity will be served thereby, subject to the limitations of this chapter, shall grant to any applicant therefor a station license provided for by this chapter.

(b) In considering applications for licenses, and modifications and renewals thereof, when and insofar as there is demand for the same, the Commission shall make such distribution of licenses, frequencies, hours of operation, and of power among the several States and communities as to provide a fair, efficient, and equitable distribution of radio service to each of the same. . . .

(d) No license granted for the operation of a broadcasting station shall be for a longer term than three years and no license so granted for any other class of station shall be for a longer term than five years, and any license granted may be revoked as hereinafter provided.

§308.

(b) All applications for station licenses, or modifications or renewals thereof, shall set forth such facts as the Commission by regulation may prescribe as to the citizenship, character, and financial, technical, and other qualifications of the applicant to operate the station; the ownership and location of the proposed station and of the stations, if any, with which it is proposed to communicate; the frequencies and the power desired to be used; the hours of the day or other periods of time during which it is proposed to operate the station; the purposes for which the station is to be used; and such other information as it may require.

The regulation of the programming of the station licensee, however, is not based upon any express statutory provision in the Communications Act of 1934 but rather upon the phrase in the Act that the Federal Communications Commission must regulate licenses in the "public interest, convenience or necessity." While the two cases discussed above, radio station *KFKB* and *Trinity Methodist Church, South,* both involved the Federal Radio Commission's efforts to deny license renewal to broadcasters who fail to operate in the "public interest," the Federal Communications Commission, as the successor agency to the Federal Radio Commission, failed for nearly 12 years to follow the latter's active and militant lead. During this period of ineffectual enforcement, the Federal Communications Commission did occasionally order hearings to be held, but the most stringent penalty the agency proscribed was either delaying license renewal until the station represented to the Federal Communications Commission that it would change its policies with respect to programming or granting "temporary" license renewals for periods of less than the statutory three years. Obviously the Federal Communications Commission was simply not exercising its authority.

After World War II, however, the Federal Communications Commission did a turnabout and issued a series of programming principles which would supplement the "public interest" guidelines, called "Public Service Responsibility of Broadcast Licensee" or, as it was generally known, "The Blue Book." Herein the Federal Communications Commission noted that the licensee had a primary responsibility for programming service, and it affirmed its own statutory duty to make absolutely certain that station licensees were themselves actually fulfilling the intent of the Communications Act of 1934. The Federal Communications Commission went on to state that it would give consideration to four factors in the granting of license renewals, to wit:

1. The broadcast of sustaining programs designed to maintain a balanced structure.
2. Use of local live talent on shows.

3. Coverage of important public events.
4. Elimination of excess advertising (some stations had more commercial than noncommercial air time).

Of the four factors, the most important was the first factor, and in elaborating upon its importance, the "Blue Book" stated:

> Since the early days of broadcasting, broadcasters and the Commission alike have recognized that *sustaining* programs also play an integral and irreplaceable part in the American system of broadcasting. The sustaining program has five distinctive and outstanding functions.
>
> 1. To secure for the station or network a means by which, in the overall structure of its program service, it can achieve a *balanced* interpretation of public needs.
> 2. To provide programs which by their very nature may not be sponsored with propriety.
> 3. To provide programs for significant minority tastes and interests.
> 4. To provide programs devoted to the needs and purposes of nonprofit organizations.
> 5. To provide a field for experiment in new types of programs, secure from the restrictions that obtain with reference to programs in which the advertiser's interest in selling good predominates." (Emphasis added.)

Thus, sustaining programming should be (a) balanced, i.e., offer "words" from all parts of the entertainment, educational, and informational spectrum, (b) free of commercials, if possible, (c) of interest to varying racial, ethnic, and religious groups, (d) a forum for charitable, educational, and other noncommercial institutions, and (e) free to develop into new unrestricted areas of endeavor.

The Federal Communications Commission, however, was as lax in effectively enforcing these newly promulgated principles as it was in the late 1930's and early 1940's. It continued to renew the licenses of stations, notwithstanding the nature of their programming. A few licenses were revoked, but these did not involve programming deficiencies or failure to operate in the "public interest." The conducting of illegal lotteries, the airing of a continued spate of obscenities, or the engaging in fraudulent advertising were the only bases for license revocation. In 1960, however, 14 years after the issuance of the "Blue

Book," the Federal Communications Commission published a new set of principles to guide radio and TV stations in establishing programming policies, to-wit: "Report and Statement of Policy re: Commission En Banc Programming Inquiry." This policy pronouncement was far less ambiguous in scope and far more succinct in detail than the "Blue Book." Nevertheless, it was more amenable to enforcement, for its basic proposition was that the station, on the one hand, has a constitutional guarantee of free speech and free press but still was a mere "steward" of its broadcast or telecast frequency and operated under statutory aegis which required governmental supervision and overseeing. The Federal Communications Commission, on the other hand, which had no existence outside of the statutory authority of the Communications Act of 1934, had to enforce its edicts and continue to maintain the respect for the constitutional rights of the stations. In this latter constitutional regard, the "Report and Statement of Policy re: Commission En Banc Programming Inquiry" stated:

> In view of the fact that a broadcaster is required to program his station in the public interest, convenience and necessity, it follows despite the limitations of the First Amendment and Section 326 of the Act [prohibiting the FCC from censoring broadcasts], that his freedom to program is not absolute. The Commission does not conceive that it is barred by the Constitution or by statute from exercising any responsibility with respect to programming. It does conceive that the manner or extent of the exercise of such responsibility can introduce constitutional or statutory questions. It readily concedes that it is precluded from examining a program for taste or content, unless the recognized exceptions to censorship apply: for example, obscenity, profanity, indecency, programs inciting to riots, programs designed or inducing toward the commission of crime, lotteries, etc. These exceptions, in part, are written into the United States Code and, in part, are recognized in judicial decisions. . . .

The Federal Communications Commission believed that there was neither absolute statutory nor absolute constitutional prohibition of its programming responsibility. But in the absence of illegality, it could not examine a program's actual content:

> A review of the Communications Act as a whole clearly reveals that the foundation of the Commission's authority rests upon

the public interest, convenience and necessity. The Commission may not grant, modify or renew a broadcast station license without finding that the operation of such station is in the public interest. Thus, faithful discharge of its statutory responsibilities is absolutely necessary in connection with the implacable requirement that the Commission approve no such application for license unless it finds that 'public interest, convenience, and necessity would be served.' While the public interest standard does not provide a blueprint of all of the situations to which it may apply, it does contain a sufficiently precise definition of authority so as to enable the Commission to properly deal with the many and varied occasions which may give rise to its application.

The "Report and Statement of Policy re: Commission En Banc Programming Inquiry" also stated that it was the licensee who must assume responsibility for everything broadcast over its frequencies or facilities:

> This duty is personal to the licensee and may not be delegated. He is obligated to bring his positive responsibility affirmatively to bear upon all who have a hand in providing broadcast matter for transmission through his facilities so as to assure the discharge of his duty to provide acceptable program schedule consonant with operating in the public interest in his community. The broadcaster is obligated to make a positive, diligent and continuing effort, in good faith, to determine the tastes, needs and desires of the public in his community and to provide programming to meet those needs and interests. This, again, is a duty personal to the licensee and may not be avoided by delegation of the responsibility to others.

The Federal Communications Commission, in essence, stated that a station could not "pass the buck" for subpar programming by blaming a network or production crew or sponsors. The broadcaster licensee himself had an affirmative responsibility to make sure that his station was operating within the principles of the "publc interest" guideline. More important, however, was the Federal Communications Commission's statement as to the major elements of programming necessary to meet the "public convenience, interest and necessity," which it delineated as 14 separate items.

(1) Opportunity for Local Self-Expression,
(2) The Development and Use of Local Talent,
(3) Programs for Children,

(4) Religious Programs,
(5) Educational Programs,
(6) Public Affairs Programs,
(7) Editorialization by Licensees,
(8) Political Broadcasts,
(9) Agricultural Programs,
(10) News Programs,
(11) Weather and Market Reports,
(12) Sports Programs,
(13) Service to Minority Groups,
(14) Entertainment Programming.

Indeed, the Federal Communications Commission noted that these fourteen elements were neither "all-embracing nor constant," but the FCC

> re-emphasized that they do not serve and have never been intended as a rigid mold or fixed formula for station operations. The ascertainment of the needed elements of the broadcast matter to be provided by a particular licensee for the audience he is obligated to serve remains primarily the function of the licensee. His honest and prudent judgments will be accorded great weight by the Commission. Indeed, any other course would tend to substitute the judgment of the Commission for that of the licensee.

One year after the issuance of the "Report and Statement of Policy re: Commission En Banc Programming Inquiry," the Chairman of the Federal Communications Commission, Mr. Newton N. Minow, author of the ennobled phrase, "television is a vast wasteland," spoke at Northwestern University School of Law in Chicago and noted that the FCC had gone one step beyond its 1960 policy statement:

> On July 13, 1961, we informed every broadcaster of a *change* in the Commission's renewal policy. In the past we granted renewals even though there had been a substantial failure to live up to the programming representations, where the applicant 'upgraded' his proposals and gave reliable assurances that these new proposals would be carried out. This will no longer be the case. We have put our licensees on notice that 'proposals versus actual operation' is of vital concern to the Commission, that licensees are not entitled to one or any license period where they do not have to make good-faith effort to deliver on their public service proposals and that if they have not been endeavoring in good faith to discharge their representations, they should take *immediate* steps to do so.

Thus, in effect, the Federal Communications Commission informed station licensees that their programming would be closely scrutinized and their past representations as to broadcasting and telecasting would be made in good faith to conform to the standard of the "public convenience, interest, and necessity".

In 1962, the courts had an opportunity to examine the Federal Communications Commission's recently promulgated programming policies in the case of *Henry v. FCC.*[7] Here Suburban Broadcasters sought to obtain a license for an FM radio station in Elizabeth, New Jersey, which is within the New York City metropolitan area. After Suburban Broadcasters announced their intention, the Metropolitan Broadcasting Company, which had a license to operate New York City's AM and FM radio station, WNEW, objected to the issuance of the Elizabeth license and requested the FCC to hold a hearing "to determine whether the program proposals of Suburban Broadcasters are designed to and would be expected to serve the needs of the proposed service area." The trial examiner for the FCC found in favor of Suburban Broadcasters, but the FCC, on appeal, *reversed,* favoring Metropolitan Broadcasting Company. Thereupon Suburban Broadcasters appealed to the Federal Circuit Court of Appeals for the District of Columbia. This Court upon reviewing the facts, found that Suburban Broadcasters had no Elizabeth, New Jersey residents as principals, had made no inquiries into the programming needs of the community, and had submitted programming proposals that were identical to those of other stations owned by the same principals in Berwyn, Illinois, and Alameda, California. The federal court concurred with the Federal Communications Commission that a radio station must be an outlet for community self-expression and community needs: "It is not sufficient that the applicant will bring a first transmission service to the community—it must in fact provide a first local outlet for community self-expression. Communities may differ, and so may their needs; an applicant has the responsibility of ascertaining his community's needs and of programming to meet those needs." Suburban Broadcasters

---

[7] 302 F2d 191, CCADC, 1962.

defended its position on the basis of the Communications Act of 1934, which, it said, required only that a prospective licensee be legally, financially, and technically qualified. But the Circuit Court opined that "this view reflects an arbitrarily narrow understanding of the statutory words 'public convenience, interest, or necessity.' It leaves no room for Commission consideration of matters relating to programming." Furthermore:

> We think these broad contentions are beside the narrow point at issue upon this record. It may be that a licensee must have freedom to broadcast light opera even if the community likes rock and roll music, although that question is not uncomplicated. Even more complicated is the question whether he may feed a diet of rock and roll music to a community which hungers for opera. These are questions, however, that we need not here decide. As we see it, the question presented on the instant record is simply whether the Commission may require that an applicant demonstrate an earnest interest in serving a local community by evidencing a familiarity with its particular needs and an effort to meet them.

The Court, upholding the Federal Communications Commission's determination here, asked whether or not the FCC could require a licensee to show that it would affirmatively take the views of the audience it served into consideration in broadcasting programming. The Court's answer, which provided the basis for all future activity of the FCC in respect to programming, was strongly in the affirmative.

Shortly after the decision in the *Suburban* case was handed down by the Court, radio and television stations all over the nation became concerned about the quality and nature of their programming. After thirty years of neglect, the Federal Communications Commission was finally going to scrutinize programming at the time of license renewal. This was of special concern to stations whose programming reflected the controversial issues of the day, such as the advocacy of extreme and radical political and social viewpoints, of both the Right and the Left. Even more important, however, was the fear on the part of these stations that ostensibly "well-meaning" local citizen groups might demand a hearing before the FCC at the time for license renewal upon the ground that the station's license should be revoked because the programming was not in the "public convenience, interest, and necessity." Many of these "intervention" requests were received by the FCC, including the celebrated case against the Pacifica Foundation, a non-profit organization which operated WBAI-FM in New York City and KPFB and KPFA-FM in Berkeley, California. In 1963, this broadcaster's license was up for renewal together with an application to operate a new station, KPFK in Los Angeles. The programming policies at the three existing Pacifica Foundation stations could be aptly described as "extremely liberal." A number of special-interest groups, believing that the nature of Pacifica's programming was "detrimental" and "offensive" to the communities which the stations served therefore sought to oppose the issuance of the new license as well as the three license renewals. Among these groups' specific objections to the programming were five programs which Pacifica had aired on its three existing stations, to wit:

1. Allegedly obscene poems by Lawrence Ferlinghetti, read by the poet himself.
2. A recording of the allegedly offensive Edward Albee drama, "The Zoo Story."
3. A group discussion, "Live and Let Live," where eight male homosexuals discussed their attitudes and problems.
4. Allegedly obscene poems by Robert Creeley, read by the poet himself, particularly his "Ballad of the Despairing Husband."
5. Readings from *The Kid,* an unfinished and allegedly obscene novel by Edward Pomerantz.

Upon presentation of all the evidence, the Federal Communications Commission found that the Albee drama, the group discussion, "Live and Let Live," and the unfinished Pomerantz novel, were unquestionably "all . . . under the public-interest standard," and "well within the licensee's judgment." The FCC questioned the other two programs, the Ferlinghetti and Creeley poems, because of their obscene words but deemed them to be merely "isolated errors" and therefore not actionable. In delivering its opinion approving the renewal and granting of a new Pacifica license, the Federal Communications Commission remarked:

We recognize that as shown by the complaints here, such provocative programming as here involved may offend some listeners. But this does not mean that those offended have the right, through the Commission's licensing power, to rule such programming off the airwaves. Were this the case, only the wholly inoffensive, the bland, could gain access to the radio microphone or TV camera. No such drastic curtailment can be countenanced under the Constitution, the Communications Act, or the Commission's policy, which has consistently sought to insure 'the maintenance of radio and television as a medium of freedom of speech and freedom of expression for the people of the Nation as a whole.' . . . In saying this, we do not mean to indicate that those who have complained about the foregoing programs are in the wrong as to the worth of these programs and should listen to them. This is a matter solely for determination by the individual listeners. Our function, we stress, is not to pass on the merits of the program—to commend or to frown. Rather, . . . it is the very limited one of assaying, at the time of renewal, whether the licensee's programming, on an overall basis, has been in the public interest and, in the context of this issue, whether he has made programming judgments reasonably related to the public interest. This does not pose a close question in the case: Pacifica's judgments as to the above programs clearly fall within the very great discretion which the act wisely vests in the licensee. In this connection, we also note that Pacifica took into account the nature of the broadcast medium when it scheduled such programing for the late evening hours (after 10 P.M., when the number of children in the listening audience is at a minimum).[8]

---

[8]In a dissenting opinion, Commissioner Robert E. Lee also felt that the discussion "Live and Let Live" was an airing not in the public interest.

> Having listened carefully and painfully to a one and one-half hour tape recording of a program involving self-professed homosexuals, I am convinced that the program was designed to be, and succeeded in being, contributory to nothing but sensationalism. The airing of a program dealing with sexual aberrations is not to my mind, per se, a violation of good taste nor contrary to the public interest. When these subjects are discussed by physicians and sociologists, it is conceivable that the public could benefit. But a panel of eight homosexuals discussing their experiences and past history does not approach the treatment of a delicate subject one could accept by a responsible broadcaster. A microphone in a bordello during slack hours could give us similar information on a related subject. Such programs, obviously designed to be lurid and to stir the public curiosity, have little place on the air.
>
> I do not hold myself to be either a moralist or a judge of taste. Least of all do I have a clear understanding of what may constitute obscenity in broadcasting.

Author's Note: There is a serious question as to whether or not Commissioner Lee would alter his viewpoint in the 1970's with respect to the fact that a discussion concerning homosexuality was not in the "public interest."

The Federal Communications Commission therefore stated that it would not condemn programming which was thought-provoking, dynamic, and colorful, if a licensee's overall programming was reasonably within the guideline phrase; nor would the FCC deny the prospective licensee the issuance of a license to operate a new station.

As the 1960's wore on and the mood of the entire nation changed, people became more concerned with pressing social issues and took on increasingly militant stands. The Federal Communications Commission did likewise, for it began to require prospective licensees, as well as stations seeking license renewals, to demonstrate affirmatively that they had ascertained the needs of the community audiences which they served. Furthermore, the FCC insisted that those seeking licenses or renewals thereof show that they translated these community needs into meaningful broadcast and telecast programs. In August, 1968, the FCC published a new policy statement titled: "Ascertainment of Community Needs by Broadcast Applicants," which prescribed four elements to show that a prospective licensee had taken active steps to learn the community's broadcasting needs, to wit:

> (a) Full information on the steps the applicant has taken to become informed of the real community needs and interests of the area to be served.
> (b) Suggestions which the applicant has received as to how the station could help meet the area's needs.
> (c) The applicant's evaluation of those suggestions.
> (d) The programming service which the applicant proposes in order to meet those needs as they have been evaluated.

Thus a prospective licensee had to show the Federal Communications Commission the steps it had taken to learn the needs and interests of the community it sought to serve, the suggestions it received, and its evaluation of these suggestions, and finally its proposed programming to meet those interests and needs. The FCC stated it belief that if these community needs were effectively ascertained, "the programming service will be rooted in the people whom the station is obligated to serve and who will be in a much better position to see that the obligation to them is fulfilled, thus lessening the enforcement burden of the Commission.

On January 14, 1970, the Federal Communications Commission issued what is perhaps the most important document with respect to radio-television programming since the enactment of the Communications Acts in 1934. This policy statement, entitled "Comparative Hearings Involving Renewal Applications," dealt with the triannual review by the FCC of the "stewardship" of station licensees and the determination of whether or not the conduct of licensees fulfilled the import of the "public interest" guideline. Furthermore, this 1970 policy statement dealt with the situation of prospective licensees contesting the reissuance of a license to the incumbent by showing the former could better serve the public interest. The Federal Communications Commission, according to Commissioner Nicholas Johnson in his dissent to the 1970 Policy Statement, noted that the Statement effectively deprived the "American people of substantial rights." The FCC, rather than expanding upon the community needs standards of the *Suburban* and *Pacifica* cases, above, and the 1968 FCC Policy Statement, determined that it would hold an incumbent licensee to a different public interest standard than the prospective licensee. The Federal Communications Commission, in 1970, expressed its conviction in these words:

> The public interest standard is served, we believe, by policies which insure that the needs and interests of the listening and viewing public will be amply served by the community's local broadcast outlets. Promotion of this goal, with respect to competing challenges to renewal applicants, calls for the balancing of two obvious considerations. The first is that the public receive the benefits of the statutory spur inherent in the fact that there can be a challenge, and indeed, where the public interest so requires, that the new applicant be preferred. The second is that the comparative hearing policy in this area must not undermine predictability and stability of broadcast operation.
>
> The institution of a broadcast service requires a substantial investment, particularly in television, and even where the investment is small, it is likely to be relatively large to the person making it. It would disserve the public interest to reward good public service by a broadcaster by terminating the authority to continue that service. If the license is given subject to withdrawal despite a record

> of such good service, it will simply not be possible to induce people to enter the field and render what has become a vital public service. Indeed, rather than an incentive to qualified broadcasters to provide good service, it would be an inducement to the opportunist who might seek a license and then provide the barest minimum of service which would permit short-run maximization of profit, on the theory that the license might be terminated whether he rendered a good service or not. The broadcast field thus must have stability, not only for those who engage in it but, even more important, from the standpoint of service to the public.

Although every challenge to an existing radio and television licensee is an incentive for that licensee "to improve his programming," it must be realized that the "public interest" can best be served by assuring the incumbent licensee of a sense of stability in protecting his enormous financial investment. Challenges, however, do encourage responsible broadcasters to provide good service to the community. Thus the incumbent licensee should be protected even if he fulfills the statutory requirement that he operate in the "public convenience, interest, and necessity" in a slightly different way than a prospective licensee might do. The FCC thereupon opined:

> We believe that . . . if the applicant for renewal of license shows in a hearing with a competing applicant that its program service during the preceding license term has been substantially attuned to meeting the needs and interests of its area,* and that the operation of the station has not otherwise been characterized by serious deficiencies, he will be preferred over the newcomer and his application for renewal will be granted. His operation is not based merely upon promises to serve solidly the public interest. He has done so. Since the basic purpose of the Act—substantial service to the public—is being met, it follows that the considerations of predictability and stability, which also contribute vitally to that basic purpose, call for renewal.

The incumbent licensee need not demonstrate that he is "completely attuned" to the needs of the community in order to be entitled to a renewal of his license, for "substantial attunement" is all that is necessary. In expectation of a possible controversy regarding the phrase "substantially attuned," the Federal Communications Commission specifically provided a footnote, delineated by the asterisk in the above quote, clarifying the words. This footnote stated:

> *We wish to stress that we are not using the term 'substantially' in any sense of partial performance in the public interest. On the contrary, as the discussion within makes clear, it is used in the sense of "solid," "strong," etc., . . . performance as contrasted with a service only minimally meeting the needs and interests of the area. In short, we would distinguish between two types of situations—one where the licensee has served the public interest but in the least permissible fashion still sufficient to get a renewal in the absence of competing applications (defined herein as minimal service) and the other where he has done so in an ample, solid fashion (defined herein as substantial service).

"Substantially" was meant to imply in a "solid fashion" and to be contrasted with "minimally" which, according to the FCC, is the least permissible way in which a station can operate and still be entitled to a license renewal. "[W]e recognize that the terms 'substantially' and 'minimally' also lack mathematical precision. However, the terms constitute perfectly appropriate standards. Thus, the word "substantially' is defined as 'strong; solid; firm; much; considerable; ample; large; of considerable worth or value; important'." One of the most constructive criticisms of this 1970 Statement has been made by Commissioner Nicholas Johnson who expressed the thought that essentially the hearing renewal was to be an adversary process with the incumbent trying to prove substantial and the prospective licensee trying to prove minimal programming service to the community:

> The Commission has made it clear that it will not permit chaos to reign, that the better broadcasters have nothing to fear, and that all can get back to the task of programming their stations in ways that serve the awesome needs of the American people for quality entertainment, cultural enrichment, continuing education, and information and analysis about life in the communities and world in which they live. The more responsible broadcasters now know they will be protected from harrassment from audience or FCC.
>
> On the other hand, the public now clearly understands that a new day has dawned; licenses will not be automatically renewed; those licensees not offering 'substantial' service are open to challenge.

> The below-average broadcasters should respond to this new state of affairs by upgrading their programming from a "minimal" to a "substantial" performance. They now have a very real incentive to purchase this "renewal insurance" against the possibility of a challenge.

Johnson believes that the new policy will reenforce the viewpoint of responsible licensees that their programming should reflect as accurately as possible the needs of the community it serves, while the subpar and borderline licensees will realize that if they want to retain their licenses, they must "shape up."

On the balance, however, Commissioner Johnson feels that this new Federal Communications Commission policy fails to give the public the very best possible programming.

> What the public loses by this statement can be summarized in the word "competition." The theory of the 1934 Communications Act was that the public would be served by the best licensees available. No licensee would have a 'right' to have his license renewal. Each would be open to the risk that a competing applicant would offer a service preferable in some way, and thereby win the license away. The FCC was to choose the best from among the applications before it, whether the incumbent's record was "mediocre" or "excellent." This is the principle of the marketplace: the public is assured the best products by opening the market to all sellers, comparing their products, and rewarding the best with the greater sales. The analogy in broadcasting is the competing application. The FCC is the public's proxy. It is we who must make the choice among competitors; it is the public that receives the benefits (or burdens) of our choice.
>
> What we have done in this policy statement is comparable to providing that there could be no new, competing magazines, automobiles or breakfast cereals unless a new entrant could demonstrate that the presently available products are not 'substantially' serving the public interest. The affected industry's arguments on behalf of such a policy would be quite similar to those presented by the broadcasters in this instance. But this country has long believed that the public will be better served over the long run by free and open competition. And after lengthy consideration it is still my belief that, on balance, the principle is equally valid in the broadcasting industry."

The most recent statement issued by the FCC in respect to programming, however, is found in an article appearing in the February 22, 1971, edition of the *New York Times*. After more than sixty years of broadcasting regulation, the Federal Communications Commission revealed that it was prepared to establish guidelines for the types of television and radio programs that a licensee *must* air, i.e. (a) television stations in large urban centers must devote a minimum of 15 per cent of their prime evening time to local shows and another 15 per cent of prime time to news and (b) stations in smaller cities must also devote specified time, though less than that required for large urban stations, to public affairs; furthermore, failure to comply with these FCC guides will constitute programming *not* "substantially attuned" to community needs and must thus affect license renewal. (Also for the first time, six months prior to the expiration of their license, stations must air once every eight days a statement to the effect that the license is expiring, that its frequency is public property, and that the public has a vital role in assessing a station's service and programming.) It should be noted that most stations affected by these standards are generally meeting or even exceeding the requirements.

Although Federal Communications Commission guides are not scheduled to become effective until the fall of 1971, the industry has "seen the light," so that passive programming regulation by the Federal Communications Commission is over. Station licensees will no longer be coddled nor allowed to saturate the public airways with unsatisfactory programming. The highest priority will be given by the FCC to assure that radio and television station licensees broadcast and telecast all their programming with the "public convenience, interest, and necessity," as their most important guiding principle.

QUESTIONS FOR REVIEW

1. What was the purpose of the Communications Act of 1934?
2. What was the significance of the *KFKB Broadcasting Ass'n.* case with respect to the powers of the Federal Radio Commission, and what reasoning did the Court use in sustaining the FRC?
3. Discuss the history of electronic communications regulation in the United States from 1910 to 1934.

4. What reasoning did the Court use in the *Trinity Methodist Church, South* case in sustaining denial of the renewal of the stations license?
5. Discuss the basic provisions of the Communications Act of 1934, with particular emphasis upon the duties and powers of the FCC.
6. What was the "Blue Book" and in what way did it involve the granting of license renewals to broadcasting stations?
7. What was the substance of the "Report and Statement of Policy re: Commission En Banc Programming Inquiry" with respect to broadcasting and telecasting licensing?
8. What are the elements of programming necessary to meet the "public interest" guidelines?
9. What were the facts of the "Suburban" situation and why did the Court in the *Henry* case uphold the FCC's licensing requirements with respect to programming?
10. What is the significance of the Pacifica Foundation case and what factors led to its programming practices being called into question in the first instance?
11. What are the steps that a prospective licensee is required to take to learn a community's broadcasting needs?
12. What was the substance of the "Comparative Hearings Involving Renewal Applications" policy statement of 1970 and how did it alter the prior practice of the FCC? What was the basis of Commissioner Nicholas Johnson's criticism of this policy statement?
13. Why was the 1971 policy statement with respect to programming of licensees such a departure from the past, and what were the substance of the new FCC guidelines?

Chapter 4

THE UNITED NATIONS GENOCIDE CONVENTION: LIFE OR DEATH FOR MANKIND

IT IS COMPLETELY UNJUSTIFIABLE and almost unforgivable for the Government of the United States to continue in 1972 to chart its course of isolationism and disinterest on the issue of ratification of the United Nations Genocide Convention.

The Convention on the Prevention and Punishment of the Crime of Genocide,[1] approved December 9, 1948 by the United Nations General Assembly contains, *inter alia,* the following nine articles:

ARTICLE I

The Contracting Parties confirm that genocide, whether committed in time of peace or in time of war, is a crime under international law which they undertake to prevent and to punish.

ARTICLE II

In the present Convention, genocide means any of the following acts committed with intent to destroy, in whole or in part, a national, ethnical, racial or religious group, as such:

(a) Killing members of the group;
(b) Causing serious bodily or mental harm to members of the group;
(c) Deliberately inflicting on the group conditions of life calculated to bring about its physical destruction in whole or in part;
(d) Imposing measures intended to prevent births within the group;
(e) Forcibly transferring children of the group to another group.

[1]United Nations Resolution 260A (III).

ARTICLE III

The following acts shall be punishable:

(a) Genocide;
(b) Conspiracy to commit genocide;
(c) Direct and public incitement to commit genocide;
(d) Attempt to commit genocide;
(e) Complicity in genocide.

ARTICLE IV

Persons committing genocide or any of the other acts enumerated in article III shall be punished, whether they are constitutionally responsible rulers, public official or private individuals.

ARTICLE V

The Contracting Parties undertake to enact, in accordance with their respective Constitutions, the necessary legislation to give effect to the provisions of the present Convention and, in particular, to provide effective penalties for persons guilty of genocide or any of the other acts enumerated in article III.

ARTICLE VI

Persons charged with genocide or any of the other acts enumerated in article III shall be tried by a competent tribunal of the State in the territory of which the act was committed, or by such international penal tribunal as may have jurisdiction with respect to those Contracting Parties which shall have accepted its jurisdiction.

ARTICLE VII

Genocide and the other acts enumerated in article III shall not be considered as political crimes for the purpose of extradition.

The Contracting Parties pledge themselves in such cases to grant extradition in accordance with their laws and treaties in force.

ARTICLE VIII

Any Contracting Party may call upon the competent organs of the United Nations to take such action under the Charter of the United Nations as they consider appropriate for the prevention and suppression of acts of genocide or any of the other tests enumerated in Article III.

ARTICLE IX

Disputes between the Contracting Parties relating to the interpretations, application or fulfillment of the present Convention, including those relating to the responsibility of a State for genocide or any of the other acts enumerated in article III, shall be submitted to the International Court of Justice at the request of any of the parties to the dispute.

It was 23 years ago on December 9, 1971,[2] that the United Nations Convention on Genocide was unanimously adopted (55-0) by the United Nations General Assembly (although genocide had been declared an international crime by United Nations General Assembly Resolution No. 96(I) on December 11, 1946). The legislation was a direct result of World War II and in particular of the realization in the mid-1940's that Hitler's vow to exterminate the Jewish people was not mere propaganda but was the expression of a systematic policy of genocide. The International Military Tribunal at Nürnberg described the mass murders of the Jews of Europe but considered these human victims of genocide to be beyond the jurisdiction of the Tribunal insofar as they were not directly related to planning and waging aggressive warfare. The international community, as represented in the United Nations, responded in 1946 with the Convention on Genocide. But the essential element of the crime of genocide (from the Greek words *genos* i.e. race, tribe or nation, and *caedere*, i.e. to kill) goes back long before the technical perfection of brutality as achieved in the twentieth century: the Romans not only conquered but destroyed the people of Carthage; Mohammed boasted that he eradicated a Jewish tribe; the Crusaders attempted to eliminate men, women, and children of other faiths; and Cortes in Mexico and Pizzaro in Peru systematically eliminated tribes of Indians.

The United Nations Convention on Genocide actually came into force on January 12, 1951, for those nations that had earlier ratified it. President Harry S Truman first submitted it to the United States Senate for ratification on July 16, 1949; but from that very moment in 1949 the embittered leadership of the House of Delegates of the American Bar Association opposed approval. This group has been successful in keeping the United

[2]On November 23, 1970, the Senate Foreign Relations Committee voted to report favorably the Genocide Convention by a vote of 10 to 2, but the full Senate took no action on the measure.

States government from membership in the Convention. Their arguments against ratification were as follows: (a) a state could not be held liable in damages for injuries inflicted by it on its own citizens; *but* this is but an expression of sovereign immunity which had been waived in 1946, for example, by the enactment of the Federal Tort Claims Act; (b) the intent to destroy must affect a substantial portion of that group; *but* the language of Article II of the Convention clearly refers to "group as such" and certainly does not delineate one or two individuals as a group; (c) mental harm, to be sufficiently delineated, must mean "permanent physical injury" to mental faculties; *but* today brainwashing and other torture techniques involving the administration of drugs leave their permanent imprints; and (d) "complicity in genocide" must include participation before and after the commission of the crime of genocide; *but* it is the active participation by perpetrators of genocide that is delineated. The full United States Senate Foreign Relations Committee, after a 1950 hearing characterized by enmity, simply tabled the matter! Twenty years later, at a mid-year meeting in Atlanta on February 23, 1970, the House of Delegates of the American Bar Association reaffirmed its position of opposition, but by the narrowest of margins, 130 to 126.

For a delineation of that eventful meeting, the following excerpts are taken from a report in the *American Bar Association Journal*[3]:

> The debate on the Genocide Convention, which took place on Monday afternoon, February 23, produced the liveliest action in the House in many years, and more than two dozen lawyers spoke, including eight former Presidents of the Association, the current President, one former Attorney General of the United States, one former Deputy Attorney General, and the Solicitor General. . . .
>
> The resolution to change the Association's position on the convention was proposed by the Section of Individual Rights and Responsibilities, and the Section Chairman, Jerome J. Shestack of Philadelphia, opened the debate. Mr. Shestack began by outlining the history of the Genocide Convention and the Association's original opposition to it.
>
> He argued that there were at least three changes in the sit-

[3]56 *A.B.A.J.*, April, 1970, 370 *et seq.*

uation since 1949 that made it desirable to reverse the position taken then. First, the convention is no longer new, but has been ratified by 75 nations, none of whom have any intention of hurting their nationals. Second, whereas in 1949 the Section of International and Comparative Law favored the convention with some reservations, the Committee on Peace and Law Through United Nations opposed it. Now all the Sections and Committees of the Association that have special cognizance of the subject matter favor it—the International Rights and Responsibilties Section, the International Law Section, the Criminal Law Section and the Committee on World Order Under Law. Finally, Mr. Shestack said, in 1949 there had been no definitive study of the effects of the convention on our own constitutional law, but since then, many constitutional authorities and four Attorneys General have discovered no constitutional problems that would arise from the convention. This convention is fully in the American tradition, Mr. Shestack declared, and its endorsement would carry out the legal profession's commitment to the rule of law.

Ben R. Miller of Baton Rouge, Louisiana replied that President Eisenhower had never urged ratification—as a military man, he knew its potential harmful effect on the military necessity of obedience to orders, since each soldier would have to decide in the heat of battle whether to risk a court martial for disobedience or face a future trial for genocide. Mr. Miller argued that the definition of 'genocide' is vague and that the convention would permit trials for the offense not only in American courts but also in foreign courts, where our concepts of a fair trial might not be recognized.

Rita E. Hauser, United States Delegate to the United Nations, was given unanimous consent to address the House. Speaking in favor of the convention, she said that the treaty had been thoroughly reviewed by the State Department only last year and that all the points raised against it had been thoroughly considered. In particular, the review had demonstrated that the convention would in no way jeopardize American soldiers fighting abroad, Ambassador Hauser stated. In fact, 'we concluded that by our ratification of the treaty, we would be able to refute in a much better way the charges that are often made by our enemies, that we are committing genocide in Vietnam,' she declared. . . .

Nicholas deB. Katzenbach, former Attorney General and former Undersecretary of State, who favored the convention, pointed out that it is normal for any crime to be tried in the place where it is committed. This includes crimes committed by members of our Armed Forces stationed overseas. It is true that Americans would be subject to extradition under the treaty, he said, but only to countries with which we have treaties of extradition, and those are countries in whose legal procedures and fairness we trust. If anything, ratification of the treaty would help American men held prisoner by North Vietnam, Mr. Katzenbach said, because if the United States Senate doesn't change its position, the North Vietnamese will say it is because the Senate knows that we are guilty of genocide.

Armistead J. Maupin of Raleigh, North Carolina, disagreed with Mr. Katzenbach, saying that he had "no intention of voting for a proposition which a Communist state would surely use as a crutch to support a kangaroo trial of the decent young manhood of this country."

Whitney North Seymour of New York City, former President of the Association, said that the treaty had been in effect in some seventy-five countries for twenty years now, and no one has reported a single episode in which any soldier of any country has been subjected to the sort of thing feared by the opponents of the convention. The national interests of the United States call for ratification, he declared. . . .

Eberhard P. Deutsch of New Orleans, another nonmember of the House who was given unanimous consent to speak, said that if the United States ratifies the convention, it will be obliged to accept the international criminal court or be charged with a breach of faith. Mr. Deutsch asserted, "It can hardly be suggested that if pre-Hitler Germany had been party to a genocide convention, there would have been no mass extermination of Germany's Jews by the Nazis. Can it be suggested with any less naiveté that Soviet Russia was deterred from her rape of Czechoslovakia by the nonaggression provisions of the Charter of the United Nations, to which she had been a party since its inception?"

The President of the Association Bernard G. Segal of Philadelphia, urged the House to vote in favor of ratification. "The question is whether this Association, and through us, the law profession in the United States, can come together in support of an international commitment to root out genocide. To this question, 75 nations . . . have signed the treaty. We alone hesitate, and we stand alone among the democratic nations of the world," he said.

Subsequently, the U.S. Senate failed again to take up the cudgel for individual rights and human dignity! Why the ultraconservative ABA should continue to be the bellwether must be deplored by freedom-loving peoples everywhere!

Though the world has greatly changed and the presumed

risks of 22 years ago have proved groundless, the United States, alone out of 75 nations including the U.S.S.R., has not yet ratified nor acceded to the Convention.[4] It is unjust for the United States to persist with "this sad record and the responsibility for it" because ultraconservative and extremist leaders continue to have "a parochial outlook on world problems." These are the very words of former Chief Justice Earl Warren in addressing the National Conference on Continuing Acts for Human Rights in Washington on December 4, 1968. He further castigated these leaders who have "failed to measure the element of change in the world. They have failed to recognize that men and their institutions do not stand still in the face of great changes."[5]

To every thinking person it is unbelievable that anyone in the 1970's should continue to contend that genocide "lies within the domestic sphere"[6] and therefore beyond the pale of international concern, or that helpless people should not be protected against tyrannical government, whenever and wherever those governments or individuals in public capacities act contrary to basic moral principles. How vacuous it is to argue that the United States Government might become the victim of charges

---

[4]Earliest ratification of the United Nations Convention on Genocide was achieved by Australia, Ecuador, Ethiopia, Iceland, and Norway in 1949. Countries which have not yet ratified the Convention include Bolivia, Dominican Republic, New Zealand, Paraguay, and the United States.

[5]The Convention on the Prevention and Punishment of the Crime of Genocide is an international commitment to decency and morality consistent with the American tradition. It does not, of course, stand alone. Like other efforts throughout history, from the Ten Commandments through the Magna Carta, the English Bill of Rights, the French Declaration of the Rights of Man and the Citizen, the United States Bill of Rights, the Thirteenth, Fourteenth, and Fifteenth Amendments to the United States Constitution, and the United Nations Charter, the Convention is a statement which advances individual rights and human dignity.

[6]Perhaps some of the misunderstanding of "international concern" and "relation to American foreign policy" has resulted because some have confused that doctrine with the very different concept of "domestic jurisdiction." In part, responsibility for this confusion may be traced to the original Circular 175 [U.S. Dept. of State, Dept. Cir. No. 175 (1955), reprinted in 50 *Amer. J. Intl. Law,* 784, 1956], promulgated by Secretary of State John Foster Dulles apparently in an effort to console the Bricker forces after the defeat of their efforts to amend the Constitution. The Circular—an instruction to the State

(continued next page)

of genocide deliberately brought against her by her enemies, should the United States become a party to the Convention. (Have we not anything to fear but fear itself?) It is similarly questionable to assert that treaties are not the proper constitutional means for the United States Government to act in such

---

Department—provided that "Treaties should be designed to promote United States interests by securing action by foreign governments in a way deemed advantageous to the United States. Treaties are not to be used as a device for the purpose of effecting internal social changes or to try to circumvent the constitutional procedures established in relation to what are essentially matters of domestic concern." The Circular, it should be noted, announced policy, not constitutional doctrine. Indeed, it was probably designed to impose as policy what the Bricker Amendment would have imposed as constitutional law but which, it was realized, was not the law of the Constitution unamended. [In fact, when President Kennedy in 1963 sent three minor human rights conventions to the Senate, it did eventually consent to one of them (113 Cong. Rec. 15750-51 (daily ed. Nov. 2, 1967)) (consent to convention on abolition of slavery)]. Still, the final clause of the Circular has apparently led some to argue that the Constitution precludes American adherence to any treaty that deals with matters "that are essentially within the domestic jurisdiction of the United States."

Whatever its intellectual origins, the argument reflects fundamental misconceptions. The concept of "domestic jurisdiction" is unknown to American constitutional doctrine; it is well known to international law. Under international law, a matter is deemed to be within a country's domestic jurisdiction if it is not governed by international law or by any treaty obligation. What is within the domestic jurisdiction of a country in the absence of treaty ceases to be so when that nation enters an international agreement on the subject. To suggest that the Constitution forbids treaties as to matters that are "essentially within the domestic jurisdiction of the United States" is to bar any treaty on any matter not already governed by customary international law or previous agreement. Such a theory would prevent the United States from participating in the development of new law by multilateral convention—the principal form of international legislation today. It would preclude many provisions in treaties of commerce, friendship, and navigation, in treaties on disarmament, extradition, nationality, the prevention of double taxation, and a host of other subjects. It seems patently absurd. In any event, it is a limitation which no one has suggested before and which is without foundation. It cannot be implied in Mr. Justice Hughes' "international concern" limitation, nor can it be derived from the character and purpose of the treaty power as an instrument of foreign relations; it has no support even in early writings on the Constitution; and it is contradicted by the history of American treaty practice. In the absence of treaty, this country's armaments, its nationality laws, its immigration policies, all lie within its "domestic jurisdiction"; yet the United States has negotiated agreements on these subjects of international concern from the beginning of its history to this date.

affairs as genocide.[7] Beginning in 1945 when the United States became signatory to the United Nations Charter, some 4,000 treaties and international agreements were entered into by the United States, without any observable diminution of American sovereignty and without any debasement of American standards or morality. It is the very arbitrariness of heinous practices of government, or of individuals utilizing the powers of government, in committing genocide that make it necessary that such government and its leaders be bound to cease their international crimes. Mass murders by people in or out of government must be immediately halted. Human rights are matters of international concern. Otherwise, what relief is there from the tyranny of man over man! The Preamble to the Convention on the Prevention and Punishment of the Crime of Genocide poignantly delineates genocide as "an odious scourge" which has "inflicted great losses on humanity."

The prophets of doom and gloom who have so selfishly fought against United States ratification of the Genocide Convention these many years center much of their argument on the fact that the original United Nations Declaration had denounced genocide whether committed on "religious, racial, *political,* or any other grounds"; but the final Declaration in Article II substituted the word "ethnical" for the word "political" because of the insistence of Communist countries. But these critics fail to grasp the pragmatics of legislative "give and take." Legislative compromise is also the essence of democracy within the United Nations as well as within the United States. Still, the final language does not condone the elimination of political

[7]While no treaty or treaty provision has ever been declared unconstitutional, it is settled that treaties are subject to constitutional limitations. There was once a myth that this was not so. The view that treaties are not subject to constitutional limitations found support in the language of the supremacy clause and in an ambiguous suggestion by Justice Oliver Wendell Holmes. But the question was thoroughly explored during the Bricker controversy, and everyone on both sides firmly rejected that view. In 1957, in *Reid v. Covert* (354 U.S. 1), Mr. Justice Black seized the occasion to lay that ghost to rest. Although there was no majority opinion of the Court, and Justice Black's statement was perhaps not necessary to his result, he stated that treaties, like laws, must be made "in pursuance of" the Constitution.

groups, with or without the complicity of government, as recently occurred in Czechoslovakia and Hungary, because clearly those acts were "committed with intent to destroy" a group of people (Article II). The reservation in Article VII that genocide is not a political crime for purpose of extradition simply assures that such perpetrators will not be allowed to hide out from prosecution.

The opponents of the Genocide Convention are perhaps rabid isolationists who are frightened by the possibility that American citizens may be subjected to injustice at the hands of a court other than an American court. These opponents have failed to heed the language of Article VI which emphasizes that "persons charged with genocide . . . shall be tried by a *competent* tribunal of the state in the territory of which the act was committed, *or* by such international penal tribunal as may have jurisdiction . . . ." All the constitutional guarantees to which the American citizen has become inured would be respected, because in the enabling legislation which must be enacted by Congress (after American ratification of the Convention), these constitutional rights would be guaranteed.[8] Congress can also withdraw at any time the conferred jurisdiction on an international penal tribunal over an American citizen. The so-called "Connally Amendment," which is a reservation of the United States in its declaration of adherence to the International Court of Justice, would not preclude submission of a United States citizen to the judicial processes of an international penal tribunal because genocide is an international crime and not a "dispute" solely within the "domestic jurisdiction" of the United States. Again, traditional American safeguards including jury trial are carefully preserved by virtue of the option to accept or reject on each occasion the international court's jurisdiction.[9]

The heart of the treaty defining Genocide is found in Article II:

---

[8]Note that the United States Constitution, Article VI, clause 2 provides in part: "This Constitution, and the Laws of the United States which shall be made in Pursuance thereof; and all Treaties made, or which shall be made, under the Authority of the United States, shall be the supreme Law of the Land. . . ."

> . . . any of the following acts committed with intent to destroy, in whole or in part, a national, ethnical, racial or religious group as such:
>
> (a) Killing members of the group;
> (b) Causing serious bodily or mental harm to members of the group;
> (c) Deliberately inflicting on the group conditions of life calculated to bring about its physical destruction in whole or in part;
> (d) Imposing measures intended to prevent births within the group;
> (e) Forcibly transferring children of the group to another group.

It should be noted that this definition goes beyond mass murder (i.e. the wanton killing of Armenians by the Turks in World War I or the fiendish murder of 6 million Jews by the Nazis), and embraces as international crimes mass sterilization, group drugging, and forced separation of children as a group from their parents. Unfortunately, "cultural genocide," i.e. destruction of cultural or religious institutions or suppression of schools is not expressly included, although it is certainly *implicit* in subparagraphs (b), (c), and (d). The thrust of Article II rests upon the criminal "intent to destroy" a group of people as in the case of the Soviet Government's anti-Semitic policies. Article III additionally covers conspiracy, direct and public incitement, attempts to commit genocide, and complicity in genocide. Article I, it should be noted, in declaring genocide to be an international crime, states that this is so, whether the crime is committed in time of peace or in time of war. Indeed, genocide is a subject of common concern to all mankind, for mass

---

[9]The basic question is not whether the United States should legislate for its own citizens by treaty or should submit actions in the United States to the scrutiny of other nations. Rather, the question is whether the United States, concerned with the treatment of individuals in other countries and its effect on international peace and security, may seek to regulate such treatment and thinks it worth the necessary price—agreement to subject actions in this country to similar international or foreign scrutiny. To suggest that human rights conventions are not of "international concern" or do not "affect American foreign relations" requires some special and narrow restriction of the natural meaning of those phrases. It necessitates a new doctrine holding that a treaty must affect American foreign relations in a particular way, that it further only certain kinds of foreign relations interests, and further them only in specific ways.

horror anywhere on earth affects everyone and every country. Genocide is, above all, a breach of international peace and security, and its ugly head must not be permitted to exist anywhere at any time.

Enforcement of the prohibition against genocide is admittedly not an easy problem; and policing, *ipso facto,* is not the *summum bonum.* It is *the universal* declaration and *the universal* warning against genocide that promises a more effective end to genocide. The world will react when the world is prepared legislatively to ban genocide, as 75 sovereign nations have demonstrated by their accession to the Convention. The destructiveness of genocide may only be compared with the destructiveness of nuclear weapons! However, the enforcement provisions of the Convention are clear: (a) the states must, under Article V, enact implementing legislation to punish *effectively* persons found guilty of genocide or the accessory crimes listed in Article III and (b) *competent* organs of the United Nations are available to supplement such enforcement, particularly against the governments involved (Article VIII). The Security Council or the General Assembly or the Economic and Social Council are all authorized to hear the complaint. Under Article IX disputes between the States may be referred to the International Court of Justice. The so-called "Nürnberg defense," whereby persons seek to escape blame for evil acts by asserting that they were only carrying out the orders of others, is expressly repudiated by Article IV, which states that no one, not "constitutionally responsible rulers," not government officials, not military officers, and not private individuals, can escape responsibility for his actions through this defense. Furthermore, punishment for perpetrators of genocide must take place in the country where the acts of genocide occurred. All signatory States must return such fleeing criminals for trial.

Today genocide is still tragically a present threat and in no sense remote. In Africa, in the Middle East, and in southeast Asia, ethnic hatreds, the war against hunger and depredation, and the brainwashing and torture in Indochina are not of the past. In the U.S.S.R., there is a stifling stagnation and atrophication imposed by the government upon its 2¾ million Jewish citizens. The United Nations Genocide Convention, when ratified by a greater number of States including the United States, will assure that these excesses will cease. Genocide is "a crime under international law, contrary to the spirit and aims of the United Nations and condemned by the civilized world." (*Preamble* to United Nations Convention on the Prevention and Punishment of the Crime of Genocide) Under Article XI even nonmember States are invited to sign and accede to the U.N. Convention.

In February, 1970, President Nixon publicly urged the United States Senate to ratify the Convention.[10] Favorable recommendations emanated from both the Secretary of State and the Attorney General, pointing out that there were "no constitutional obstacles to United States ratification." But the isolationists again mounted their offensive, erringly arguing that ratification is not within the treaty-making powers of the United States Constitution. The treaty-making power under Article II, Section II of our Constitution is indeed very broad: "It is not perceived that there is any limit to the questions which can be adjusted on any matter which is properly the subject of negotiations with a foreign country."[11] Antisocial conduct and the denial of human rights have been for a hundred years proper subjects of international negotiation. American treaties prohibit white slave traffic, narcotic drugs, arms shipments, and have suppressed slave trade and slavery (from 1926 to 1967), for example. The United States has signed treaties dealing with every form of antisocial conduct, including even the protection of the lives of seals and migratory birds! How much more valuable is the life of a human being!

And so in February, 1970, the powerful House of Delegates

---

[10]Article II, Section 2 of the Constitution provides that the President "shall have Power, by and with the Advice and Consent of the Senate, to make Treaties, provided two-thirds of the Senators present concur." The Constitution does not define treaties; the framers knew what treaties were and, no doubt, did not see any need to define what was well known in international law and practice. Nor does the Constitution state that there are matters which cannot properly be the subject of a treaty or that there are other limitations on treaties and the treaty power.

[11]Geofroy v. Riggs, 133 U.S. 258, 267, 1890.

of the American Bar Association by the very close vote of 130-126 once again failed to understand that human rights must be protected everywhere. The ugly spectre of the war in Vietnam clouded the issue because some narrow-minded Americans were fearful that charges of genocide would be brought against the United States for its involvement in Vietnam. The United Nations Convention on Genocide is one of the most important Conventions which this country could ratify, and every American citizen should be concerned that his country is not ostracized from its international responsibilities by perverted views of what is America's self-interest.[12] Again, genocide is not an internal nor a domestic matter but purely and simply an international crime. Ratification of the Convention by the United States Senate must still be followed by implementing federal legislation making the crimes specified punishable under United States law. Failure by Congress to enact such legislation would leave the United States in breach of international obligation. Thus the immediate step is for the United States Senate to ratify the Convention, per the draft below (prepared by the Section of Individual Rights and Responsibilities of the American Bar Association) of the recommended implementing legislation.

AN ACT TO IMPLEMENT THE CONVENTION ON THE PREVENTION AND PUNISHMENT OF THE CRIME OF GENOCIDE

Be it enacted by the Senate and House of Representatives of the United States of America in Congress assembled. That title 18 of the United States Code is amended by adding the following new Section.

Sec. 000 *Genocide*

(a) Whoever, with the intent to destroy, in whole or in part, a national, ethnical, racial or religious group as such, wilfully

(i) kills members of the group;

[12]The United States, which was founded on the basis of protest against governmental excesses and which grew great in substantial measure because it was a haven and the hope for oppressed persons everywhere, should be in the lead in joining in the declaration of revulsion at any organized effort to eliminate a whole people and of determination that genocide shall not be undertaken ever again.

(ii) causes serious harm to the body or mind of members of the group;

(iii) inflicts on the group conditions of life calculated to bring about its physical destruction in whole or in part;

(iv) enforces measures intended to prevent births within the group; or

(v) transfers children of the group by force to another group shall be guilty of genocide.

(b) Whoever is guilty of genocide, or of conspiracy to commit genocide, or of attempt to commit genocide, or of aiding, abetting, counseling, commanding, inducing, procuring commission of genocide or of publicly inciting to genocide shall be punished [by such punishment as the Congress shall determine to be appropriate].

QUESTIONS FOR REVIEW

1. Why is "genocide" a life or death issue for mankind today?
2. When did the United Nations first adopt the Convention on Genocide. Name several countries which have not yet ratified it.
3. Explain the American Bar Association's opposition to the United Nations Convention on Genocide. List the arguments pro and con.
4. Can "genocide" be purely an issue which "lies within the domestic sphere" of any nation? Should there be "international concern" for purely domestic matters?
5. What is the purpose and scope of a treaty with foreign governments? How many treaties has the United States signed since 1945?
6. Has any treaty or treaty provision ever been declared unconstitutional?
7. Are treaties subject to constitutional limitations?
8. Under the United Nations Convention, is genocide a "political" crime? Is genocide a "religious" crime, a "racial" crime, an "ethnical" crime? Explain.
9. Could the United States Congress withdraw jurisdiction from an international penal tribunal over an American citizen charged with the crime of genocide?

10. Is "cultural genocide" a crime under the United Nations Convention? Can the United Nations act against the utter suppression of Soviet Jewry, for example?
11. What is the "Nürnberg defense"? Does it apply to the genocide issue?
12. List instances of "genocide" during the past ten years which qualify for action by the United Nations.

Chapter 5

DECLARATION OF WAR: WHO WIELDS THE POWER, THE CONGRESS, THE PRESIDENT, OR THE PEOPLE?

ARTICLE I, SECTION 8 of the United States Constitution provides that Congress shall have the power "to declare war." Furthermore, the President "shall be Commander in Chief of the Army and Navy of the United States" (Article II, Section 2). Apparently the intent of the framers of the Constitution was to *divide* the nation's war-making power between the President and the Congress, although there is constitutional opinion to the contrary. Unfortunately, from the earliest days of the Republic, the United States has engaged in armed hostilities with a foreign power without a congressional declaration of war. Our history is replete with instances of "undeclared wars," from the war with France in 1798 to the current Vietnamese war. The Fifth United States Congress passed a law (contained in the first book of the Statutes at Large) authorizing President John Adams to "instruct the commanders of the public armed vessels which are, or which shall be, employed in the service of the United States, to subdue, seize and take any armed French vessel, which shall be found within the jurisdictional limits of the United States, or elsewhere, on the high seas. . . . " President Adams proceeded to carry out congressional instructions, and such naval seizures were not uncommon during the period of the undeclared war with France. The United States Supreme Court, in a case arising out of this undeclared war, recognized the differences between what it called "solemn war," which required a declaration by Congress, and "imperfect war," which did not, in *The Eliza* case.[1] It simply will not do, then, either as a matter of constitutional

1 4 Dall. 37, 1800.

law or as a matter of historical practice, to say that armed hostilities engaged in by the United States in the absence of a declaration of war by Congress are unlawful. To say this by no means answers the question as to what the President may do without congressional authorization, but it does focus attention upon matters of substance rather than form.

Thus the power of the President as Commander in Chief implies substantial authority *to declare and to make war.* Chief Justice John Marshall, writing for the United States Supreme Court in *Little v. Barreme*[2] spoke of the power of the President to order the seizure of a ship on the high seas in a situation where Congress has not specified the procedure.

> It is by no means clear that the President of the United States, whose high duty it is to 'take care that the laws be faithfully executed' and who is Commander in Chief of the Armies and Navies of the United States, might not without any special authority for that purpose, in the then-existing state of things, have empowered the officers commanding the armed vessels of the United States, to seize and send into port for adjudication, American vessels which were forfeited by being engaged in this illicit commerce.

Mr. Justice Grier, speaking for the United States Supreme Court in its famous decision in the *Prize Cases,*[3] likewise argued in favor of Presidential authority on which he might rely in putting down a rebellion.

> Whether the President in fulfilling his duties, as Commander in Chief, in suppressing an insurrection, has met with such armed hostile resistance and a civil war of such alarming proportions as will compel him to accord to them the character of belligerents is a question to be decided *by him* and this court must be governed by the decisions and acts of the political departments of the government to which this power was entrusted. 'He must determine what degree of force the crisis demands.'

Presidents throughout American history have exercised the power (a) to deploy armed forces outside of the United States, (b) to engage United States armed forces in conflict with a foreign nation, and (c) to determine how a war, once initiated,

---

[2] 2 Cranch. 170, 1804.
[3] 2 Black 635, 1863.

shall be conducted. In 1801, President Thomas Jefferson sent a small squadron of American naval vessels into the Mediterranean to protect United States commerce against the Barbary pirates. But he was of the view that for these ships to take offensive, as opposed to defensive, action congressional action would be necessary. In 1845, President James K. Polk ordered military forces to the coast of Mexico and to the western frontier of Texas in order to prevent any interference by Mexico with the proposed annexation of Texas to the United States. Following annexation, President Polk ordered General Zachary Taylor to march from the Nueces River, which Mexico claimed as the southern border of Texas, to the Rio Grande River, which river Texas claimed as her southern boundary. While so engaged, Taylor's force encountered Mexican troops, and hostilities between the two nations commenced on April 25, 1846. Note that there had been no prior authorization by Congress for General Taylor's march south of the Nueces River. In April, 1861, President Abraham Lincoln called for 75,000 volunteers to suppress the rebellion by the southern states, and proclaimed a blockade of the Confederacy. These actions were taken *prior* to their later ratification by Congress in July, 1861. (The United States Supreme Court upheld the validity of the President's action in proclaiming a blockade in the *Prize Cases,* above.) In 1900, President William McKinley sent an expedition of 5,000 United States troops as a component of an international force during the Boxer Rebellion in China. While Congress recognized the existence of the conflict by providing for combat pay, it neither declared war nor formally ratified the President's action. Similar incidents in Central America took place under the administrations of Presidents Theodore Roosevelt, William Howard Taft, and Woodrow Wilson. Naval or armed forces were sent to Panama, Nicaragua, and twice to Mexico in the first two decades of the twentieth century. On none of these occasions was there prior congressional authorization. In 1950, following the invasion of South Korea by the North Koreans and a request for aid by the United Nations Security Council, President Harry S. Truman ordered air and sea forces to give South Korean troops cover and support and furthermore ordered the Seventh Fleet to guard

Formosa. Ultimately 250,000 troops were engaged in the Korean War, which lasted for more than three years. President Truman relied upon the United Nations Charter as a basis for his action, as well as his power as Commander in Chief. The fact that his actions were authorized by the United Nations Charter, however, does not reduce the value of the incident as a precedent for executive action in committing United States armed forces to extensive hostilities *without* a formal declaration of war by Congress.

Congress has on some of these occasions acquiesced in the President's action without formal ratification; on others, it has ratified the President's action; and on still others Congress has taken no action at all. On several of the occasions, individual members of Congress and, at the close of the Mexican War, one House of Congress on a preliminary vote, protected executive use of the armed forces. While a particular course of executive conduct to which there was no opportunity for the legislative branch to object effectively cannot conclusively establish a constitutional precedent in the same manner (as it would be established by an authoritative judicial decision), nevertheless a long-continued practice on the part of the executive, acquiesced in by the Congress, is itself some evidence of the existence of constitutional authority to support such a practice by a President.

The speed and subtlety of international events today have all but made a Congressional declaration of war obsolete. Indeed, it is the executive branch of government, i.e. the President as Commander in Chief, that truly wields the power to make war. Congress has for all intents and purposes surrendered its control over the initiation of military hostilities, although it is Congress that must pay the bill, to wit: appropriate the monies necessary to carry on *presidentially ordered* wars, most recently in Korea, Lebanon, Santo Domingo, and Vietnam. This unilateral expansion of Presidential power in war-making has reached dangerous limits and could undermine the whole system of checks and balances underpinning our constitutional system of government. It could leave the nation solely dependent on the good judgment and benign intent of the incumbent President. While we have had, throughout our history, a high standard for eminence in our Presidents, experience has shown that our liberties require firmer institutional safeguards if they are to survive. The point has been reached where any effort simply to check the further expansion of Presidential war powers is regarded by some defenders of the Presidency as an encroachment on the office itself. And yet recent history confirms that executive-military leaders tend to embroil their nations into wars for bad or nonexistent reasons, and that it is a danger to a nation to entrust basic war and/or peace decisions to decision-makers who do not have to justify their actions (upon a rational basis) to representatives of the people. This is true irrespective of party affiliations or personal ideologies of the executive-military leaders. The framers of our Constitution, mindful of the war-making activities of English and continental monarchs in the sixteenth, seventeenth, and eighteenth centuries, wrote into the Constitution the requirement that only Congress has the power to declare war and to raise and support armies and navies. The almost insurmountable problem begs for a solution!

United States Senator Jacob K. Javits of New York introduced a bill in the Senate in November, 1970, to curb presidential power to initiate war by limiting the President to act only in four instances, to wit: (a) to repulse a sudden attack against the United States, its territories and possessions, (b) to repulse an attack against the Armed Forces of the United States on the high seas or where lawfully stationed on foreign territory, (c) to protect lives and property, as may be required, of United States nationals abroad, and (d) to comply with a national commitment affirmatively undertaken by Congress and the President. Under the Javits bill, the President must *otherwise* report fully and immediately to the Congress the circumstances and details of any military action he may initiate. His authority to sustain such military actions terminates wthin 30 days unless affirmatve legislative action is taken by Congress to sustain for a longer period of time the military actions initiated by the President. The Javits bill has not yet been acted upon by the Congress.

The question of the executive usurpation of the power to declare war has been faced in several recent court decisions. In

Berk v. Laird,[4] decided on June 19, 1970, by the Second United States Court of Appeals, a private first class who enlisted in the United States Army refused to report for induction. He argued that the "executive officials of the United States Government have exceeded their constitutional authority by commanding him to participate in military activity NOT properly authorized by Congress." The Court disagreed, pointing out that "the power to commit American military forces under various sets of circumstances is shared by Congress and the executive." In the case of the Vietnam war, "Congress definitely has acted, in part expressly through the Gulf of Tonkin Resolution and impliedly through appropriations and other acts in support of the project over a period of years. . . ." Furthermore, according to the Court:

> It is more difficult for Berk to suggest a set of manageable standards and escape the likelihood that his particular claim about this war at this time is a *political question.* It may be that he will be able to provide a method for resolving the question of when specified joint legislative-executive action is sufficient to authorize various levels of military activity, but no such standard has as yet been presented to us . . . (Italics added.)

Accordingly, the resolution of a "political question" must be made by Congress and the President, *not* by the judiciary. "The political question doctrine itself requires that a court decline to adjudicate an issue involving 'a lack of judicially discoverable and manageable standards for resolving it.'" It should be noted, however, that the Second United States Court of Appeals found no difficulty in hearing Berk's suit:

> Sovereign immunity is no bar to this action, since the complaint alleges that agents of the government have exceeded their constitutional authority while purporting to act in the name of the sovereign. . . . The requested relief does not require affirmative governmental action but only that the agent involved cease certain allegedly improper conduct. . . . Although the rule has long been that the alleged 'illegality' of a war may not be raised as a defense to prosecution for refusal to submit to induction into the armed forces . . . this court indicated in *Bolton* that 'any question as to the legality of an order sending men to Korea to fight in an 'undeclared war' should be raised by someone to whom such an order has been

[4]No. 900, CCA2, 1970.

directed.' The rule should be the same for a soldier ordered to Vietnam under allegedly similar circumstances.

In contrast to the *Berk* case is the decision of the United States Court of Military Appeals in *U.S. v. Averette,*[5] decided on April 3, 1970. Here the question was whether a civilian employee of an Army contractor was subject to the military jurisdiction of a court-martial. Article 2(10) of the Uniform Code of Military Justice subjected to military jurisdiction "persons serving with or accompanying an armed force in the field *in time of war.*" Averette argued that in the absence of a formal declaration of war by Congress, he could not be tried by a court-martial, and the Court agreed.

> The words 'in time of war' mean, for the purposes of Article 2(10) . . . a war declared by Congress. . . . As a result of the most recent guidance in this area from the Supreme Court we believe that a strict and literal construction of Article 2(10) would open the possibility of civilian prosecutions by military courts whenever military action on a varying scale of intensity occurs . . . . We emphasize our awareness that the fighting in Vietnam qualifies as a war as that word is generally used and understood. . . . But such a recognition should not serve as a shortcut for a formal declaration of war, at least in the sensitive area of subjecting civilians to military jurisdiction.

However, in *Davi v. Laird,*[6] decided on October 9, 1970 by a federal court in West Virginia, it was agreed that the Government's authority to conduct a war in Vietnam without formal declaration by Congress was a nonjusticiable *political* question. District Judge Widener, at the outset, stated that "by its very nature, the issue raises questions concerning the relationship between the judiciary and the coordinate branches of government. It is therefore necessary for this court to make a threshold inquiry into whether the issue involves a nonjusticiable political question." Accordingly, the Court opined:

> Examining the question of the separation of the three branches of government in its historical setting, we find that the power to commit American military forces under various sets of circum-

[5]38 Law Week 254, Ct. M.I. App., 1970.
[6]39 Law Week 2228, USDC WVa., 1970.

> stances is shared by Congress and the Executive. The House of Representatives, where all revenue bills must originate, was viewed by the Framers as the bulwark against encroachment by the other branches (The Federalist, No. 58 (Hamilton or Madison)). It was realized that the House alone can propose the supplies requisite for the support of government. Nor is Congress without other means of control. To an extent, it can restrict and qualify a president's conduct of foreign relations through resolution and other forms of legislation. If it so chooses, Congress may even resort to the drastic measure of impeachment. Against this array of congressional checks upon presidential prerogative, the question arises, of what practical significance, by itself, is the power to declare war? It has been suggested that formal declarations of war belong to an earlier age and are seldom appropriate today. . . . Authoritative sources report that since the Constitution was adopted, there have been as many as 125 instances of armed action initiated by American presidents without prior formal congressional declaration. . . . It is an established fact that Congress has participated actively with respect to the military effort in Vietnam. Since 1964, the southeast Asian conflict has been the subject of continuing debates on the floors of both Houses. Recently there have been various measures debated in both Houses concerning limitation of our military participation in southeast Asia. In view of this, it is abundantly clear that Congress is aware both of its responsibility regarding foreign policy and of the constitutional means afforded it to carry them out.

Thereupon Judge Widener concluded that "the issue of whether a certain instance of hostilities requires a formal declaration for its legitimization inescapably presents a *political* question." "By their claim that the conflict in Vietnam is a form of war which may be prosecuted only under authority of formal congressional declaration, plaintiffs pose an issue which, in the opinion of this court, portrays the very substance of a nonjusticiable political question." The West Virginia federal court reasoned that "adjudication of plaintiffs' claim would require this court to make an initial policy determination of a kind clearly non-judicial in nature; that is, a judgment as to whether the war may be maintained in its present posture . . ." and "resolution in favor of plaintiffs would admit of a judicial supervisory power over Congress' and the President's foreign policy-making authority by establishing a rule defining when, and if, a declaration is required. . . ." The Court concluded: "It is crystal clear that if there is one political question in the fabric of government of the Republic, it is whether or not to maintain a war, and if so, whether to maintain it as an imperfect or declared war. Into this seamless web of national and international politics, the courts should *not* intrude."

The Commonwealth of Massachusetts on April 1, 1970, sought to determine whether it is constitutional to require its citizens to fight in a foreign war, without congressional declaration of war. On that day the antiwar bill[7] passed both houses of the Massachusetts legislature (Senate vote 29 to 3, and House vote 127 to 97), and was signed into law by the Governor by the following day. The bill provided that no inhabitant of Massachusetts inducted into or serving in the armed forces "shall be required to serve" abroad in an armed hostility that has not been declared a war by Congress under Article I, Section 8 of the United States Constitution. Exceptions were made for an

---

[7]In his book, *The People vs. Presidential War* (Dunellen Company, 1970) Dr. John M. Wells wrote:

> I live in a historic house. It belonged to one of the Minute Men, Jonathan Harrington. He was engaged in the first battle of the Revolution, which took place in his front yard, now the Battle Green in Lexington. He died on April 19, 1775. It does something to one to live in such a house. Every morning, I look out the window on the Green where the flag flies day and night in commemoration of the place where the American Revolution began. What was it all about? It was for the right of people to participate in the decision-making process, in what the government does. And the process of government that most involves people, their lives, their pocketbooks, is war.

This book then recounts how the Massachusetts antiwar bill was "born." A remarkable rallying of forces against the Vietnam War occurred. Steve Worth, a professor at Northeastern University, was convinced that the war was unconstitutional and offered assistance; Larry Adler, a Boston lawyer and member of Dr. Wells' church, helped to draft the original bill; David Lustig, a graduate student, enlisted press support; many others used their talents to keep up the pressure on the Statehouse. And Representative James Shea, Jr., of the Massachusetts legislature called for "intellect and guts" by candidates to demand the "immediate withdrawal of our troops from Southeast Asia." The book provides a raw and fighting account of who and what was behind one of the most daring efforts to confront the Federal Government's death-making authority. The Shea-Wells bill was the work of a score of citizens—ministers, housewives, teachers, lawyers, journalists and, yes, politicians. Their recollections of how the bill became law are assembled here by the moving spirit, John M. Wells, a Unitarian minister with a law degree and a background of service as a judge advocate and Pentagon legal consultant. It was Dr. Wells who enlisted Representative James Shea, Jr., to introduce the bill.

"emergency" or when the President is acting as Commander in Chief of the Armed Forces. A further provision of the bill ordered the state Attorney General to bring appropriate legal action on behalf of Massachusetts and on behalf of its servicemen who are required to serve abroad in an undeclared war. All servicemen notifying the Attorney General under this bill are to be joined as parties in the legal action. The Attorney General was directed to bring action directly in the United States Supreme Court as a matter of original jurisdiction but should this fail, to bring another such action in an inferior federal court. This antiwar bill clearly focused upon the immense cost to the American economy and the morale of American youth of the undeclared war in Vietnam and was an attempt to secure United States Supreme Court adjudication of the illegality of unilateral executive action which brought this country into the Vietnam entanglement in the first place. Similar or identical bills have been introduced into the legislature of Illinois, Ohio, Maine, New York, Rhode Island, and California.

The United States Supreme Court was thereupon asked on November 9, 1970, in *Massachusetts v. Laird,*[8] to declare that United States participation in the Indochina war was "unconstitutional in that it was not initially authorized or subsequently ratfied by Congressonal declaration." Inherent in the suit were possible answers to the following questions: (a) Is it constitutional for a State to pass such a bill? (b) Does not the bill "interpose" the State against the federal government? (c) What is the "political" purpose of the bill? (d) Would not the bill hamstring the President? Recent U. S. Supreme Court decisions, like *Baker v. Carr*[9] in 1965, involving the gerrymandering of political districts, and *Powell v. McCormack*[10] in 1969, involving the fortunes of a former Congressman from Harlem in New York City, have not denied review of the issue of constitutionality on any theory of "political questions," so at least there is a precedent for deciding the issue. Furthermore, in 1958 in *Kent v. Dulles,*[11]

---

[8]39 Law Week 3196, 1970.
[9]369 U.S. 186, 1965.
[10]395 U.S. 486, 1969.
[11]359 U.S. 116, 1958.

the highest court scrutinized very carefully an alleged congressional delegation to the executive of power to control passports, without raising the political question barrier. If that case did not involve a political question where there was nothing specific in the Constitution giving Congress a power in the first instance over passports, then *a fortiori*, there should be no political question on the issue of an undeclared war when the Constitution in Article I, Section 8 states that "The Congress shall have Power . . to declare war." Mr. Justice Stewart, while dissenting in the 1967 case of *Mora v. McNamara*,[12] realistically approached the problem. "We cannot make these problems [of the constitutionality of the Vietnam war] go away simply by refusing to hear the case. . . ." The Massachusetts antiwar bill does not appear to shackle the President in the area of foreign relations; the bill recognizes an exception for "emergencies" or for Presidential action as Commander in Chief. Surely if the United States were territorially attacked, the President would respond without first checking with Congress.

And so a majority of the United States Supreme Court on November 9, 1970, refused to hear the case, i.e. denied *certiorari*. Mr. Justice Douglas vehemently *dissented*, pointing out that the question is justiciable, is not "political," and involves the same issues as the presidential war-making which the United States Supreme Court had entertained in the *Prize Cases*[13] involving the legality of President Lincoln's blockade, and in the *Steel Seizure Cases*,[14] *Youngstown Sheet & Tube Co. v. Sawyer*. Both Mr. Justices Harlan and Stewart also dissented, but the 6-3 vote of the Court precluded the necessary judicial decision-making. It is terrifying that the highest United States Court abdicated its responsibility because today there is no more fundamental constitutional doubt arising in the mind of the American public than the legality of the war in Indochina. In this day when the concept of "law and order" has a hollow ring in the minds of many of the youth of this nation,

---

[12]389 U.S. 934, 1967.
[13]67 U.S. 635, 1863.
[14]343 U.S. 579, 1952.

largely because of Vietnam, it is vital for the executive branch of our government to behave strictly according to the letter of the law and the Constitution. When a substantial popular doubt arises as to the legality of executive action, the President should indeed welcome a definitive interpretation from the United States Supreme Court. But even if the President fears an adverse resolution of the issue, the Court should take the realistic view required by the ideal of a "government under law" and hear the case on its merits. Perhaps the United States Supreme Court will again entertain the suit as it progresses this time through the lower federal court system. If the Court holds that the undeclared war in Vietnam is constitutional, most doubts on this particular issue will be allayed and public confidence will be restored. If the Court holds the other way, the President will have no choice but to dismantle forthwith the military effort in Southeast Asia, unless Congress passes a formal declaration of war. If the President has to dismantle the military effort, he can persuasively claim that he is doing his duty under law, even though he personally would have not done so had he not been legally compelled. There can be no embarrassment for a statesman in such a position. In either case, the Chief Executive can only gain in stature and in respect.

On September 10, 1970, the lower federal district court for the Northern District of California in *Mottola v. Nixon*[15] answered the question of the constitutionality of the Vietnam war. It declared that the time has come for the judicial authorities to rule on the question. (The Court indicated that the reason why the US Supreme Court has not yet decided the issue is because the lower federal courts have avoided the necessity for the ruling by disposing of such cases on technical, jurisdictional, or procedural grounds.) Accordingly, this lower federal court ruled that the petitioning military reservists have standing to challenge the constitutionality of the war since their case presents the kind of "personal stake in the outcome" and "concrete adverseness" required as the test by the United States Supreme Court in *Flast v. Cohen.*[16] As members of the Reserve, these plaintiffs are vulnerable to an order to report to the Vietnam War area. (However, a draft registrant is denied "standing," since a compulsory draft system without a war declaration would not necessarily be illegal.) The challenge of the military reservists, said the Court, rested not merely on the ground that President Nixon exceeded his general executive powers, but that he acted in violation of a specific limitation on his powers, to wit: Article I, Section 8 (II), vesting in the Congress the power to declare war. Furthermore, the doctrine of sovereign immunity is no bar to the challenge by the military reservists because the essence of that challenege is that the President, although purporting to act in the name of the sovereign, really exceeded his constitutional authority. In such a case, the court need not require affirmative governmental action, but only that the executive cease its continuance of the war until war has been declared by Congress. As for contention that the "political question" issue bars the present action, the Court stated that to strike down as unconstitutional a President's wartime seizure of a few private steel mills, as in *Youngstown v. Sawyer*,[17] but to shy away from interfering with a Presidential war itself, "would be to strain at a gnat and swallow a camel." Obviously, the United States Supreme Court will have the last say on the subject when that Court faces this issue in the Massachusetts antiwar bill case in the near future.

The issue of the power to declare war has been timely raised in two recent articles appearing in the important *American*

---

[15]39 Law Week 2228, USDC Cal., 1970.

[16]Flast v. Cohen [392 U.S. 83] modified the doctrine of standing which, since Frothingham v. Mellon, [262 U.S. 477, 1923], had barred suits by federal taxpayers to enjoin allegedly unconstitutional federal expenditures. In Flast, the United States Supreme Court *reversed* (8-1) a dismissal of a taxpayer's complaint and ruled that a federal taxpayer has standing to challenge the constitutionality of a congressional expenditure that is an exercise of Congress' Article I, Section 8 taxing and spending power, on the ground it violates the establishment clause and the free exercise of religion clause of the First Amendment. In Flast, the majority ruled that "standing," as a basis for invoking federal judicial power, requires merely that the party suing have "a personal stake in the outcome of the controversy [sufficient] to assure that concrete adverseness which sharpens the presentation of issues upon which the Court so largely depends for illumination of difficult constitutional questions" [392 U.S. at 99, quoting Baker v. Carr (369 U.S. 186, 204, 1962)].

[17]343 U.S. 579, 1952.

Bar Association Journal. Attorney Eberhard P. Deutsch of Louisiana takes the position that the President has full plenary power to conduct military operations during a war, declared or undeclared. The second article by attorney Charles B. Blackmar of Missouri argues that the President cannot conduct military operations unfettered by Congressional control. These articles[18] are reproduced for their timeliness.

THE PRESIDENT AS COMMANDER IN CHIEF

EBERHARD P. DEUTSCH

Recent extended debate in the Senate on the Cooper-Church Amendment to the Foreign Military Sales Act, the Hatfield-McGovern Amendment to military procurement legislation, and the deployment, not long ago, of segments of the Armed Forces into Cambodia in the course of the war in South Vietnam, with widespread public discussion, have accentuated the question as to the powers under the Constitution of the President of the United States as commander in chief of those forces vis-à-vis those of the Congress.

While all United States forces have since been withdrawn from Cambodia and such legislation as sought to restrict Presidential authority over the Armed Forces has either been defeated or is in limbo, the over-all military necessities of the situation in Southeast Asia, as well as possible exigencies of other restless areas in a troubled world, require careful consideration of the constitutional issues involved in what may be the need for prompt action to protect important interests of the United States.

That the United States is "at war" in Vietnam can hardly be disputed, despite repeated recent assertions that there can be no war in the absence of an unequivocal declaration thereof by the Congress.

Formal Declarations Are Not Always Used

Historically, Presidents of the United States, in their con-

[18]Reprinted with permission of the American Bar Association Journal.

stitutional capacity as commanders in chief of our Armed Forces, have, on innumerable occasions, deployed those forces into troubled areas involving armed conflict in combat conditions without any Congressional declarations of war,[1] and the Supreme and other courts of the United States have recognized the existence of a "state of war" under the Constitution in such cases. For instance, hostilities were conducted against France in 1798, and troops were deployed in recent years to Santo Domingo, without any declaration of war in support thereof. In 1945, President Truman, in an unprecedented move—one of the most significant war measures ever taken by a commander in chief—ordered, without Congressional sanction or even knowledge, the dropping of the terrifying atom bomb on Hiroshima. In 1962, President Kennedy established a blockade of Cuba against the importation and installation of Russian missiles without Congressional authority, and more recently, both the Korean and Vietnam Wars have been conducted without formal declarations.[2]

In Tucker on *The Constitution*, it is stated that even "in Greece and Rome, and even in the European countries in the Middle Ages, public declaration of war was uniformly made and was obligatory, but since the middle of the Eighteenth Century, formal declarations have not been universal and have fallen into disuse."[3]

As early as 1800, the Supreme Court had occasion to pass

Note: Reprinted from 57 *A.B.A.J.* 27-32, 1971.

[1]"The occupation of Iceland was but one of 'at least 125 incidents' in our history in which Presidents, 'without Congressional authorization, and in the absence of a declaration of war [have] ordered the armed forces to take action or maintain positions abroad'." Vinson, C.J., dissenting in Youngstown Company v. Sawyer, 343 U. S. 579 at 694 (1952).

[2]"Of course, a state of war may in fact exist without a formal declaration." Jackson, J., concurring in Youngstown Company v. Sawyer, 342 U.S. 579 at 642 (1952). "Neither in the language of the Constitution, the intent of the framers, the available historical and judicial precedents, nor the purposes behind the clause" giving Congress the exclusive authority to "declare war", is support to be found for the claim that "nothing short of a formal declaration of war will satisfy the Constitution's demand for congressional control of the war power." Note, Congress, The President, and the Power To Commit Forces to Combat, 81 Harv. L. Rev. 1711, 1801-1802 passim (1968).

on the question as to whether the United States was actually involved "in war" without a formal declaration thereof. Congress had, by two statutes enacted in 1798 and 1799 respectively, provided salvage allowances for recapture of vessels of the United States which had been taken "from the enemy" (France).

All of the Justices concurred in the holding by the Court, each in a separate opinion, to the effect that the United States was actually "at war," as recognized by the Congress through the statutes in question, despite the fact that there had been no declaration of war against France.

One of the opinions was written by Mr. Justice Washington (nephew of the President). He stated that the question before the Court was whether "there subsisted a state of war between the two nations. . . . If it be declared in form it is called *solemn* . . . but hostilities may subsist . . . limited as to places, persons and things; and this is more properly termed *imperfect* war. . . . Still, however, it is public war, because it is an external contention by force." And Justice Washington concluded his opinion on this point with the statement that "as to *America*, the degree of hostility meant to be carried on, was sufficiently described without declaring war, or declaring that we were at war. . . . In fact and in law, we are at war."[4]

Four years later, the Supreme Court had occasion to rule on a related point, the opinion being written by Chief Justice Marshall. The statute involved in that case authorized the seizure of vessels of the United States proceeding *to* emborgoed French ports. Such a vessel was seized en route *from* such a French port. The Court held that the statute had to be construed strictly and did not authorize the seizure of the vessel in question.

However, in the course of his opinion, the great Chief Justice had occasion to say:

---

[3]2 Tucker, The Constitution 576 (1899). "Use of the Congressional power to declare war, for example, has fallen into abeyance because wars are no longer declared in advance." Executive Department Report Prepared For Use of Joint Committee of Senate Committee on Foreign Relations and House Committee on Armed Services, 82d Cong., 1st Sess., Powers of the President To Send the Armed Forces Outside the United States 27 (Comm. Print 1951).

[4]The Eliza, 4 Dall. 307, 340-341, 342 (1800).

> It is by no means clear that the President of the United States, whose high duty it is to 'take care that the laws be faithfully executed', and who is Commander-in-Chief of the Army and Navy of the United States, might not, without any special authority for that purpose, in the then-existing state of the times, have empowered the officers commanding the armed vessels of the United States to seize and send into port for adjudication, American vessels which were forfeited by being engaged in this illicit commerce.[5]

In December, 1900, while troops of the United States were stationed in China, having been deployed for the protection of American and other interests in the course of the Boxer uprising there, an American soldier was tried and convicted by court martial for the murder of another soldier. The conviction was under an Article of War covering such an offense when committed "in time of war". It was contended that because the American forces had been deployed to China without a declaration of war, the offense had not been committed "in time of war" and that the judgment of the court martial was accordingly invalid. The case came before a circuit court of the United States in the District of Kansas, which held expressly that a formal declaration of war "is unnecessary to constitute a condition of war."[6] The court pointed out that extensive military forces, both of the United States and of other nations, had been deployed into China and that "many engagements resulting in considerable loss of life" had taken place; "military zones were formed"; and "by act of Congress the pay of the officers and men in the military service of this country during the time they were occupied in China was increased to the amount paid in time of actual war . . . notwithstanding the further fact that at no time was there any declaration of war on the part of this government against the government of China. The court accordingly con-

---

[5]Little v. Barreme, 2 Cranch. 170 at 177 (1804).

[6]Early in our constitutional history, Alexander Hamilton, while recognizing the exclusive power of Congress under the Constitution "to declare war", submitted that nevertheless, "when a foreign nation declares, or openly and avowedly makes war upon the United States, they are then by the very fact *already at war,* and any declaration on the part of Congress is nugatory; it is at least unnecessary." Hamilton, Works 747 (J. Hamilton ed. 1851).

cluded that "at the time the homicide in question was committed there prevailed in China a condition of war. . . . "[7]

Congress Has Approved Presidential Action

The point here under discussion has already been adjudicated several times directly as to the war in Vietnam. In the first of these cases, a man convicted of willful failure to report for induction into the Army claimed "that with respect to the War in Viet Nam the Universal Military and Service Training Act is being unconstitutionally applied, because Congress has not declared war; [and] and that the Executive, in effect, has declared war. . . ."

The court held that

> "while Congress has not formally declared war with respect to the military action in Vietnam, nor did it in Korea, it has given its wholehearted approval to the action of the President by appropriations and other implementing help. The President, as Commander-in-Chief, has always exercised the power to begin hostilities. . . . Unquestionably the President can start the guns at home or abroad to meet force with force; he is not only authorized, but bound, to do so.[8]

The same point was raised in defense of the recall of some soldiers to active duty; and the court held again "that the United States of America has the right to, and may, make war under

---

[7]Hamilton v. McClaughry, 136 Fed. 445 at 450-451 (C.C. Kan. 1905). The Senate Foreign Relations Committee has itself recently said that "it does not believe that formal declarations of war are the only available means by which Congress can authorize the President to initiate limited or general hostilities." S. Rep. No. 797, 90th Cong. 1st Sess. 25 (1967).

[8]United States v. Mitchell, 246 F. Supp. 874 at 897, 898 (1965); aff'd, 369 F. 2d 323 (3d Cir. 1966). Former President and Chief Justice William Howard Taft, in the course of a lecture in 1916 at Columbia University, said that while "under the Constitution, only Congress has the power to declare war", the President can, as commander in chief under the same instrument, "order the Army and Navy anywhere he will", and thus "can take action such as to involve the country in war and to leave Congress no option but to declare or to recognize its existence". Taft, Our Chief Magistrate and His Power 94-95 (1916).

the Constitution without the necessity of a formal declaration of the Congress".[9]

Shortly after the outbreak of hostilities in Korea, Senator Paul Douglas of Illinois, in an address on "The Constitutional and Legal Basis for the President's Action in Using Armed Forces To Repel the Invasion of South Korea", stated: "The acts of the President in helping to protect Southern Korea from Communist aggression were in thorough harmony with the legislative intent of the framers of the Constitution, in line with sound historical precedent, in conformity with international law and the rules of the United Nations, and in the best interests of our own ultimate security and the peace of the world."[10]

President Is Bound To Resist Force by Force

In the *Prize Cases,* decided by the Supreme Court early during the War Between the States, the question was whether, since there had been no Congressional declaration of war, it could be said that the United States were actually "at war" in the sense that seizures of vessels as prize for blockade running could be justified under international law.

Speaking for the Supreme Court, Mr. Justice Grier held that "if a war be made by invasion of a foreign nation, the President is not only authorized but bound to resist force by force. He does not initiate the war, but is bound to accept the challenge without waiting for any legislative authority. . . . " The conflict, the learned Justice went on, "sprung forth suddenly from the parent brain, a Minerva in the full panoply of *war.* The President was bound to meet it in the shape it presented itself, without waiting for Congress to baptize it with a name. . . ."[11]

---

[9]Ali v. United States, 289 F. Supp. 530, 531 (D.C. C.D. Cal. 1968). Two very recent opinions in the Eastern District of New York are to the same effect: Orlando v. Laird, 39 Law Week 2069 (July 1, 1970), and Berk v. Laird, 39 Law Week 2201 (September 16, 1970). And see Weissman v. Metropolitan Life Insurance Company, 112 F. Supp. 420 (D.C. S.D. Cal. 1953).

[10]96 Cong, Rec. 9647, 9649 (1950).

[11]Prize Cases, 2 Black 635, 668-669 (1862). "As long as the United States is not the initial aggressor, the President's actions will remain 'defensive' requiring no further Congressional action to enable him to wage war thrust on the country." Note, Congress, The President and the Power To Commit Forces to Combat, *supra* note 2 at 1779-1780.

It can hardly be contended, in light of the foregoing authorities, so clearly recognizing that a state of war may exist under the Constitution without a formal declaration thereof by the Congress, that the United States has not been at war in Vietnam since 1965. The Presidents who have been in office during that time have acted accordingly, and Congress has invariably supported the action of the President in his conduct of the Vietnamese conflict.[12]

Constitutional Authority: Deployment of Troops

The next—and perhaps the more interesting—question at issue concerns the division of constitutional authority in the matter of the deployment of troops, once a state of war—declared or undeclared—has come into being, as it has in Indochina. When the Constitution was being framed, there was no objection whatever to the provision that the President, even though he was likely to come generally from civilian life, was to be commander in chief of the Armed Forces. This provision grew out of the difficulties which Washington had experienced with the Continental Congress during the Revolution.

> This action of the Convention was probably due to some particular consideration, and none seems more reasonable than the fact that during the Revolution, Washington experienced great trouble and embarrassment resulting from the failure of Congress to support him with firmness and dispatch. There was a want of directness in the management of affairs during the period which was attributable to the absence of centralized authority or command. The members of the Convention knew this, and probably thought they could prevent its recurrence by making the President Commander-in-Chief of the Army and Navy.[13]

The original intent of the framers of the Constitution as to its detailed provisions can best be gained from contemporaneous writings, largely pamphlets, circulated while the instrument

---

[12]It has recently been suggested that a "formal declaration of war in the modern context is often deliberately avoided precisely because of the apparent commitment to total victory and the general hardening of attitudes likely to result". Note. Congress, The President and the Power to Commit Forces to Combat, *supra* note 2 at 1772-1773.

[13]2 Watson, The Constitution 912.

was being considered by the states for ratification. Thus, Alexander Hamilton, writing with reference to the power and authority of the President as Commander in Chief under the Constitution, said:

> Of all the cares or concerns of government, the direction of war most peculiarly demands those qualities which distinguish the exercise of power by a single hand. The direction of war implies the direction of the common strength; and the power of directing and employing the common strength forms a usual and essential part in the definition of the executive authority.[14]

In another of his essays, Hamilton expounded somewhat more fully on the principle underlying this provision of the Constitution, which places broad power in the hands of the President as Commander in Chief:

> In the legislature, promptitude of decisions is oftener an evil than a benefit. The differences of opinion, and the joinings of parties in that department of the government, though they may sometimes obscure salutary plans, yet often promote deliberation and circumspection, and serve to check excesses in the majority . . . . But no favorable circumstances palliate or atone for the disadvantages of dissension in the executive department. . . . They constantly counteract those qualities in the Executive which are the most necessary ingredients in its composition,—vigor and expedition, and this without any counterbalancing good. In the conduct of war, in which the energy of the Executive is the bulwark of the national security, everything [hurtful?] would be to be apprehended from its plurality.[15]

Some years later, in his renowned *Commentaries on the Constitution*, Justice Joseph Story, in part at least, in the identical words used a half century earlier by Alexander Hamilton, gave expression to the same principle:

> Of all the cares and concerns of government, the direction of war most peculiarly demands those qualities, which distinguish the exercise of power by a single hand. Unity of plan, promptitude, activity and decision, are indispensable to success; and these can scarcely exist, except when a single magistrate is entrusted exclu-

---

[14]The Federalist No. 74 (Hamilton).
[15]*Id.*, No. 70.

> sively with the power. Even the coupling of the authority of an executive council with him in the exercise of such powers, enfeebles the system, divides the responsibility, and not unfrequently defeats every energetic measure. Timidity, indecision, obstinacy and pride of opinion, must mingle in all such councils, and infuse a torpor and sluggishness, destructive of all military operations.[16]

The foregoing principle, so strongly emphasized by these eminent authorities, will be found stated and restated in various forms in practically all works on the Constitution. For instance, in his *Commentaries*, Judge Kent wrote:

> The command and application of the public force to execute law, maintain peace, and resist foreign invasion, are powers so obviously of an executive nature, and require the exercise of qualities so characteristic of this department, that they have always been exclusively appropriated to it, in every well-organized government upon earth.[17]

"War Power" Is Invested in the President

Again, in Watson on *The Constitution*, it is stated:

> The power of the President under this clause is commonly called the "War Power" of the President. It is an immense power to exercise and might be used in a most dangerous manner by an unwise Executive, as there does not seem to be any limitation prescribed by the Constitution to the exercise of the power by the President in the field of military operations.
>
> By this clause he is made commander of the military and naval forces of the United States, for the whole time that he is President. No other department of the government, and no other officer of the government can exercise this power or assume to command either the Army or the Navy, unless designated by the President to do so. Congress can legislate relative to the number of the Army or the Navy, the compensation of the officers and men, and the term of their service, as well as many other matters, but the command of the Army and Navy is vested in the President, and Congress can neither command them or take that power from the President.
>
> The power is vested in the President to dispose of or arrange the component parts of the Army and Navy at his pleasure. In practice he does this through the military and naval departments of the government, but this action is his action. While Congress can

---

[16]Story, *Commentaries on the Constitution* 546-547.
[17]1 Kent, *Commentaries* 295.

make rules for the Army and Navy, it can not interfere with the President's power as commander of such forces. The line between the exercise of his power as commander and that of Congress is plain, and neither can rightfully or legally invade the other.[18]

At this point in his treatise, Watson quotes from the opinion of the Supreme Court of the United States in the famous case of *Ex parte Milligan,* involving the constitutional validity of a military commission sitting in Indiana during the War Between the States, in which it was stated in the opinion of the Chief Justice:

Congress has the power not only to raise and support and govern armies but to declare war. It has, therefore, the power to provide by law for carrying on war. This power necessarily extends to all legislation essential to the prosecution of war with vigor and success, except such as interferes with the command of the forces and the conduct of campaigns. That power and duty belong to the President as commander-in-chief. Both these powers are derived from the Constitution, but neither is defined by that instrument. Their extent must be determined by their nature, and by the principles of our institutions.

The power to make the necessary laws is in Congress; the power to execute in the President. Both powers imply many subordinate and auxiliary powers. Each includes all authorities essential to its due exercise. But neither can the President, in war more than in peace, intrude upon the proper authority of Congress, nor Congress upon the proper authority of the President.[19]

Powers of President and Congress Are Separate

Watson, in his notable work, then goes on to state:

The power of Congress, and that of the President over the Army and Navy are separate and distinct, neither can impair or invade the authority of the other. The powers of the President under this clause are only those which may be called "military." He can direct the movements of the Army and Navy so as to injure the enemy in the most effective way, and to do this may order an invasion of the enemy's country, and if possible establish the authority of the United States over it.[20]

---

[18] 2 Watson, *The Constitution* 913-914.
[19] 4 Wall. 2, 139 (1866).
[20] 2 Watson, *The Constitution* 915-916.

The language of the Supreme Court of the United States in *Fleming v. Page,* involving a question of import duties dependent on the national status of Tampico while under occupation by military forces of the United States in the Mexican (undeclared) War, parallels Watson's foregoing dictum:

> As Commander-in-Chief, [the President] is authorized to direct the movements of the naval and military forces placed by law at his command, and to employ them in the manner he may deem most effectual to harass and conquer and subdue the enemy. He may invade the hostile country, and subject it to the sovereignty and authority of the United States.[21]

Quite recently, the United States Court of Appeals for the District of Columbia Circuit had occasion to express itself forcefully on this point. The case involved an action against the Secretary of Defense to compel him to permit "the use of newsstand facilities of military post-exchanges in the Far East" for the sale of certain newspapers whose character had been put in question. In the course of its opinion, the court said:

> With respect to this first category, we note that we deal here with a matter far removed from what is ordinarily subsumed under the head of military operations. It is—and must be—true that the Executive should be accorded wide and normally unassailable discretion with respect to the conduct of the national defense and the prosecution of national objectives through military means. The power of the armed services to make their disposition of men and materiel, and to take measures for the safeguarding of each does not admit of fragmentation.[22]

Swaim v. United States involved an action by a Judge Advocate General of the Army who had been sentenced by a court martial convened by the President of the United States to forfeiture of half of his pay for a period of years on being found guilty of "conduct prejudicial to good order and military discipline." General Swaim sued in the Court of Claims for restoration of his pay on the ground, *inter alia,* that the President had no authority, under the Constitution, to convene the court.

---

[21]9 How. 603, 615 (1850).

[22]Overseas Media Corporation v. McNamara, 385 F. 2d 308 at 314. See also *Exparte* Quirin, 317 U.S. 1 at 26 (1942).

Court Upholds Presidential Power

In the course of its opinion upholding the Presidential power, the Court said:

> Congress may increase the Army, or reduce the Army, or abolish it altogether; but so long as we have a military force, Congress can not take away from the President the supreme command. It is true that the Constitution has conferred upon Congress the exclusive power "to make rules for the government of the land and naval forces" but the two powers are distinct; neither can trench upon the other; the President can not, under the disguise of military orders, evade the legislative regulations by which he in common with the Army must be governed; and Congress can not in the disguise of "rules for the government" of the Army impair the authority of the President as commander in chief.[23]

This decision was expressly and unanimously affirmed by the Supreme Court, which held: "We approve the opinion of the Court of Claims. . . ."[24]

In *Ex parte Quirin,* 317 U.S. 1, 28 (1942), it was held that the order of the President creating a military commission to try the German saboteurs who landed by submarine on Long Island and Florida beaches was a proper exercise of "such authority as the Constitution itself gives the Commander in Chief, to direct the performance of those functions which may constitutionally be performed by the military arm of the nation in time of war."

A decade later, Mr. Justice Jackson, concurring in the *Steel Seizure* case, and agreeing with Mr. Justice Douglas that "our history and tradition rebel at the thought that the grant of military power carries with it authority over civilian affairs," nevertheless felt constrained to concede that he "should indulge the widest latitude of interpretation to sustain" the power of the President as commander in chief, in "his exclusive function to command the instruments of national force, at least when turned against the outside world for the security of our society."[25]

A tremendously significant statement is found in a note

---

[23]Swaim v. United States, 28 Ct. Cl. 173 at 221 (1893).
[24]Swaim v. United States, 165 U. S. 553 at 558 (1897).
[25]Youngstown Company v. Sawyer, 342 U. S. 579 at 632 and 645 (1952).

sent in 1861 to Lord Lyons, British Minister to the United States, by William H. Seward, then Secretary of State. In that note, Seward clearly, concisely, and emphatically defines this phase of power of the President as Commander in Chief:

> It seems necessary to state that Congress is by the Constitution invested with no executive power or responsibility whatever, but on the contrary the President of the United States is, by the Constitution and laws, invested with the whole executive power of the government and charged with the supreme direction of all ministerial agents as well as of the whole land and naval forces of the United States . . . .
>
> If it be said that these acts of the President in time of war are unconstitutional, the answer is that as Commander-in-Chief of the Army and Navy, the President has the constitutional power to employ the means recognized by the laws of war as necessary to conquer the enemy.
>
> Congress can pass no law which can deprive the President of the power conferred in creating him Commander-in-Chief.[26]

In the course of a debate on the floor of the Senate in 1922, Senator Reed of Missouri suggested that Congress had constitutional authority to compel the President to withdraw American forces stationed in Europe. To that suggestion, Senator Borah of Idaho replied:

> We could not make the President do it. He is Commander-in-Chief of the Army and Navy of the United States; and if in the discharge of his duty he wants to assign them there, I do not know of any power that we can exert to compel him to bring them home. We may refuse to create an Army, but when it is created he is the Commander.[27]

Some question has at times been raised as to the authority of the President, as commander in chief of the country's Armed Forces, to deploy them into foreign combat areas pursuant to treaties by which the United States have assumed the obligation, in advance, to come to the aid of another country if attacked, without the express consent of Congress as a whole.

---

[26]Quoted in Woodburn, *American Republic* 181.

[27]64 Cong. Rec. 933 (1922). "It is clear that Congress may not usurp the functions of the Executive . . . by forbidding or directing the movement of the Army and Navy. Taft, The Boundaries Between the Executive, the Legislative and the Judicial Branches of the Government, 25 Yale L. J. 599 at 606 (1916).

Under Section 2 of Article II of the Constitution, the President is not only designated as commander in chief of the Army and Navy, but he is also given "Power, by and with the Advice and Consent of the Senate, to make Treaties, provided two thirds of the Senators present concur." Then, under Article VI of the Constitution, that instrument, the laws made "in pursuance thereof" and "all Treaties made, or which shall be made, under the Authority of the United States, shall be the supreme Law of the Land." Finally, under Section 3 of Article II, the President is charged to "take care that the Laws [presumably including treaties as "the supreme Law of the Land" under Article VI] be faithfully executed."

When, therefore, a treaty, duly approved by the Senate, which has thus become "the supreme Law of the Land," requires the United States to come to the military aid of a foreign country under attack, the President, as constitutional commander in chief, must, without awaiting Congressional sanction, deploy the Armed Forces of the United States into the foreign combat area in compliance with his constitutional obligation, as President to "take Care that the Laws be faithfully executed."[28]

Following consideration of the United Nations Participation Act[29] by the Senate Foreign Relations Committee, it reported its conviction

> that any reservation to the Charter, or any subsequent congressional limitation, designed to provide, for example, that employment of the Armed Forces of the United States to be made available to the Security Council under special agreements referred to in Article 43 could be authorized only after the Congress has passed on each individual case would . . . violate the spirit of the United States Constitution under which the President has well-established powers and obligations to use our Armed Forces without specific approval of Congress.[30]

---

[28]Executive Department Report Prepared for Use of Joint Committee of Senate Committee on Foreign Relations and House Committee on Armed Services, 82d Cong., 1st Sess., Powers of the President To Send the Armed Forces Outside the United States 2 (Comm. Print 1951).

[29]59 Stat. 621, 22 U.S.C. § 287 (1945).

[30]S. Rep. No. 717, 91st Cong., 2d Sess. 8 (1945). The House Foreign Affairs Committee expressly concurred in the report of the Senate Foreign Relations Committee.

When the bill reached the floor of the Senate, Senator Wheeler of Montana insisted that it sought to override the exclusive constitutional power of Congress to declare war, and he offered an amendment to preserve that Congressional authority unimpaired, as follows:

> Nothing in such agreement or agreements shall authorize the President, and the President shall have no authority, to make available to the Security Council any armed forces to enable the Security Council to take action under Article 42 of said Charter, unless the Congress has by appropriate act or joint resolution authorized the President to make such forces available. . . .[31]

Senator Taft opposed Senator Wheeler's amendment on the ground that in his view the President already had the power under the Constitution to use troops without Congressional sanction. The amendment was defeated, 65 to9.[32]

This constitutional drama was repeated less than four years later, when the North Atlantic Treaty was submitted to the Senate for its advice and consent. Following consideration of the treaty, the Senate Foreign Relations Committee reported that nothing in it, "including the provision that an attack against one shall be considered an attack against all, increases or decreases the constitutional powers of either the President or the Congress or changes the relationship between them."[33]

On the floor of the Senate, Senator Watkins of Utah introduced a proposed reservation to the treaty to the effect that "the United States assumes no obligation to . . . employ" its Armed Forces "unless in any particular case the Congress which, under the Constitution, has the sole power to declare war or authorize the employment of" those forces, "shall by act or joint resolution so provide."[34]

The reservation was rejected by a vote of 84 to 11, and the treaty was approved without the reservation, by 82 to 13.[35]

It is interesting to note in this connection that the consti-

[31]91 *Cong. Rec.* 11,392 (1945).
[32]*Ibid.*
[33]S. Exec. Doc. No. 8, 81st Cong., 1st Sess. 14 (1949).
[34]95 *Cong. Rec.* 9898 (1949).
[35]*Id.* at 9916.

tutional powers of the President under the first section of Article II, which provides simply that the "executive Power shall be vested" in him, are far broader than those of Congress under Section 1 of Article I, which restricts its "legislative Powers" only to those "herein granted."

From all the foregoing, it certainly seems abundantly clear that whenever a state of war exists – whether declared or undeclared–the President of the United States has, under the Constitution, as commander in chief, full and plenary power to conduct military operations in prosecution of the war, unhampered by anything in the nature of strategic legislative restrictions.

Any other construction of the Constitution would so hamper the conduct of a war as to portend ultimate military defeat. The Constitution of the United States was never meant to be construed as a suicide pact.

THE PRESIDENT AS COMMANDER IN CHIEF: ANOTHER VIEW

Charles B. Blackmar

For more than a decade, the United States has been involved in armed combat in Indochina. Several Presidents have dispatched hundreds of thousands of men, many of them involuntary inductees. There have been aerial bombing and naval operations, and these have been directed in several countries in support of strategic or tactical objectives.

Our forces first entered the Republic of Vietnam (South Vietnam) at the request of its government to aid in the suppression of an insurrection. It was evident that the insurrection was heavily supported by troops and material supplied by the Democratic Republic of Vietnam (North Vietnam) and, through that conduit, by other Communist nations. President Johnson ordered strategic bombing operations deep inside North Vietnam. These were suspended in the hope of facilitating the pending peace negotiations in Paris, but with reservation of the possibility of renewal if the negotiations did not proceed in a satisfactory manner. The Nixon Administration has asserted the authority to engage in aerial operations wherever these are considered necessary for the protection of American forces, and the President has directed bombing missions in North Vietnam, Laos, and Cambodia.

North Vietnamese forces had made free use of the territory of Cambodia, which had a "neutral" government lacking either the force or the will to inhibit the operations. Then there was a change in the government of Cambodia, and the United States embarked on ground operations in "sanctuaries" along the border between Cambodia and South Vietnam. The new government apparently felt that it could not express approval of the operations, but it certainly did not protest. President Nixon stated that his purpose was to protect American forces in Vietnam, so that they could continue in the Vietnamization program and be withdrawn sooner. He promised a strict limitation on the venture, with obvious deference to American public opinion, but made it clear that the limitation was a voluntary one and that he might resume operations or probe more deeply if he thought it necessary.

The entire venture in Indochina has proceeded without any express declaration of war. The Presidents have taken the initiative. There have been consultations with Congressional leaders and committees, but the Presidents usually have been in the position of telling Congress what they are going to do rather than of seeking advice. Congress has shown virtually complete acquiescence, especially in the earlier stages of the operation. It has appropriated money and enacted draft laws and other supporting legislation, and at times it has prescribed severe penalties for unlawful manifestations of dissent.[1] The 88th Congress adopted the now repealed Tonkin Gulf Resolution, giving the President very broad authority for the use of ground and air forces in Southeast Asia.[2] Until late in 1967, the overwhelming

---

Note: Reprinted from 57 A.B.A.J. 335-339, 1971.

[1]See, *e.g.*, 50 App. U.S.C. § 462(b), prescribing a sentence of up to five years for burning or mutilating draft cards.

[2]This resolution, adopted August 7, 1964, because of information about attacks against attacks on American warships in the Gulf of Tonkin, gave the President the authority "to take all necessary measures to repel any armed attack against the forces of the United States and to prevent further aggression."

weight of public opinion seemed to be behind the Indochina operations.

Then there was a dramatic change. The expected military successes did not materialize. Opposition to the war grew, both inside and outside Congress. Dissent became respectable. The war situation was surely the predominant factor in President Johnson's decision in 1968 not to seek another term. President Nixon promised the total withdrawal of American forces, while declining to specify a detailed timetable because of his fear of interfering with the Paris peace negotiations. Vocal opposition to the war became less intense until the tranquility was shattered, at least temporarily, by the entry of American ground troops into Cambodia in May of 1970.

Cambodia gave rise to a series of Congressional proposals designed to limit the scope and duration of operations in Indochina. For almost the first time in history, there was substantial Congressional support for the enactment of restrictions that would affect the President in his direction of military operations. Defenders of Presidential authority not only challenged the merits of the restrictive proposals but asserted that they would amount to an unconstitutional interference with the authority conferred upon the President by Article II, Section 2 of the Constitution: "The President shall be commander in chief of the army and navy of the United States, and of the militia of the several states when called into the actual service of the United States. . . ."

My purpose is not to argue the merits of our involvement in Southeast Asia, or its possible extensions, but rather to discuss the constitutional problems presented by such proposals as Cooper-Church,[3] McGovern-Hatfield,[4] and other proposals that surely will be presented so long as American involvement in Indochina continues. The specific occasion for my writing is Eberhard P. Deutsch's scholarly article, "The President as Commander in Chief," in the January, 1971, issue of this *Journal* (page 27), in which he expresses the following conclusion: ". . . whenever a state of war exists—*whether declared or undeclared*—the President of the United States has, under the Constitution, as commander in chief, full and plenary power to conduct military operations in prosecution of the war, unhampered by anything in the nature of strategic restrictions. (Emphasis supplied.)"

Mr. Deutsch suggests that attempted limitations by legislative action and similar proposals that may be made in the future are in derogation of the President's constitutional authority. His analysis necessarily gives rise to corollaries, as follows: (a) The President may order the Armed Forces into action in any part of the world, in support of his conception of the national interest, (b) he may extend the scope of operations by means of aerial bombing, naval bombardment, firing of missiles or other means, (c) Congress is without power to restrict the President in the exercise of his powers respecting the deployment and operations of the Armed Forces, except by disestablishing the forces or failing to furnish necessary material and supplies.

These broad propositions are contrary to the concept of popular government. The legislature has a proper concern with any sustained military operation. Congress would be acting within the scope of its authority in proscribing operations in a particular nation or area. It would have the power to specify a date for the cessation of a particular military involvement. It could properly limit the dispersal of the Armed Forces, and, especially, could restrict the areas in which drafted soldiers could be compelled to serve. The power to appropriate connotes the power to place restrictions on the appropriations in a manner designed to give effect to Congressional policies. Future debate over measures on the order of Cooper-Church or McGovern-Hatfield should deal with the merits of continuing, extending or restricting operations and not with fine points of constitutional authority or doctrine.

The "Intent of the Framers" Balances President and Congress

Discussion of problems of constitution interpretation logically begins with the language of the document and the available evidence about the intent of the members of the Constitutional Convention.

It perhaps proves too much to suggest that the framers would be horrified at the suggestion that the document they proffered would give the President the power to conduct a sustained military operation in a distant land, using what is essentially a conscript army, and without any authority in Congress to limit the scope of disestablishment of the Armed Forces. The framers had no conception of a situation in which there could be a military position bearing resemblance to Vietnam.

We must always remember, however, that the framers sought to design "a constitution, intended to endure for ages to come, and consequently to be adapted to the various crises of human affairs."[5]

The constitutional language is quite emphatic in stating that there is a distribution of power between the executive and the legislature with regard to military matters. The "executive power" (Article II, Section 1) and "commander in chief" (Article II, Section 2) provisions are balanced by the language of Article I, Section 8, which give Congress basic and substantial authority over military matters. Of prime importance, of course, is the express power to declare war. The power "to raise and support armies" is qualified by the injunction that "no appropriation of money to that use shall be for a longer term than two years." No other power of Congress is restricted in this manner. The restriction, interestingly, does not apply to the provision giving Congress power "to provide and maintain a navy." The two-year restriction necessarily means that Congress was expected to exercise surveillance over the Army in operation and, inevitably, over the President's stewardship in his capacity of commander in chief. Congress would not be able, at the commencement of a President's term, to appropriate funds for Army purposes for the duration of that term. Nor could one Congress bind a future

---

[3]The ultimate form of this proposal is embodied in the Special Foreign Assistance Act of 1971 and reads as follows: "[Federal funds are not to be used] to finance the introduction of United States ground combat troops into Cambodia, or to provide United States advisors to or for Cambodian military forces in Cambodia."

[4]The purpose of this proposal, which assumed several forms in the 91st Congress, was to set a date for the termination of the involvement of American forces in Vietnam.

[5]McCulloch v. Maryland, 4 Wheat. 316 (1819).

Congress to a program of appropriation for maintenance and support of armies.

The essential purpose of specifying that the President is to be commander in chief of the Army and Navy is to maintain civilian control over the military. The clause also prevents Congress from investing a rival to the President by designating some person other than the President as commander of the military forces. Nothing in this particular clause, however, may be construed as a limitation on Congress in the exercise of its express powers, nor does the language of the clause give the President the authority to determine the scope and extent of military operations free from Congressional limitation or control. The Constitution says, in effect, that Congress may determine the ends of military operation and that the President has control of the means. Available contemporary authority seems to support this conclusion.[6]

"Commander in Chief" in History and Opinion

The interpreters of a viable constitution must give account to history as well as to language. The expectations of the framers have not always worked out in practice. The élite electoral college, for example, became a puppet body, and any elector who departed from his voting pledge would surely be subject to severe criticism. President Washington made one futile attempt to secure the "advice" of the Senate in the negotiation of a treaty, and since that time he and his successors have done the negotiating themselves, through their chosen agents, and have then submitted the completed document for ratification.[7] Prescription plays an important role in constitutional history and constitutional interpretation.

History shows many instances in which Presidents have directed the Armed Forces to engage in hostile operations without prior Constitutional authorization. Such uses of force have

---

[6]The Federalist No. 69 (Hamilton) states that the Presidential power is less substantial than the power of the British Crown because it does not include the power to "declare war" or to "raise armies." The Federalist No. 74 (Hamilton) emphasizes the need for unitary command of operations, as justification for the power.

generally been approved by Congress, by public opinion, and by historians. There are cases in which advance approval is impracticable and is not a condition precedent. (Whether the use of force is justified, of course, is a question of judgment.) The historical incidents do not support the claim that the Presidential authority must necessarily be free from Congressional limitation. It will facilitate analysis to classify the several incidents.

Limited Operations

Presidents have often directed the use of armed force for specific and limited purposes. In the early days of our history, there were incidents arising from the Napoleonic Wars, with attendant threats to American neutrality, and also the operations against the Barbary pirates.[8] During the first three decades of the twentieth century, our forces were dispatched to Latin American countries with some regularity.[9] More recently, in 1962, President Kennedy proclaimed the missile blockade of shipments to Cuba, and President Johnson directed troops into the Dominican Republic in 1965 to maintain the status quo during a revolutionary uprising. The incidents in this category did not result in prolonged military operations, and there were no substantial attempts at restriction through Congressional action.[10]

Resistance to Invasion

It is evident that the President may use forces under his control to repel an invader. The Pearl Harbor raid is the prime example of hostile attack against American territory, but it furnishes little in the way of precedent, since a declaration of war by Congress followed almost immediately and came before effective resistance could be offered to the invader. President Polk asserted hostile invasion as the occasion for commencing

---

[7]See Corwin, *The President: Office and Powers* 209-211 (4th ed. 1957).

[8]See 1 Morrison and Commager, *The Growth of the American Republic,* 373-374, 388-389 (3d ed., New York, Oxford, 1942).

[9]Herring, *A History of Latin America,* 429-432 (1961), 429-432 (Haiti), 464-466 (Nicaragua), 473-478 (Panama).

[10]See *The Constitution of the United States of America, Revised and Annotated,* 540-542 (G.P.O., 1963).

hostilities against Mexico.[11] The power to repel invasion undoubtedly includes the power to pursue the invader or to attack his homeland, especially under modern conditions. The President is not limited to beating the enemy forces back from our shores. But this is not the same thing as extending and maintaining foreign operations when our country has not been invaded.

The Civil War

The Civil War, from the federal point of view, was an insurrection which developed into a war. The courts have had difficulty with the resulting legal problems, and their answers have not been wholly consistent.[12] An insurrection is a treasonable act, but if it becomes widespread, then the rebels are normally accorded some of the rights of belligerents.[13] President Lincoln felt that his oath of office imposed the duty to preserve the Union and to use the Armed Forces in the discharge of this duty.[14] Although there was substantial contemporaneous opposition to his theory and practice, there are few today who would disagree with his conception of the Presidential duty. It is not helpful, however, to try to translate domestic precedents into authority for foreign operations.

Recent Undeclared Wars

President Truman ordered American troops into Korea in 1950 without prior Congressional authorization, and Congress never entered into a subsequent declaration of war. President

---

[11] Corwin, *op. cit.* note 7, at 200-201. Congress declared that "by the act of the Republic of Mexico, a state of war exists between that Government and the United States." Morrison and Commager, *op. cit.* Note 8, at 592.

[12] In the Prize Cases, 2 Black 635 (1863), the Court recognized a right of "prize and capture" appropriate under the laws of war, saying: "As a civil war is never publicly proclaimed, *eo nomine,* against insurgents, its actual existence is a fact in our domestic history which the court is bound to notice and to know. . . ." In Texas v. White, 7 Wall. 700 (1869), the Court held that Texas had never truly left the Union, and that the acts of its legislature in attempting secession were "absolutely null."

[13] See 2 Warren, The Supreme Court in United States History 485-487 (1929). Case of Jefferson Davis, 7 Fed. Cas. 63 (No. 3621d.). Davis was never brought to trial on the charges against him.

[14] Corwin, *op. cit.* note 7, at 228-234.

Johnson likewise directed massive ground forces to South Vietnam and instituted the bombing of military and industrial targets deep inside North Vietnam, without declaration of war.[15] Both the Korean and Indochina conflicts have all the external indicia of war. In both instances, operations have been limited by barriers that may seem to be artificial from the military standpoint, but these have been imposed by Presidential decision rather than because of legislative restriction. Congress has generally acquiesced in whatever the Presidents in charge have thought necessary in these operations and certainly has not objected to the state of *de facto* war. Even though there was no advance approval, there has certainly been ratification of the situation which developed. There may be a state of war, in fact, without formal declaration, and Congress may effectively recognize the existence of a state of war by legislating in aid of the operation, although it makes no formal declaration. Under these circumstances, the President may direct operations as commander in chief, on the basis of implied Congressional approval.

Congressional Approval Is Expressed or Implied

Incidents of the type described above have been the subject of litigation at various times. There have also been theoretical debates in Congress over the nature and extent of Presidential power. The general tendency of the judicial opinions and legislative discussions has been to support executive action. In almost all instances, however, there has been express or implied Congressional approval. There have been criticisms over details, but seldom has Congress sought to place restrictions on the President with respect to operations in progress. In recent years, particularly, the President has taken the initiative and Congress has usually acquiesced.[16] There is a dearth of authority about what Congress may lawfully do to restrict the President

---

[15]There is merit in Mr. Deutsch's suggestion that a declaration of war may be omitted because Congress does not want to indicate total commitment. As to North Korea and North Vietnam, moreover, there are theoretical problems because the United States does not recognize the existence of either as a separate nation.

[16]Corwin, *op. cit.,* note 7, at 171, 184-193, 201-204.

in the maintenance and extension of military operations. The problems that could arise, moreover, might not lend themselves to adjudicatory settlement.

It is clear that the President does not acquire power simply because he believes that a particular course of action is necessary or desirable in the efficient conduct of current hostile military operations. The *Steel Seizure Cases* arose in the setting of the Korean War. Steel production was interrupted by a labor dispute, and the President directed the Secretary of Commerce to take possession of the steel mills involved so that production would not be interrupted while Congress was considering possible legislative solutions to the problem. The majority of the Supreme Court (six to three) held that the President had acted in excess of his authority, since there was no legislative authorization for the seizure.[17] The several opinions spoke in eloquent terms about the division of governmental power as set out in the Constitution and about the binding effect of the separation of powers under all conditions. Even Chief Justice Vinson's dissenting opinion emphasized the authority of Congress and sought to justify the seizure on the basis of other expressions of Congressional intent. None of the Justices would have sustained the seizure in the fact of an express Congressional prohibition.

There is neither legal nor historical support for the proposition that Congress would be trespassing on the Presidential prerogative if it should assume to forbid sustained military operations in particular areas or to direct that a specific military venture be brought to an end.

Presidential Authority Subject to Legislative Restriction

Questions of Congressional power to delimit or to terminate a war, declared or *de facto*, are not foreclosed by prior authority. They are open for consideration and should be considered in the light of the principles underlying the Constitution. It is

[17]Youngstown Sheet & Tube Company v. Sawyer, 343 U. S. 579 (1952). The Court gave substantial attention to the failure of Congress to include seizure authority in the Taft-Hartley Act of 1947, in spite of suggestions, and to the President's failure to make use of the methods provided in the act for avoiding strikes.

fundamental that our government is a popular government, with power distributed among the several branches and with the legislature as repository of the public will.

The Nixon Administration opposed the Cooper-Church amendment on the claim that it interfered with the Presidential prerogative. It has sought, however, to comply with the literal terms of the inhibition against use of ground forces and advisers in Cambodia.[18] If this resolution were in violation of the Constitution, there would be no need to observe it. The attempts at compliance indicate the legitimacy of the exercise of Congressional authority.

The Nixon Administration sought to justify the initial entry into Cambodia on the ground that it protected American troops in South Vietnam, and it indicates that it might take similar action in the future for this same purpose, if necessary. If a military operation were in progress with the express or implied consent of Congress and if American troops were threatened by hostile forces in a neutral nation, then the President undoubtedly would have the authority to direct operations against these forces in the absence of legislative restriction. He, of course, would have to weigh the dangers of violating neutrality, but this is irrelevant in a discussion of the extent of Presidential power.

In Cambodia, however, the President could have eliminated any threat to the American troops by withdrawing them. The danger was not directly to the troops but to the "presence" which the administration considered it desirable to maintain. If the presence were lawful, then the President would have the right to protect that presence. It by no means follows that he would have the authority to maintain the presence in the face of a contrary Congressional direction.

Why should Congress not be able to say to the President: "We do not want any ground operations by American forces in

---

[18]It has been suggested that the administration has made use of legalism and subterfuge in trying to assist the Cambodian government, while maintaining apparent compliance with the restrictions on American ground forces and advisers. See Dudman, *U. S. Deception in Cambodia,* St. Louis Post Dispatch, January 28, 1971, at 1-C. As to the use of American troops in Laos, see *Time,* February 22, 1971, page 24.

Cambodia. If our troops in Vietnam are threatened by hostile forces in Cambodian sanctuaries, then you should withdraw them to safe positions, but should not go into Cambodia?" If Congress does not have authority to give this direction, then the President may sustain hostile operations in a remote theater in derogation of the popular will.

Congress, furthermore, should be able to direct the President to bring hostilities in a particular theater to an end, either immediately or within the confines of a specified schedule. Why should the power to declare or to recognize war not connote the power to call for the end of a conflict? The President has no inherent power to direct that a conflict be continued until it is "won"—in the sense that American objectives are fulfilled.

Nor would the presence of a treaty obligation inhibit Congress in the exercise of its authority. Treaties along with statutes are the "law of the land," but a treaty may be abrogated by legislative enactment.[19] The President may have the power to use military force to effectuate the obligations of an existing treaty, but his authority is clearly subject to legislative restriction.[20]

Commander's Authority Is Not Always Exclusive

No war, declared or otherwise, may be maintained without Congressional support. There must be provision for men and material. Congress may necessarily use its appropriation power in the control of military involvements and commitments. It may say that certain funds are to be used for urban renewal rather than for armament, and the President must comply with the instruction. It may forbid the use of an appropriation for a particular item of material, and the President could not violate the

[19]The Constitution of the United States of America, Revised and Annotated (G.P.O., 1963), at 470-473; Whitney v. Robertson, 124 U.S. 190 (1888).

[20]It is going too far to assert that the President is necessarily bound to use military force in support of another nation pursuant to a treaty obligation. Surely he has the authority to consider the situation as it is presented at the time decision is necessary. Might he not conclude that available forces are inadequate in view of other commitments, or that conditions had changed since the adoption of the treaty so that intervention would not be in the national interest, or that the use of force should be considered by Congress?

instruction even though he thought it unwise. It follows that Congress may say in so many words that its appropriations are not to be used for operations in specified nations or for operations in a particular theater beyond a designated date.

The decision to make and to sustain declared or undeclared wars is one properly referable to the popular will and to the legislature as the agent of the popular will. The President may direct operations as commander in chief, and Congress may not ordain or establish a rival. The commander's authority, however, does not connote exclusive power to determine the extent and duration of operations.

A conclusion that this authority is lodged in the President free from legislative control is inconsistent with the nature of popular government, and a power so maintained in the face of Congressional inhibition could be challenged as illegitimate.

QUESTIONS FOR REVIEW

1. Under the Constitution, which branch of government has the power "to declare war?" Is there a difference between "declaring" and "making" war? Explain.
2. Cite some historical examples of "undeclared wars" in which the United States has been involved.
3. Has the United States Supreme Court generally supported or rejected the President's authority in declaring and/or making war? Explain.
4. What was the legal basis upon which President Truman acted in the Korean War?
5. List the four limitations on Presidential war-making powers proposed by the Javits bill. Are these limitations realistic?
6. Was Private First Class Berk successful in his refusal to report for induction into the Armed Forces? Is the "illegality" of a war a valid defense to Berk's crime?
7. When is a "political question" *not* a "political question," vis-a-vis a declaration of war? Why should a court refuse to decide "political questions"?
8. In the *Averette* case, the civilian employee of an Army contractor won his suit not to be tried by a military court. Distinguish this decision from the *Berk* case.

9. Is it significant that the Commonwealth of Massachusetts, as opposed to one or more citizens, has petitioned the court for a decision that the Vietnamese War is "illegal," absent a congressional declaration of war? Explain.
10. Why did the United States Supreme Court initially refuse to hear the Massachusetts antiwar bill case? Explain.
11. Does the decision of the lower federal court in the *Mottola* case bid well for the future? Will the highest United States court follow that lead?
12. Do you agree with attorney Deutsch in his article that a state of war may exist under the Constitution without a formal declaration of war?
13. Do you agree with attorney Blackmar in his article that the Constitution's designation of the President as the Commander in Chief of the Armed Forces means only that no rival Commander in Chief may be established?
14. Is there a "third position" between the views of attorneys Deutsch and Blackmar? Explain.

Chapter 6

ANTI-SEMITISM AND THE CHRISTIAN COMMUNITY: A CHANGE FOR THE BETTER

As this Sacred Synod probes the mystery of the Church, it remembers the spiritual bond that ties the people of the New Covenant to Abraham's stock.

Thus the Church of Christ acknowledges that, according to God's saving design, the beginnings of her faith and election go back as far as the days of the patriarchs, of Moses and the prophets. She affirms that all who believe in Christ—Abraham's sons according to faith (cf. Gal. 3:7)—are included in the call of this patriarch; she also affirms that her salvation is mysteriously prefigured in the exodus of the chosen people from the land of bondage. The Church, therefore, cannot forget that she received the revelation of the Old Testament through the people with whom God, in that loving-kindness words cannot express, deigned to conclude the Ancient Covenant. Nor can she forget that she draws sustenance from the root of that well-cultivated olive tree onto which the wild shoots of the Gentiles have been grafted (Rom. 11:17-24). For the Church believes that by His cross, Christ, who is our Peace, reconciled Jews and Gentiles, making the two one in Himself (cf. Eph. 2:14-16).

The Church keeps ever before her eyes the words of the Apostle about his kinsmen: "Theirs is the sonship and the glory and the covenants and the law and the worship and the promises: theirs are the patriarchs and from them is the Christ according to the flesh" (Rom. 9:4-5), the Son of the Virgin Mary. Furthermore, she recalls that the Apostles, the Church's foundation-stones and pillars (cf. Apoc. 12:14; Gal. 2:9) sprang from the Jewish people as did most of the early disciples who proclaimed Christ's Gospel to the world.

As the Holy Scriptures testifies, Jerusalem did not recognize the time of her visitation (cf. Lk. 14:44), nor did the Jews in large number accept the Gospel; indeed, not a few opposed its dissemination (cf. Rom. 11:28). Nevertheless, now, as before, God holds them most dear, for the sake of the patriarchs; He has not withdrawn His gifts or calling—such is the witness of the Apostle (Rom. 11:28-29). In company with the prophets and the same Apostle, the Church awaits that day, known to God alone, on which all peoples will address the Lord in a single voice and 'serve Him with one accord' (Sph. 3:9, cf. Is. 66:23; Ps. 65:4; Rom. 11:11-32).

Since the spiritual patrimony common to Christians and Jews is so rich, this Sacred Synod wishes to encourage and further their mutual knowledge of, and respect for, one another, a knowledge and respect born principally of biblical and theological studies, but also of fraternal dialogues.

True, the Jewish authorities and those who sided with them pressed for the death of Christ (cf. Jn. 19:6); still what happened in His passion cannot be attributed without distinction to all Jews then alive, nor can it be attributed to the Jews of today. Certainly the Church is the new people of God; nevertheless, the Jews are not to be presented as rejected or accursed by God, as if this followed from Holy Scripture. May all, then, see to it that nothing is taught, either in catechetical work or in the preaching of the Word of God, that does not conform to the truth of the Gospel and the spirit of Christ.

The Church, moreover, rejects any persecution against any man. For this reason and for the sake of her common patrimony with the Jews, she decries hatred, persecutions, displays of anti-Semitism, staged against the Jews at whatever time in history and by whomsoever. She does so, not moved by political reasons, but impelled by the Gospel's pure love.

One thing remains: Christ underwent His passion and death freely and out of infinite love because of the sins of all men so that all may obtain salvation. This the Church has always held and holds now. Sent to preach, the Church is, therefore, bound to proclaim the cross of Christ as the sign of God's all-embracing love and as the fountain from which every grace flows.

The above statement entitled "The Declaration on the Jews" delineates the Catholic Church's bond to the Jewish people and is part of the Vatican Council's Declaration on the Relationship of the Church to Non-Christian Religions. It was adopted on October 15, 1965. In the United States, this basic document was expanded upon by the National Conference of United States Bishops in "Guidelines for Catholic-Jewish Relations" in March 1967. Hereinafter set forth are pertinent excerpts from this latter document:

In its Declaration on the Relationship of the Church to Non-Christian Religions of 1965, the Second Vatican Council issued a historic Statement on the Jews and summoned all Catholics to re-

> appraise their attitude toward, and relationship with, the Jewish people.
>
> The call of the Council to a fraternal encounter with Jews may be seen, further, as one of the more important fruits of the spirit of renewal generated by the Council in its deliberations and decrees.
>
> More specifically, the Council's call is an acknowledgment of the conflicts and tensions that have separated Christians and Jews through the centuries and of the Church's determination, as far as possible, to eliminate them. Well does it serve both in word and action as a recognition of the manifold sufferings and injustices inflicted upon the Jewish people by Christians in our own times as well as in the past. The statement speaks from the highest level of the Church's authority to serve notice that injustices directed against the Jews at any time from any source can never receive Catholic sanction or support.
>
> The Church in America is faced with a historic opportunity to advance the cause of Catholic-Jewish harmony throughout the world. . . . In the United States lives the largest Jewish Community in the world. In the United States, a land that has welcomed immigrants and refugees from persecution, the Church has committed herself without reserve to the American ideal of equal opportunity and justice for all. In such a setting the Church in America today is providentially situated to distinguish itself in pursuit of the purposes of the Council's statement.

The problem of anti-Semitism is not of recent origin, for it arose in the earliest Christian times as Christianity developed as a sect *within* Judaism to a separate and competing religion *outside* of Judaism. The writings of the early Church fathers contain many instances of anti-Semitic sentiments, including the charge of deicide. Christian teaching also stressed that Jews could not be saved until they accepted Jesus as the Messiah, and the Jewish failure to do so caused the Christian world to place the severest restrictions on Jews, not only in their opportunities to make a living but in the more basic, physical security, as Christians conducted massacres, burnings, widespread pogroms, and even genocide. Beginning with the First Crusade in 1096, wholesale massacres of Jews, among others, were perpetrated by the Crusaders on their way to capture Jerusalem from the pagans. Jews were accused of many "crimes," i.e. they were deemed to be ritual murderers who used the blood of Christians for the making of "matzot"; they were called prisoners of the wells in the time of the Black Plague; and they were labeled evil persons. Jews were the victims of preposterous accusations that were readily believed by the Christian masses. It was not until the beginning of the 18th century that some enlightenment began to permeate Christian communities, with the result that there was a loosening of the restrictions against the Jewish population; but pogroms and massacres continued, only at a slower pace. Immigrants from Europe to the United States unfortunately brought with them these seeds of anti-Jewish prejudice. But the American brand of anti-Semitism never reached the intensity of the European vintage. Yet a significant proportion of the American population, even today, harbors unfriendly attitudes toward the Jew. Most of these people are shocked when violent anti-Jewish acts occur, but they do not relate their own prejudices to these outrageous actions. The "polite" variety of anti-Semitism, in the form of discrimination in housing, in education, in employment, and in social interplay, is somehow tolerated. Although both overt and covert acts of anti-Semitism have in recent years generally diminished, it is a recognized fact that there is an innate prejudice against Jews, as well as other minority groups, that is ever present as a potential menace to our free society. Paradoxically the greater the Jewish contribution to the economic and cultural welfare of this country, the greater the manifestation of anti-Semitism. The Jew is stereotyped as an overly ambitious person obsessed with the acquisition of tangible wealth, and as demeaning physical labor in favor of the professions, the financial, business, and managerial positions.

In our present-day pervasive climate of strife and tumult, rising crime rate, changing moral codes, rebellious youth, decaying cities, and the Vietnam war, there is a continuing threat that latent anti-Semitism may become overt and virulent. The very conditions that breed ignorance, want, frustration, and alienation generate anti-Semitism because a scapegoat must be found. The lunatic, extremist fringe of our population can fan the flames and precipitate the irrational acts of the multiude. And yet anti-Semitism is, in Christian theology, a grave sin, i.e. it is a direct violation of the supreme Christian law to love thy neighbor (Mark 12:31). Anti-Semitism is a sin against justice. Proverbs 21:3 tells us: "To do justice . . . is more than acceptable to the Lord than sacrifice." Yet to blindly dislike or disrespect a person because he or she is of a certain origin or faith is surely an injustice. Anti-Semitism is a sin of hate and anger, a sin against the Fifth Commandment (also John 2:11 and 4:20). Anti-Semitism directly violates the scriptures and the words of Jesus (John 15:12, Romans 11:28) and the scriptural teachings of the unity of man (Romans 10:12). Anti-Semitism is also disobedience to the Church, i.e. Vatican Council II, and other documents, have explicitly condemned such hatred, prosecutions, and displays of anti-Semitism "at any time and by anyone." In the beautiful booklet, "Our Spiritual Heritage" (printed in 1966 by the Olive Tree Press of The John XXIII Center of Fordham University, and bearing the imprimatur of the Bishop of Providence) there is eloquent testimony to the evils of yesteryear:

> Christianity did not suddenly appear, exploding onto the earth as a shooting star. You today have a deep, spiritual heritage . . . the heritage of your Church, the heritage of Christianity. This heritage has come to you from the people of Israel.
>
> Judaism is the root from which Christianity grew.
>
> This root is at once spiritual, historical and very real. It lives today, and today the Church wants you to know and understand the ties which connect you and your Jewish brothers.
>
> That mutual heritage is a spiritual bond too often unrecognized, too seldom respected.
>
> For nearly 2,000 years the Christian and Jewish peoples have existed together. Their histories are interwoven in belief, in worship, hope and responsibility and in tears and tragic misunderstandings.

Fortunately, since 1965 there has been a meeting of the minds between Jewish leaders and leaders of the Catholic Church, in particular. Everywhere there are ecumenical endeavors which encompass seminars, dialogues, exchange of professorships, and even occasional support for the survival of the State of Israel. The thrust of this current ecumenism is to recognize the mutual differences in the respective religions and at the same time to gain understanding of these differences because they do not impinge upon nor threaten the existence of the other religions. (Even cooperative social action between members of the religious communities is deemed a *summum bonum.*) Specifically, the "Guidelines for Catholic-Jewish Relations, above, spells out numerous *themes* to be considered by Christians and Jews engaged in the dialogue: (a) joint scholarly studies and educational efforts to show the common historical, biblical, doctrinal, and liturgical heritage of Judaism and Christianity, (b) presentation of the Crucifixion story in such a way as not to implicate all Jews of Jesus' time nor of today in a collective guilt for the Crucifixion, and (c) the strongest repudiation of anti-Semitism by frank and honest treatment in textbooks, courses, and curriculum on the history of Christian anti-Semitism. Implicit in these themes is a mutual recognition of the vitality of the faiths which precludes the necessity for any proselytizing, as well as a recognition of the contrary positions on secular issues taken by large numbers of Jews and Christians.

The vitality of Judaism, for example, is sometimes misunderstood; the late and revered Rabbi Morris Adler in a 1963 *Harper's Magazine* article touched base upon "this thing called Jewishness":

> Judaism has never developed an official statement as to what one must believe to be accounted a Jew. There is no Jewish equivalent of the Nicene Creed honored by Catholics, the Apostles' Creed of the Episcopalians, the Westminster Confession of the Presbyterians, or the Augsburg Confession of the Lutherans. The Jew is not taught any catechism and is not bound by an ironclad formula. The Talmud, whose interpretations, applications, and enlargements have shaped Jewish deeds and practices even more than the Bible, records the clashing views of differing schools and scholars, preserving minority opinions along with the binding majority dicta. Even the thirteen articles of faith drawn up by Maimonides in the twelfth century, which are still printed in traditional prayer books, have not gained universal acceptance and approval.
>
> To be sure, profound affirmations are implicit in the tradition. But these have never been formalized as an authoritative creed. It is only a slight exaggeration to say that in Judaism the deed is the reflection of one's theology. "Believe and be saved" is the Christian approach; "Do and you will believe," the Jewish. Being the culture of a community rather than the faith of a church, Judaism never found it necessary to make uniformity of belief its central cohesion.

It is perhaps this heterogeneity of the Jewish tradition which

Christians have not grasped and which incongruity has been the source of vitality and will to survive on the part of the Jews for the past 3,000 years. The Nazi holocaust, which involved the systematic slaughter of 6 million Jews, is still a central trauma of Western civilization because the Christian world has been unable to rationalize its avoidance. It is one thing to condemn the Nazi holocaust as the product of sadist and psychotics; yet it is much more important to remember the lesson of history so as to insure that genocide will never reoccur.[1] The right to be different is the right to exist as a minority in the community of peoples. The Christian world generally in June, 1967, gave little support to the State of Israel; Christian leaders were morally lax in failing to condemn Arab threats of genocide against Israel. Hopefully, current progress in ecumenism will be directed toward amelioration of the conditions of man in a world seeking to dehumanize him. The State of Israel is more than a bulwark of democracy against Communism; it is the central strand out of which and about which all aspects of Judaism are spun, and Christian acceptance of this fact bids well for the future.

The Olive Tree Press of The John XXIII Center of Fordham University in 1966 published six beautifully illustrated booklets for distribution to Catholics, entitled "The Declaration on Non-Christian Religions," "The Outline of Truth," "The Anguish of a People," "The Face of Sin," "To Talk Together," and "Our Spiritual Heritage." The following excerpts taken from the first of these booklets reflect the beauty of these writings.

> Super-sonic jets, space-travel, automobiles, these and other things have made man realize he is no longer isolated from how his fellow-man thinks and acts. Today we realize that, if for no other reason than self-interest, we have a *collective responsibility* toward each other.
>
> The Church says you also have a spiritual and moral collective responsibility toward your neighbor because you are more than neighbors . . . you are brothers.
>
> The Church draws attention to your spiritual heritage in Judaism, to the spiritual ties which bind the Christian and Jewish

---

[1]See Chapter IV concerning the United Nations Genocide Convention.

> peoples together. It is this heritage which brings a special brotherhood between you and your Jewish neighbors.
>
> The Church reminds you that this heritage is 'of the flesh,' that Jesus, Mary, Joseph, the apostles, were not Jewish in name only but in origin and in thought and outlook.
>
> So your bond is not just of faith but of people, of the spirit and of the flesh.
>
> With these words, the Church cries out for simple, common justice for your Jewish neighbors. She proclaims that the Jewish people of today cannot be held guilty for something a few of their ancestors may have taken part in, no more than you can be held guilty for something some of your ancestors may or may not have done.
>
> The Church recognizes the unreasoning, inflammatory poison of the mind and spirit which is anti-Semitism, a poison which can turn differences into dislikes, misunderstanding into mistreatment. The Church attacks the evil of anti-Semitism as a thought as well as an act.
>
> Take part in organized dialogues should you have the opportunity; be aware of new theological interpretations and insights; read the writings of eminent Catholic thinkers. Do all these things, but remember that love and respect are things of people, not organizations, of you and your neighbor finding out about each other in openness and trust.

In 1969, the Vatican Secretariat for the Promotion of Christian Unity promulgated a far-reaching document on relations between Roman Catholics and Jews. Among its recommendations were the following: (a) Catholics should recognize the religious significance of the State of Israel for Jews and attempt to "understand and respect" the "link between the people and the land"; (b) the Jewish religion should not be seen as a steppingstone to Christianity, and the Old Testament should be recognized for its "proper validity"; and (c) the Catholic view of the Jewish religion should recognize that it is one of justice and possesses love and freedom. Throughout this 1969 document are references to Judaism as a growing faith that continues to this day to enrich itself "and develop in a rich spiritual tradition." Also, the document stressed the desirability of altering Catholic texts and Catholic education in general to conform to the guidelines, including the establishment of a chair on Judaism in Catholic colleges. Specifically, Judaism should occupy an important place in Christian curriculum because (a) a full understanding of the Old Testament is basic to a vital Christianity, as is a knowledge of the 3000-year-old tradition of biblical interpretation in Judasim; (b) Judaism has a significant role to play in providing an understanding of the background of Jesus, the Apostles, Paul, and the early Church; (c) Jews and Judaism must be understood as living elements of the modern world and not as some fossilized relic of a decadent society; and (d) Christian teaching must have an adequate understanding of contemporary Jewry, including the history and ethnology of anti-Semitism, the moral and theologfical implication of the Nazi holocaust, and the spiritual, ethnic, and cultural unity of the State of Israel and the Jewish people.

The Anti-Defamation League (ADL) of B'nai B'rith (organized in 1913 and having 28 offices throughout the United States) has been in the forefront of ecumenical endeavors bringing Jew and Christian to the meeting place. The ADL has sought to root out, to expose, and to educate; the ADL has attacked the complacency, lack of knowledge of the problem, and the hesitancy of people to stand up and oppose what is indecent and immoral. The philosopher, Dr. H. A. Overstreet, eloquently posed the problem:

> He who permits evil commits evil. This is what makes the haunting sense of guilt in our culture. Many a member of the dominant group will earnestly aver that *he* never intended it that Negroes should be insulted and maltreated on buses, on railroad stations, and on public streets; that *he* never intended it that the Mexican-Americans should be brutally beaten up; that *his* heart is sore and ashamed when he reads of the defiling of Jewish synagogues by hoodlums. He did not intend these things. *But he created the social sanction for these things.* By adopting a twisted principle of human association he and the people like him opened the Pandora's box out of which have flown the intolerances and cruelties that have defiled our culture.

All organizations working in the field of ecumenism must not permit the evil of anti-Semitism nor create the social sanction for anti-Semitism. Synagogue and Church, Jew and Christian, can work side by side and escape the haunting sense of guilt, for anti-Semitism must be truly eradicated on the American scene.

QUESTIONS FOR REVIEW

1. Is anti-Semitism the product of Christian teaching? Explain.
2. List some of the "spiritual bonds" which tie the people of the New Testament to the the people of the Old Testament.
3. Is the "Church in America" better able "to advance the cause of Catholic-Jewish harmony throughout the world?" Explain.
4. Is *latent* anti-Semitism a factor in the United States today? Cite some examples of the "gentleman's agreement."
5. Does ecumenism foster mutual respect for the differences in the respective religions? Explain.
6. What "ecumenical endeavors" are indicative of the mutual goodwill between Christian and Jew? What issues separate the respective groups?
7. Is the fear of proselytizing a realistic one?
8. Is Judaism monolithic, i.e. is uniformity of belief its central cohesion? Explain by reference to the words of Rabbi Morris Adler.
9. Do you agree or disagree with the statement that today "the Church cries out for simple, common justice for your Jewish neighbors?"
10. Why is a recognition of the Jewish link to the State of Israel so integral a part of the modern ecumenical movement?
11. Why is an awareness by Christians of the Nazi holocaust so vital to an understanding of the Jew?
12. Explain why "exposure" of the evils of anti-Semitism can negate its unfortunate social sanction.

Chapter 7

AIRPLANE HIJACKING: A FAILURE OF INTERNATIONAL DETERRENTS

DURING THE REIGN of the Emperor Justinian, an accepted maxim of Roman law was "pirata est hostis humani generis"—"a pirate is an enemy of the human race." These words remain as truthful today as they were 1400 years ago, except that contemporary man must deal with a brand new variety of the loathesome marauder—the air pirate, whose escapades adversely affects countless thousands of people.

Perhaps the first recorded hijacking of an airplane in the twentieth century is to be found in James Hilton's 1933 novel, *Lost Horizon,* where the hijacked airplane was brought down in the earthly paradise of Shangri-La. Today, however, hijacked aircraft are forced to put down at inhospitable José Martí Airport in Havana, Cuba, or on same uninhabited strip of a Middle Eastern desert. Since the first American airliner was hijacked above the Florida Keys on May 1, 1961, nearly 10,000 passengers from all over the world have been, during the ensuing ten years, victims of air pirates.[1] President Richard M. Nixon, in a speech to the United Nations in 1969, called the problem of air hijacking an issue involving "the interests of every nation, the safety of every traveler and the integrity of that structure of order on which a world community depends." What started out as simply a localized dilemma in countries involved in revolutionary upheavals, as in the Caribbean and Central American areas, has infected every part of the world, including Ethiopia, Kashmir,

[1]Non-American aircraft hijackings were first recorded during 1948 when seven were reported. From 1948 to 1950, the first flurry of hijack activity occurred and generally involved Communist takeovers of nations in eastern Europe and mainland China. Other frequent acts of piracy developed as a result of Castro's revolution against the Batista regime in Cuba during the late 1950's and 1960.

and the Soviet Union. The international community outside of the Western Hemisphere at first tended to regard air piracy as merely disagreeable, uncomfortable, and rather remote. It was not until 1958 that the Geneva International Conference of Plenipotentiaries to Examine the Law of the Sea (after 30 years of relentless urging by the United States and other western nations) reluctantly broadened the then-existing legal definition of "piracy" to include "Any illegal violence, detention or any act of depredation, committed for private ends by the crew or passengers of a private ship or private aircraft, and directed: (a) On the high seas, against another ship or aircraft, or against persons or property on board such ships or aircraft." This definition simply outlawed air piracy by one aircraft against another. It completely failed, however, to allude to a situation that in a few years was to become depressingly rampant, i.e. the hijacking of the aircraft on which the pirate was himself a passenger!

Just three years later, on May 1, 1961, a man calling himself Elpir Cofrisi[2] purchased a ticket from National Airlines for its Convair 440 flying from Miami to Key West. Sometime later, prior to takeoff, the passenger asked the ticket agent to add the suffix "ata" at the end of his first name making it Elpirata Cofrisi. *El pirata is* Spanish for "the pirate" and Cofrisi was a Caribbean buccaneer of the 18th century, so that the translation was "the pirate Cofrisi." After the plane left Marathon in the Florida Keys for its next stop, Cofrisi (later identified as Antulio Ramirez Ortiz) forced his way into the cockpit, brandished a pistol and knife, and compelled the pilot, Captain Francis X. Riley, to fly to the San Antonio de Bañas Airbase, southwest of Havana, Cuba. After the plane landed, the pilot, two other crewmembers, and seven passengers remained aboard for three hours until Cuban authorities allowed them to take off for the return flight to Key West. Cofrisi remained in Cuba.

---

[2]The information regarding the Cofrisi hijacking is reported in the statement of Elmer E. Jones, Jr., Vice President for Public Affairs of National Airlines, Inc. It is affixed as Appendix E to a Report on "Aircraft Hijacking in the Carribbean" of the Subcommittee on Inter-American Affairs, Committee on Foreign Affairs, House of Representatives.

Subsequent to this first act of sky piracy in 1961 against an American carrier, three other seizures were attempted within the following four months, only two of which were successful. A frustrated attempt on August 3, 1961, involved Leon Bearden and his fourteen-year-old son, Cody, who tried to hijack to Cuba a Continental Airlines 707 jet with 74 pasengers aboard. The flight, which originated in Los Angeles, was scheduled to arrive at Houston, Texas, after a stop in El Paso, where the Beardens boarded the plane. Shortly after the plane was airborne, the father-son hijacking team commandeered the plane, but the pilot convinced them that refueling was necessary and so the plane was permitted to land at El Paso. Bearden permitted all but six of the passengers to deplane. Immediately, border policemen surrounded the aircraft and flattened the plane's tires and damaged its engines with gunfire. Both Beardens were apprehended. Since there was no federal antihijack law in force at the time of the crime, Leon Bearden was tried, convicted and sentenced to 20 years imprisonment for, among other federal crimes, the obstruction of commerce by extortion. (The younger Bearden pleaded guilty to juvenile delinquency.) Bearden's sentence was subsequently upheld by the appellate court.[3]

Soon thereafter, in 1961, Congress promptly passed amendments to the Federal Aviation Act of 1958 and created the capital offense of aircraft piracy, as well as other antihijack laws:

49 U.S.C.§1472
Aircraft Piracy

(i) (1) Whoever commits or attempts to commit piracy, as herein defined, shall be punished—

(A) by death if the verdict of the jury shall so recommend, or, in the case of a plea of guilty, or a plea of not guilty where the defendant has waived a trial by jury, if the court in its discretion shall so order; or

(B) by imprisonment for not less than twenty years, if the death penalty is not imposed.

(2) As used in this subsection, the term 'aircraft piracy' means any seizure or exercise of control, by force or violence or

---

[3]Bearden v. U.S., 320 F2d 99, CCA5, 1963.

threat of force or violence and with wrongful intent, of an aircraft in flight in air commerce.

Interference with flight crew members or flight attendants

(j) Whoever, while aboard an aircraft in flight in air commerce, assaults, intimidates, or threatens any flight crew member or flight attendant (including any steward or stewardess) of such aircraft, so as to interfere with the performance by such member or attendant of his duties or lessen the ability of such member or attendant to perform his duties, shall be fined not more than $10,000 or imprisoned not more than twenty years, or both. Whoever in the commission of any such act uses a deadly or dangerous weapon shall be imprisoned for any term of years or for life. . . .

Carrying weapons aboard aircraft

(l) Except for law enforcement officers of any municipal or state government, or the Federal government, who are authorized or required to carry arms, and except for such other persons as may be so authorized under regulations issued by the Administrator, whoever, while aboard an aircraft being operated by an air carrier in air transportation, has on or about his person a concealed deadly or dangerous weapon, shall be fined not more than $1,000 or imprisoned not more than one year, or both.

False Information

(m)(1) Whoever imparts or conveys or causes to be imparted or conveyed false information, knowing the information to be false, concerning an attempt or alleged attempt being made or to be made, to do any act which would be a crime prohibited by subsection (i), (j), (k), or (l) of this section, shall be fined not more than $1,000 or imprisoned not more than one year, or both.

(2) Whoever willfully and maliciously, or with reckless disregard for the safety of human life, imparts or conveys or causes to be imparted or conveyed false information, knowing the information to be false, concerning an attempt or alleged attempt being made or to be made, to do any act which would be a crime prohibited by subsection (i), (j), (k), or (l) of this section, shall be fined not more than $5,000 or imprisoned not more than five years, or both.

These four statutory sections, in effect, create four different federal crimes involving the hijacking of aircraft. The most severe, and the only one carrying the death penalty, is "aircraft piracy" [§1472 (i)]; it describes the actual, attempted or threatened forceful takeover of an aircraft while in flight.

Less severe a crime, carrying a 10,000 dollar fine, and/or 20 years imprisonment, is the actual or threatened interference with a member of a flight crew, including stewardesses or the pilot, while the plane is in flight [§1472 (j)]. If the hijacking assailant uses a dangerous weapon to effectuate his ends, he is liable for life imprisonment. The remaining two crimes consist of carrying a concealed weapon aboard a plane [§1472 (1)] and knowingly giving false information in respect to any of the crimes noted above [§1472(m)]. Unfortunately, all four of these penal statutes have proved incapable of successful enforcement, though not due to any inadequacy in their drafting. The problem is that the air pirate cannot be brought to trial, since the country to which he generally directs the hijacked craft is more often than not a nation such as Cuba or Algeria which will not extradite him, and frequently openly welcomes him. More than 70 per cent of the hijackings from 1961 through 1968, and certainly more than 80% from 1969 to the present, have been successful. Of the few hijacking perpetrators that have been tried for the federal crime under Title 49 U.S.C.§1472, almost all have either voluntarily returned to the United States or were apprehended by American peace officers on domestic soil. Few hijackers have been extradited[4] to the United States. In one case, two men forced at gunpoint the pilot of a small, private Cessna' plane to fly to Cuba. Sometime later, both men voluntarily returned to Florida and were indicted by the federal authorities for air piracy. Prior to trial, however, the indictments were dismissed by the Federal district court on the grounds that the "Air Piracy" Statute *above,* referred only to commercial airlines and not to private planes. The Federal Government took a direct appeal to the United States Supreme Court and the de-

[4]Extradition is the process whereby a convicted or accused criminal who has sought refuge in a foreign state or nation is surrendered to the state or nation in which he committed or is accused of having committed a crime, so that the criminal can be subjected to the laws of the state or nation from which he has fled. For example, if a man hijacks a plane in Detroit, Michigan, and has it land in Toronto, Canada, in order for the courts of the United States to prosecute the hijacker, our federal government must request the Canadian government to *extradite* him to the United States.

cision was promptly reversed in *U.S. v. Healy.*[5] The highest court found that acts of piracy aboard private airplanes were indeed within the intent of Congress in enacting the law, and thus the "air piracy" statute passed its first judicial test.

Another aspect of the new statute was approved by the Tenth United States Circuit Court of Appeals in *U.S. v. Mimms.*[6] Here, a passenger on a small, four-passenger Mooney Mark plane had a bit too much to drink and he began to scuffle with the pilot as the pilot tried to land the aircraft. The Court affirmed Mimms' conviction of "interference with flight crew members" and held that the pilot was indeed protected by the words of the statute.

Between 1961 and 1971, 28 persons have been convicted by Federal courts for violations of various sections of the federal antihijacking laws. According to the Federal Aviation Administration, the sentences meted out by the courts number a total of 350 years in prison. As of June 1, 1971, twelve other accused air pirates were awaiting either trial or the results of mental examinations, and charges against at least eight others have been dismissed after they were committed to psychiatric institutions. Currently, 92 individuals are listed as fugitives who will face prosecuton for aircraft hijacking if they are returned to the United States from their sanctuaries abroad. None of the nations granting asylum to these fugitives have as yet agreed to extradition.

Among other unsuccessful hijackers *not* indicted for air piracy was a teenage boy who attempted the deed with a toy pistol. (He was referred to a juvenile court as a youthful offender).[7] A few mentally disturbed persons who attempted hijackings were judged to be incapable of being tried and were

---

[5]376 U.S. 75, 1964.

[6]379 F2d 888, 1964.

[7]On March 9, 1971, the *New York Times* reported that a 16-year-old Alabaman high school sophomore, Thomas Kelly Marston, allegedly drew a pistol and forced a National Airline's jet to be flown to Canada. Although all 38 passengers and four stewardesses were allowed to deplane, the youth changed his mind about the hijacking while the plane was flying over Tennessee and allowed the crew to fly to Miami. Marston was charged with aircraft piracy.

therefore committed to institutions. There was also the case of an Army Sergeant who was having domestic difficulties. He hijacked a plane to Cuba with his two-year old daughter, and subsequently both returned to the United States. Another case involved the apprehension by federal authorities of a relative of a former deceased Vice-President of the United States. The problem was noted by Assistant Attorney General Will Wilson in his testimony before the House Commerce Committee:

> Where we have been able to establish identity with enough certainty, indictments have been immediately returned. . . . We have found difficulty in maintaining prosecutions, but our problem, as you know, is obtaining jurisdiction over the person. These individuals remain outside the boundaries of the United States and therefore prosecution has not been successfully completed in most of the cases.

The House Committee on Foreign Affairs, Subcommittee on Interamerican Affairs, has stated that "the main deterrent to piracy of United States carrier aircraft . . . is to place the hijacker in the hands of United States Courts for trial." Clearly this opinion is beside the mark because the threat of the death penalty or a long prison term is not enough to deter air piracy. The odds of the hijacker succeeding are in his favor, and he is reasonably certain that the country in which he lands will neither prosecute nor extradite him.

The first attempt to obtain international cooperation, especially after hijacking had become well-entrenched as a loathesome deed for the deranged, the attention seeker, and the political extremist, was a meeting of the International Civil Aviation Organization (ICAO) in Tokyo in 1963. The ICAO, a specialized agency of the United Nations with headquarters in Montreal, Canada, and composed of more than a hundred sovereign states, "provides the machinery for the achievement of international co-operation in the air." At the Tokyo meeting, the member nations agreed upon a document called the *Convention on Offenses and Certain Other Acts Committed on Board Aircraft,* although the document was not to become effective for more than five years, until December 4, 1969, when the requisite twelve members would ratify the agreement.[8] Even today, in 1971, the effect of the document is nil, as none of those nations most often involved in plane hijackings, such as Cuba, Algeria, and certain Arab States (projected landing zones), had ratified the document. The words of Article II of this *Convention* clearly denote the attitude of the majority of the world:

> 1. When a person on board has unlawfully committed by force or threat thereof an act of interference, seizure, or other wrongful exercise of control of an aircraft in flight or when such an act is about to be committed, Contracting States shall take all appropriate measures to restore control of the aircraft to its lawful commander or to preserve his control of the aircraft.
> 2. In the cases contemplated in the preceding paragraph, the Contracting State in which the aircraft lands shall permit its passengers and crew to continue their journey as soon as practicable, and shall return the aircraft and its cargo to the persons lawfully entitled to possession.

Thus, whenever a hijacker threatens or in fact takes over an aircraft in flight, the signatories to the Convention must take appropriate measures to thwart the pirate. If the hijacked plane is landed within their boundaries, the signatories must allow the plane and passengers to continue their scheduled flight as soon as practicable. But Article 11 does have glaring deficiencies, such as the absence of any provision providing for the extradition of the successful air pirate or, in the alternative, punishment of the pirate by the country in which he has landed. According to Robert P. Boyle and Roy Pulsifier in their leading article, "*The Tokyo Convention on Offenses and Certain Other Acts Committed On Board Aircraft*[9]:

> The approach taken by this Article to the crime of unlawful seizure of aircraft avoids attempting either the description of an international crime or the attempt to make such action a crime under international law. Instead, the Article provides that the contracting States have certain obligations whenever a person on board an aircraft has unlawfully committed by force or

---

[8]The twelve original ratifiers were the Republic of China (Nationalist China), Denmark, Italy, Mexico, Niger, Norway, Philippines, Portugal, Sweden, United Kingdom, United States and Upper Volta. The United States ratified on September 5, 1969.

[9]30 *J. Air Law Commerce* 305, 345, Autumn, 1964.

threat thereof an act of interference, seizure, or other wrongful exercise of control. The question of whether a particular act is lawful or unlawful is to be judged by the law of the State of registration of the aircraft or the law of the State in whose airspace the aircraft may be in flight. By the use of this technique, it is unnecessary for the Convention to attempt by international law to proscribe a particular act as criminal; instead the Convention relied upon the existing applicable criminal codes of the contracting States. While there was considerable debate at the Tokyo Conference over the question of whether the act must not only be unlawful but also must encompass either the use of force or the threat of force, the fact that in the final analysis the unlawfulness is to be measured by the law of either the State of registry or the territorial State seems to make such consideration somewhat academic.

It is clear that the mere approval by the ICAO of the *Convention* has had scant effect on the discontinuance of hijackings. Between 1963 and 1967, there were 20 attempted seizures; and in June, 1967, a group of pirates even went so far as to kidnap former Congolese premier Moise Tshombe while he was a passenger aboard a chartered flight to the Baleric Islands from his exile in Europe. The pirates took him and the plane to Algeria where Tshombe later died in prison. In July, 1968, an Israeli El Al jet was seized by members of the Popular Front for the Liberation of Palestine and also taken to Algeria. All Israeli passengers were detained there for six weeks until the International Federation of Airline Pilots Association (IFALPA) persuaded certain European airlines to boycott Algeria if the detention continued. Nine months later, the IFALPA authorized the boycott of flights into any country which refused to punish airplane hijackers. IFALPA also threatened a 24-hour world-wide strike if Syria refused to release Israeli passengers who had been detained on a flight hijacked to Damascus in August, 1968. Other incidents included the hijacking of a Boeing 707 by an American Marine who was a Vietnam veteran; he was wanted as a burglary suspect and had directed the pilot to fly from Fresno, California to Rome, Italy. Being of Italian parentage, he was unfortunately treated almost like a hero when he landed in the Eternal City of Rome. He was not extradited, as requested by the United States Government, but subsequently tried by an Italian court and given a light sentence. Perhaps the most bizarre hijacking of all occurred when a passenger aboard a jet aircraft (landing at Dulles International Airport outside of Washington, D.C.), demanded 100 million dollars in cash as ransom for the airplane. After the hijacker was given 100,000 dollars, FBI agents shot at the plane's tires in an attempt to abort a takeoff, but the hijacker shot the pilot, was himself wounded, and subsequently captured.

In September, 1968, at the 16th Assembly of the 116 members of the ICAO (it now has more than 120 members) in Buenos Aires, Argentina, the United States delegation was successful in obtaining unanimous approval of a resolution calling for ratification of the Tokyo Convention of 1963. In addition, the delegates resolved to enforce Article 11 of the *Convention* as if it were, in fact, in force. Strangely, the Cuban delegate to the Assembly joined in approval of both aspects of the resolution. Similarly, at the meeting of the Permanent Council of ICAO in Montreal in November, 1968, the United States initiated and the group adopted a resolution urging all members to take all possible measures to prevent hijackings and to cooperate with aircraft that have already been hijacked. Frank E. Loy, a member of the United States delegation, noted in his article, "Some International Approaches to Dealing with Hijacking of Aircraft"[10] that:

> To the end of inducing concerted international action against hijacking in November, 1968—against the background of the ICAO Assembly resolution of the preceeding September—we proposed in the Council of ICAO a protocol to the Tokyo Convention which would require Member States to return a hijacker to the state of registration of the hijacked aircraft without regard to considerations of political asylum. Almost needless to say, we ran into rather heavy going when it became clear that our proposal abrogated the historic right to political asylum in relation to hijackers.
>
> Frankly, we crossed this bridge ourselves only after considerable soul-searching. But it had become our judgment, after many weeks of mental and moral agonizing, that the magnitude of this 20th Century crime outweighed the right of political asylum which had come to us sacrosanct through the ages. When the November meeting of ICAO broke up, we stood almost alone in our conten-

[10] 4 *Intl. Lawyer* 450, 1970.

> tion that hijackers were not entitled to political asylum. The position of the great majority of states was that the state in which the hijacker landed had the prerogative of determining whether political asylum should be granted; and that this prerogative should not be abridged by an international commitment.

Unforunately, no concerted international action was taken, and the piracies of aircraft continued into 1969. A Japanese airliner was hijacked and flown to North Korea, although the passengers were allowed to leave the plane at the Seoul, South Korea airport when the Japanese Minister of Transportation agreed to act as a hostage. A Boeing 747, the world's largest commercial jetliner, was hijacked on a flight to San Juan, Puerto Rico and its arrival in Havana drew no less a personage than Fidel Castro, who was curious to see the new jumbo jet!

But on Sunday, September 6, 1970, a man and a woman failed in an attempt to hijack an Israeli El Al jet scheduled to fly from London to Tel Aviv. The man was killed by El Al security guards aboard the aircraft, but the woman was subdued and then jailed in the British capital. Her name was Leila Khaled, a 24-year old Arab who had taken part in a successful hijacking a year earlier. That same Sunday afternoon, three other synchronized attempts did not fail! One, a Pan American 747, was rerouted to Beirut while on its way to New York from Amsterdam and was flown to Cairo. In the middle of the Cairo Airport, the airliner was dynamited two minutes after all the passengers had scurried through the emergency exists. Those aboard two other planes however, were not as lucky. Both of these planes, a TWA round-the-world flight leaving Frankfurt, West Germany, and a Swissair jet flying from Zurich to New York, were flown to the Jordanian desert 25 miles from Amman and landed next to each other on a deserted World War II airstrip. The Popular Front for the Liberation of Palestine (PFLP) was behind all three piracies and with undisguised pride announced to the world the political reasons for these inhumane and savage deeds. The Palestinians explained that they had seized the United States planes as a protest against the "American peace plan" for the Middle East and had blown up the Boeing 747 in Cairo because the Egyptian government had accepted the plan. The Swissair jet was hijacked, they claimed, because three Palestinian commandoes had been jailed in Zurich after an unsuccessful attempt upon an El Al plane there in 1969. A similar reason was given for the seizure of the TWA plane as it left Frankfurt, as West German authorities were holding three PFLP guerrillas for an attack upon Israelis in the Munich airport. Four days later, the PFLP seized a third jet, a BOAC VC-10, and had it flown to join the other jets in the Jordanian desert. Thus the PFLP had found a way in which to compel the British government to release the pirate Leila Khaled. Although the world was horrified at the unmitigated extortion engaged in by this bandit organization, it was far more concerned with the fate of the nearly 400 passengers and crew of the hijacked airplanes. Negotiations were immediately begun by such renowned individuals as U Thant, Secretary General of the United Nations, and Andre Rochat of the International Red Cross to arrange for release of the hostages. Eventually this was accomplished but not before the planes were blown up and the conscience of the world completely horrified at the hijacking outrages of the PFLP.

The next month, the U.S.S.R. experienced its first international hijacking as two Lithuanians seized an Antonov-24 turboprop and had it flown to Trebizond, Turkey, where the air pirates asked for political asylum. Unfortunately, the hijackers killed the Russian stewardess and wounded three people aboard the plane prior to commandeering it, and Turkey was placed in a political quandry. The Soviet Union demanded the return of the hijackers-murders, but the Turks were reluctant to accede, since a crime had been committed on Turkish soil. A Turkish court found that Lithuanians were guilty of political rather than criminal hijacking and thus extradition was unavailable. The court did, however, charge the two men with homicide.[11]

[11]On March 9, 1971, the *New York Times* reported that the Turkish Supreme Court of Appeal reversed the lower court ruling that the two hijackers were not liable to extradition and held that hijacking is a criminal offense. The question of whether or not Pranas Brazinskas-Koreivo and his son Algierdas will be returned to the Soviet Union must now be determined by the government of Turkey.

With this recent history as a background, the ICAO's annual assembly met at the Hague, and on December 16, 1970, approved the *Convention For the Suppression of Unlawful Seizure of Aircraft.* (The entire text is reproduced at the end of this chapter.) In essence, this Convention makes piracy of an aircraft in flight an "offense," and requires all Contracting States (those ratifying the Convention) to make such offense punishable under its own national laws. It also requires that the offense be deemed "extradictable" and included in any current extradition treaty between Contracting States. If no treaty exists, a State may consider the Convention as the legal basis for extradition. Furthermore, and this is perhaps the most vital of the provisions, if a Contracting State does not choose to extradite the pirate to another Contracting State which would have jurisdiction over the offense, it must, *"without exception,"* prosecute the pirate under the nation's own laws. Thus, for example, in the above-mentioned case where the two Lithuanians hijacked the Soviet airliner, if both the U.S.S.R. and Turkey were Contracting States, Turkey would not have to extradict the pirates so long as they prosecuted them for hijacking.

Serious political implications, of course, may follow the effectuation of these provisions. A refugee from a state with a different ideology than that of the haven state must nevertheless be prosecuted as a pirate or extradited to the state from which he has just escaped. And if he is prosecuted by the haven state, care must be exercised so that he may not be allowed mercy and a reduced punishment simply because his daring exploits and escape have enhanced the ideology of the haven state. If airplane hijacking is to be stopped, it must be totally discredited as means for all brigands of all political persuasions to achieve asylum. When and if a situation occurs wherein a Contracting State is faced with prosecuting a political "friend" for air piracy, the validity of the Convention will show its true mettle and reliability and the entire world community will be watching.

QUESTIONS FOR REVIEW

1. What was the definition of "piracy" agreed upon by the

Geneva Conference of 1958 and what were this definition's principal defects?
2. What was the substance of anti-air-piracy laws passed by Congress in 1961?
3. Why did these new federal criminal laws prove inadequate?
4. What was the Tokyo Convention of 1963 and how did the member nations attending attempt to combat air piracy?
5. What were the shortcomings of the Tokyo Convention of 1963?
6. What acts and circumstances prompted the passage of the Hague Convention of 1970?
7. What were the principal terms of the Hague Convention of 1970?
8. How did the Hague Convention of 1970 improve upon the principles adopted by the Tokyo Convention of 1963?

CONVENTION FOR THE SUPPRESSION OF UNLAWFUL SEIZURE OF AIRCRAFT

Preamble

THE STATES PARTIES TO THIS CONVENTION

CONSIDERING that unlawful acts of seizure or exercise of control of aircraft in flight jeopardize the safety of persons and property, seriously affect the operation of air services, and undermine the confidence of the peoples of the world in the safety of civil aviation;

CONSIDERING that the occurrence of such acts is a matter of grave concern;

CONSIDERING that, for the purpose of deterring such acts, there is an urgent need to provide appropriate measures for punishment of offenders;

HAVE AGREED AS FOLLOWS:

Article 1

Any person who on board an aircraft in flight.

(a) unlawfully, by force or threat thereof, or by any other form of intimidation, seizes, or exercises control of, that aircraft, or attempts to perform any such act, or

(b) is an accomplice of a person who performs or attempts to perform any such act

commits an offence (hereinafter referred to as "the offence").

Article 2

Each Contracting State undertakes to make the offence punishable by severe penalties.

Article 3

For the purpose of this Convention an aircraft is considered to be in flight at any time from the moment when all its external doors are closed following embarkation until the moment when any such door is opened for disembarkment. In the case of a forced landing, the flight shall be deemed to continue until the competent authorities take over the responsibiltiy for the aircraft and for persons and property on board.

2. This Convention shall not apply to aircraft used in military, customs or police service.

3. This Convention shall apply only if the place of take-off or the place of actual landing of the aircraft on board which the offence is committed is situated outside the territory of the State of registration of that aircraft; it shall be immaterial whether the aircraft is engaged in an international or domestic flight.

4. In the cases mentioned in Article 5, this Convention shall not apply if the place of take-off and the place of actual landing of the aircraft on board which the offence is committed are situated within the territory of the same State where that State is one of those referred to in that Article.

5. Notwithstanding paragraphs 3 and 4 of this Article, Articles 6, 7, 8 and 10 shall apply whatever the place of take-off or the place of actual landing of the aircraft, if the offender or the alleged offender is found in the territory of a State other than the State of registration of that aircraft.

Article 4

1. Each Contracting State shall take such measures as may be necessary to establish its jurisdiction over the offence and any other act of violence against passengers or crew committed by the alleged offender in connection with the offence, in the following cases:

(a) when the offence is committed on board an aircraft registered in that State;

(b) when the aircraft on board which the offence is committed lands in its territory with the alleged offenders still on board;

(c) when the offence is committed on board an aircraft leased without crew to a lessee who has his principal place of business or, if the lessee has no such place of business, his permanent residence, in that State.

2. Each Contracting State shall likewise take such measures as may be necessary to establish its jurisdiction over the offence in the case where the alleged offender is present in its territory and it does not extradite him pursuant to Article 8 to any of the States mentioned in paragraph 1 of this Article.

3. This Convention does not exclude any criminal jurisdiction exercised in accordance with national law.

Article 5

The Contracting States which establish joint air transport operating organizations or international operating agencies, which operate aircraft which are subject to joint or international registration shall, by appropriate means, designate for each air craft the State among them which shall exercise the jurisdiction and have the attributes of the State of registration for the purpose of this Convention and shall give notice thereof to the international Civil Aviation Organization which shall communicate the notice to all State Parties to this Convention.

Article 6

1. Upon being satisfied that the circumstances so warrant, any

Contracting State in the territory of which the offenders or the alleged offenders is present, shall take him into custody or take other measures to ensure his presence. The custody and other measures shall be as provided in the law of that State but may only be continued for such time as is necessary to enable any criminal or extradition proceedings to be instituted.

2. Such State shall immediately make a preliminary enquiry into the facts.

3. Any person in custody pursuant to paragraph 1 of this Article shall be assisted in communicating immediately with the nearest appropriate representative of the State of which he is a national.

4. When a State, pursuant to this Article, has taken a person into custody, it shall immediately notify the State of registration of the aircraft, the State mentioned in Article 4, paragraph 1 (c), the State of nationality of the detained person and, if it considers it advisable, any other interested States of the fact that such person is in custody and of the circumstances which warrant his detention. The State which makes the preliminary enquiry contemplated in paragraph 2 of this Article shall promptly report its findings to the said States and shall indicate whether it intends to exercise jurisdiction.

Article 7

The Contracting State in the territory of which the alleged offender is found shall, if it does not extradite him, be obliged, without exception whatsoever and whether or not the offence was committed in its territory, to submit the case to its competent authorities for the purpose of prosecution.

Those authorities shall take their decision in the same manner as in the case of any ordinary offence of a serious nature under the law of that State.

Article 8

1. The offence shall be deemed to be included as an extraditable offence in any extradition treaty existing between Contracting States. Contracting States undertake to include the offence as

an extraditable offence in every extradition treaty to be concluded between them.

2. If a Contracting State which makes extradition conditional on the existence of a treaty receives a request for extradition from another Contracting State with which it has no extradition treaty, it may at its option consider this Convention as the legal basis for extradition in respect of the offence. Extradition shall be subject to the other conditions provided by the law of the requested State.

3. Contracting States which do not make extradition conditional on the existence of a treaty shall recognize the offence as an extraditable offence between themselves subject to the conditions provided by the law of the requested State.

4. The offence shall be treated, for the purpose of extradition between Contracting States, as if it had been committed not only in the place in which it occurred but also in the territories of the States required to establish their jurisdiction in accordance with Article 4, paragraph 1.

Article 9

1. When any of the acts mentioned in Article 1 (a) has occurred or is about to occur, Contracting States shall take all appropriate measures to restore control of the aircraft to its lawful commander or to preserve his control of the aircraft.

2. In the cases contemplated by the preceding paragraph, any Contracting State in which the aircraft or its passengers or crew are present shall facilitiate the continuation of the journey of the passengers and crew as soon as practicable, and shall without delay return the aircraft and its cargo to the persons lawfully entitled to possession.

Article 10

1. Contracting States shall afford one another the greatest measure of assistance in connection with criminal proceedings brought in respect of the offence and other acts mentioned in Article 4. The law of the State requested shall apply in all cases.

2. The provisions of paragraph 1 of this Article shall not affect obligations under any other treaty, bilateral or multilateral, which governs or will govern, in whole or in part, mutual assistance in criminal matters.

Article 11

Each Contracting State shall in accordance with its national law report to the Council of the International Civil Aviation Organization as promptly as possible any relevant information in its possession concerning:

(a) the circumstances of the offence;

(b) the action taken pursuant to Article 9;

(c) the measures taken in relation to the offender or the alleged offender, and, in particular, the results of any extradition proceedings or other legal proceedings.

Article 12

1. Any dispute between two or more Contracting States concerning the interpretation or application of this Convention which cannot be settled through negotiation, shall, at the request of one of them, be submitted to arbitration. If within six months from the date of the request for arbitration the Parties are unable to agree on the organization of the arbitration, any one of those Parties may refer the dispute to the International Court of Justice by request in conformity with the Statute of the Court.

2. Each State may at the time of signature or ratification of this Convention or accession thereto, declare that it does not consider itself bound by the preceding paragraph. The other Contracting States shall not be bound by the preceding paragraph with respect to any Contracting State having made such a reservation.

3. Any Contracting State having made a reservation in accordance with the preceding paragraph may at any time withdraw this reservation by notification to the Depositary Governments.

Article 13

1. This Convention shall be open for signature at The Hague on 16 December 1970, by States participating in the International Conference on Air Law held at The Hague from 1 to 16 December 1970 (hereinafter referred to as The Hague Conference). After 31 December 1970, the Convention shall be open to all States for signature in Moscow, London and Washington. Any State which does not sign this Convention before its entry into force in accordance with paragraph 3 of this Article may accede to it at any time.

2. This Convention shall be subject to ratification by the signatory States. Instruments of ratification and instruments of accession shall be deposited with the Governments of the Union of Soviet Socialist Republics, the United Kingdom of Great Britain and Northern Ireland, and the United States of America, which are hereby designated the Depositary Governments.

3. This Convention shall enter into force thirty days following the date of the deposit of instruments of ratification by ten States signatory to this Convention which participated in The Hague Conference.

4. For other states, this Convention shall enter into force on the date of entry into force of this Convention in accordance with paragraph 3 of this Article, or thirty days following the date of deposit of their instruments of ratification or accession, whichever is later.

5. The Depositary Governments shall promptly inform all signatory and acceding States of the date of each signature, the date of deposit of each instrument of ratification or accession, the date of entry into force of this Convention, and other notices.

6. As soon as this Convention comes into force, it shall be registered by the Depositary Governments pursuant to Article 102 of the Charter of the United Nations and pursuant to Article 83 of the Convention on International Civil Aviation (Chicago, 1944).

Article 14

1. Any Contracting State may denounce this Convention by written notification to the Depositary Governments.

2. Denunciation shall take effect six months following the date on which notification is received by the Depositary Governments.

IN WITNESS WHEREOF the undersigned Plenipotentiaries, being duly authorised thereto by their Governments, have signed this Convention.

DONE at The Hague, this sixteenth day of December, one thousand nine hundred and seventy, in three originals, each being drawn up in four authentic texts in the English, French, Russian and Spanish languages.

Chapter 8

CHRONIC ALCOHOLISM AS A DISABILITY AND A SOCIAL AND ECONOMIC PROBLEM

THE PROBLEM OF chronic alcoholism as a disability has come into increasing economic prominence with our growth of a sense of social responsibility. It has been estimated that perhaps 6 million persons in the United States are chronic, excessive drinkers who either risk chronic alcoholism or are already chronic alcoholics. In the December 1970 issue of *Manpower* magazine (United States Department of Labor) it was stated that chronic alcoholism costs American industry 3 billion dollars a year in tardiness, accidents, bad decisions, lost contracts, and medical bills. In New York State in January, 1960, according to the Public Health Committee of the State Bar Association, there were over 675,000 alcoholics, or 5,850 alcoholics above the age of 20 for each 100,000 persons; needless to say, during the past ten years, the numbers have more than doubled. The economic loss in wages, crime, accidents, and hospital and medical care in New York probably runs to one-half billion dollars a year. The experience of insurance companies generally attests to the fact that almost one half of all disability claims come from chronic disabilities such as chronic alcoholism. The problem is further highlighted by the fact that an insured person who has become a chronic alcoholic must prove in court his right to insurance proceeds based upon the occurrence of a disease; his right to insurance proceeds is barred if the injury is "self-inflicted." Unfortunately, the chronic alcoholic is treated not by the "medical branch" of government but by the judiciary! The well-known sports columnist, Jimmy Cannon, some years ago colorfully described the need for change:

> The medical profession now estimates the lush to be a sick man and not a frivolous escapist whose degradation is comical and enjoyable. Such a diagnosis does not apply to the careful drinker who moistens his appetite with a soupspoon full of cocktails before dinner or livens up his coffee with a smash of brandy. Immune also are those who get loaded at conventions and house parties and insist upon playing the drums when they visit a cafe. The rum pail who depends upon liquor as an ally to quiet his fear or to soothe his misery is a mental case. Instead of being judged by a magistrate, the bum eventually will be treated by the medicinal branch of government and will not have to account to the judiciary when his behavior becomes obnoxious. They will in time be treated with the same care given to those who have broken their legs or fractured their skulls. In our generation public intoxication will be no more a crime against society than pneumonia. The course is already planned and it requires only sensible legislation to make it acceptable.[1]

And, like the traditional moral treatment of the insane, the courts have *not* yet approached chronic alcoholism with understanding geared to scientific knowledge and medical experience. Uninformed generally and ever conscious of legal precedent, many judges have castigated the chronic alcoholic as a person who had intentionally self-inflicted the injury for which he unjustly seeks compensation from an insurance company. The typical disability insurance policy provision provides for waiver of premiums and for monthly payments to the beneficiary when the insured has become totally and permanently disabled, i.e. a disability resulting from bodily injury or disease which wholly prevents the insured from engaging in his or any occupation for compensation or profit. The only case to reach the United States Supreme Court in this limited field was the 1943 case of *Gaines v. Sun Life Assurance Co. of Canada;*[2] although the highest court denied certiorari, and in effect placed its blessings upon the determination of the highest Michigan court. Here a successful rhinolaryngologist with a yearly income of 18,000 dollars commenced drinking, and after years of consumption became "incoherent, irritable, depressed, and slovenly." He had, up to 1939, managed to continue the practice of his medical profession but had failed to make premium payments on his policy

---

[1]*N.Y. Post,* Dec. 30, 1948, p. 32.

[2]306 Mich. 192, *cert. den.,* 321 U.S. 789.

in 1935 during the period of his inebriety, upon which ground the insurer denied liability. In an action to recover disability payments, the Michigan court found no proof that this doctor was mentally or physically ill ("there is no such thing as latent inebriety") and so denied recovery because as a doctor he "knew" the consequences of his drinking, and therefore his disability was "self-inflicted." In a large moralistic opinion, the Michigan court declared:

> We are not impressed by the reasoning . . . that it must appear to the insured that the drinking of intoxicating liquor might develop from a harmless indulgence into a baneful disease of chronic alcoholism. It is common knowledge and the warning is evident that indulgence in intoxicating liquors, unless restrained . . . leads to excessive indulgence and one need not be warned that if continued, the craving for alcoholic liquor may lead to habitual drunkenness and the unfortunate self-imposed consequences.

Such a narrow-minded, intemperate opinion of "restraint" and "craving" hardly accords with reality in modern society, where consumption of alcoholic beverages is commonplace. Surely the sipping of liquor at a social gathering, though it may lead to chronic alcoholism years later, cannot be deemed a "self-imposed" act which caused such unfortunate consequences. Yet similar court opinions, endowed with the virtues of the temperance movement of yesteryear, label the chronic alcoholic disability as "self-inflicted," and by "relation back" penalize the insured for ever taking his first drink!

The chronic alcoholic is characterized by the lack of a volitional limit to his drinking, an inability to control his craving for intoxicating liquor. A person who has developed a bodily or mental disorder as a definite consequence of an extended period of heavy drinking is regarded by medical opinion today as a chronic alcoholic. One who drinks heavily but who has no discernible physical or mental ailment is an "alcohol addict" if he can maintain an interest in life only by consuming large quantities of alcohol. Compulsive drinkers cannot control their intensive craving for alcohol. The *Gaines* case unfortunately made no effort to understand these scientific categories, and simply characterized the alcoholic as an immoral creature hell-bent upon self-infliction. On the other hand, a Maryland court in 1938 in *Hurst v. Mutual Life Ins. Co.*[3] demonstrated a gratifying familiarity with the medical and psychiatric rationale of chronic alcoholism and unqualifiedly rejected the insurance company's contention that alcoholism was a self-inflicted malady. Here the insured began to drink several years after he had taken out the policy, until he became a dypsomaniac. Dangerously ill of chronic alcoholism, he received medical and psychiatric treatment in a sanitarium for seven months. The prognosis was that he would never recover from his disability. The Maryland court held that there was no question of fact for the jury, and that, as a matter of law, the disease of chronic alcoholism was *not* self-inflicted:

> There is no evidence on the record legally sufficient for the jury to find that the chronic alcoholism of the insured is the result of his conscious purpose or design . . . on the contrary, the testimony tends to show that he had vainly exercised his will to restrain and control his desire. The result of his *disease* is a weakness of will and of character which caused him to yield to the temptation of an overmastering appetite for intoxicating liquors. The drinking in the first stages was voluntary but there was no testimony that the drinker was then aware of the latent danger in his habit; and so while his consumption of liquor was a voluntary act, yet his ignorance of its insidious effect does not make the act a voluntary exposure of himself to the unapprehended and unexpected danger of the disease of chronic alcoholism. The *result* of the indulgence of an appetite does not necessarily determine that the result was self-inflicted because if the actor does not apprehend or is ignorant of the danger of his act, he may not be held to have voluntarily inflicted upon himself the consequences.

The motivational patterns of drinking do not reveal willful drives toward self-destruction. A survey by three Rutgers University sociologists (reported in December 1948 issue of the *Quarterly Journal of Studies on Alcohol*) emphasized the "social pressure" feared by young adults if they do not drink. Over 43 per cent of the drinkers interviewed gave social reasons for their drinking, while 41 per cent gave such reasons as "thirst,"

---

[3]174 Md. 596, 1938.

a liking for alcoholic beverages, and belief in its appetizing and medicinal values. The lack of a specfic intent to inflict self-injurious consequences by drinking was notably evident. But many courts, in deciding whether or not alcoholism is such an injury, *in an individual case,* have used the rather ineffective, ambiguous test of the dangers of excessive drinking. These courts were obviously assuming that there is a *stage* on the road between occasional moderate drinking and excessive habitual drinking where the person realizes the possible danger ahead of him of becoming a chronic alcoholic and still has sufficient will power left to be able to act according to his insight—and thereupon stop drinking! The weight of medical and psychiatric learning denies that there is always such a "stage" of realization or awareness. Powerful psychic drives and urges are responsible for chronic alcoholism and not lack of will power or even moral turpitude. Fortunately, recent judicial decisions have liberalized the definitions of "permanent" and "total" and "any occupation" in defining permanent and total disability which precludes the insured from practicing his or any occupation. The chronic alcoholic insured today has a more reasonable chance for recovery.

The United States Supreme Court in a *criminal* case had occasion in 1966 to review once again this problem of the chronic alcoholic. Thomas F. Budd was convicted under Sec. 647(f) of the California Penal Code, which provided, in part, that any person "found in any public place under the influence of intoxicating liquor . . . in such a condition that he is unable to exercise care for his own safety or that of others" is guilty of a misdemeanor. Mr. Budd argued that punishment under this California statute constituted "cruel and unusual punishment" in violation of the Eighth Amendment to the United States Constitution. But again the highest United States Court refused to hear the case (denied a writ of certiorari); Mr. Justices Fortas and Douglas, however, took a strong stand that an "alcoholic addict, like a drug addict, is beyond the reach of the criminal law." Mr. Justice Fortas pointed out that there was "abundant evidence" that Mr. Budd was "an alcoholic, that he suffers from an illness which results in inability to control either his drinking or certain aspects of behavior after he has been drinking." Mr. Justice Fortas then opined:

> It is time for this Court to decide whether persons suffering from the illness of alcoholism and exhibiting its symptoms or effects may be punished criminally therefor. The Court has already held that a State may not punish for narcotics addiction, that to do so would violate the constitutional prohibition of cruel and unusual punishment . . . Mr. Justice Stewart's opinion for the Court in *Robinson* makes it clear that a State may not constitutionally inflict punishment for an illness, whether the illness be narcotics addiction or "the common cold."

Mr. Justice Fortas further stated that Mr. Budd's record of countless incarcerations for drunkenness "admonish that punishment of alcoholics does society no good":

> It can be applauded only by the uninformed or the sadistic. It is neither a deterrent nor a cure for those afflicted. On the contrary, as testified here, it is not only ineffective, but "particularly antitherapeutic because it increases the feelings of worthlessness that all alcoholics have . . . ." This does not, of course, mean that alcoholics need be, or should be, permitted to endanger themselves and others or to be public nuisances. Each of the 50 States has some sort of non-criminal procedure for dealing with alcoholics, and in each State some procedure exists or can be provided for intelligent, purposeful handling of the various aspects of the problem. Our morality does not permit us to punish for illness. We do not impose punishment for involuntary conduct, whether the lack of volition results from 'insanity,' addiction to narcotics, or from other illnesses. The use of the crude and formidable weapon of criminal punishment of the alcoholic is neither seemly nor sensible, neither purposeful nor civilized.

In the *Budd* case, Mr. Justice Fortas made reference to an earlier, lower federal court decision, *Easter v. District of Columbia,*[4] in which that court had "agreed that Congress intended that alcoholics not be punished for the offence of public drunkenness." Mr. Easter was a chronic alcoholic convicted under Sec. 25-128(a) of the District of Columbia Code: "No person shall . . . be drunk or intoxicated in any street, alley, park or

---

[4]361 F.2d 50 USDC DC, 1964.

parking." The evidence showed that since 1937, Mr. Easter had been arrested for intoxication 70 times, 12 times in 1963 alone. The conviction was therefore *reversed* upon the ground that chronic alcoholism is a defense to the criminal charge of public intoxication. The federal district court stated that their conclusion was based upon an examination of the District of Columbia's Rehabilitation of Alcoholcs Act (passed in 1947 but never implemented by the appropriation of funds for facilities), which stated that "the courts of the District of Columbia are hereby authorized to take judicial notice of the fact that a chronic alcoholic is a sick person and in need of proper medical, institutional, advisory, and rehabilitative treatment. . . ." The Act defines a "chronic alcoholic" as a "person who chronically and habitually uses alcoholic beverages to the extent that he has lost the power of self-control with respect to the use of such beverages. . . ." These statutory provisions

> preclude attaching criminality in this jurisdiction to intoxication in public of a chronic alcoholic. An essential element of criminal responsibility is the ability to avoid the conduct specified in the definition of the crime. . . . To be guilty of the crime, a person must engage responsibly in the action. In the case of a chronic alcoholic Congress has dealt with his condition so that in this jurisdiction he too cannot be held to be guilty of the crime of being intoxicated because, as the act recognizes, he has lost the power of self-control in the use of intoxicating beverages.

As the result of the *Easter* decision (supported also by a federal court decision in Virginia), several states and cities have endeavored to build hospital-like treatment facilities for alcoholics. But the funds have not been available to assure this treatment of the alcoholic. In a 1966 message to Congress, President Lyndon Johnson made this statement: "The alcoholic suffers from a disease which will yield eventually to scientific research and adequate treatment. . . . Even with the present limited state of our knowledge, much can be done." A National Center for Studies of the Control and Prevention of Alcoholism was then set up as a part of the National Institute of Mental Health. Today a majority of states have enacted laws that recognize alcoholism as a *medical* problem.

In *Driver v. Hinnant,*[5] the Fourth United States Court of Appeals considered the case of a 59-year-old man convicted of chronic alcoholism for the 200th time since he was 24 years of age! The Court observed: "Driver's chronic alcoholism is a disease which has destroyed the power of his will to resist the constant, excessive consumption of alcohol; his appearance in public in that condition is not his volition but a compulsion symptomatic of the disease; and to stigmatize him as a criminal for this act is cruel and unusual punishment." Accordingly, the Court ruled that chronic alcoholism

> is now almost universally accepted medically as a disease. The symptoms . . . may appear as "disorder of behavior." Obviously, this includes appearance in public, as here, unwilled and ungovernable by the victim. When that is the conduct for which he is criminally accused, there can be no judgment of criminal conviction passed upon him. To do so would affront the Eighth Amendment, as cruel and unusual punishment in branding him a criminal, irrespective of consequent detention or fine.

(The Court warned that its conclusion did not destroy the thesis that voluntary drunkenness is no excuse for crime, and the Court did not annul the state statute.) A state may deter and punish public drunkenness to secure others against annoyances and intrusions, the Court declared, "but the Constitution intercedes when on arraignment the accused's helplessness comes to light. Then it is that no *criminal* conviction may follow. . . . [N]othing we have said precludes appropriate detention of him for treatment and rehabilitation so long as he is not marked a criminal."

It is regrettable that criminal arrests of the chronic alcoholic is the established modus operandi. The Advisory Committee of the American Law Institute (which prepared a Model Penal Code for adoption by the states), however, frowns upon the handling of nondisorderly drunks through the usual facilities of law enforcement, i.e. police stations and jails. The Committee recommended that such persons be taken to their homes, public shelters, or to hospitals where drunkenness can be differentiated from epileptic attacks or other pathological conditions.

[5]356 F2d 761, CCA4, 1966.

Indeed, the plight of the drunken derelict is a grave public health problem, not a penal problem. Modern therapy and a humane program of day-to-day care and relief is required. Police have the duty to escort the drunken derelict to his home or to a public shelter. There is no moral justification for wholesale criminal arrests of drunken derelicts.

Today, over 2 million American citizens are arrested each year for public drunkenness under laws that are seldom enforced uniformly. The typical drunkenness statute contains two elements: (a) the fact of the defendant's intoxication and (b) the defendant's intoxication in a public place. The police prefer to handle middle- and upper-class intoxicants through informal means such as transporting them to their home. On the other hand, arrest and criminal prosecution are commonplace in lower class and especially "Skid Row" sections of a city. In non-Skid-Row areas, handling the publicly intoxicated resident is regarded as a sidelight, an insignificant and bothersome protective task. In Skid Row areas, enforcement of the drunkenness laws is frequently the primary job of a specialized squad of officers and represents the most visible and extensive system of providing social services and controlling the men. These laws are virtually the only law that the Skid Row man knows. This differential enforcement has been explained as resulting from the fact that there is no way other than an arrest to protect the Skid Row drunk. Although the explanation is certainly more complex, this statement does emphasize one important factor about the enforcement of the drunkenness laws: the purpose behind the enforcement of these laws is not found in the common criminal law rhetoric of deterrence, punishment, or even rehabilitation. Thus, what is commonly referred to as the "public drunkenness problem" is best understood in its Skid Row context. Although the policies followed and the level of enforcement vary, several concerns reoccur among the jurisdictions. Arrests of nondisorderly but usually intoxicated derelict men allegedly provide the men with a brief respite from the extended drinking which can be one facet of a Skid Row way of life. In some cities, enforcement practices establish the jail as a substitute for nonexistent municipal shelter facilities providing the men with free housing for one night. Additionally, they deal with medical problems of the men and serve the law enforcement concern of protecting them from the possibility of violent assault and robbery. Often the arrests are employed primarily to service a perceived community concern to remove the unsightly derelict men from the sight of the "normal" populace, and these pressures can lead to an extremely high arrest rate. Despite some arguably laudable motives, the criminal process provides no more than minimal temporary assistance. Arrests are processed on a mass basis, frequently as a result of the operations of a specially designated "bum squad." The arrestees are herded into cells with inadequate size and almost no facilities to treat the medical and other problems that arise. Long before the men are led into the courtroom, the cells become filthy and permeated with the stench of dried blood, sweat, and vomit. The court procedure is based upon "mass production," as perhaps 100 men are "processed" within an hour. The procedure is only a stopgap measure costing municipalities huge sums of money and with little prospect of "curing" the problem. The city of St. Louis, Missouri, has a Detoxification and Diagnostic Center for Intoxicated Men (which is a medically oriented facility to which public intoxicants are taken). This "hospital" succeeds in removing the criminal label, although it is not "a panacea for the ills of the criminal system in processing the public intoxicant."[6]

> The upshot of these observations is not that the detoxification model should be abandoned but that its use and structure should be subjected to more incisive scrutiny. The difficult policy questions involved in choosing intake source, treatment emphasis and problem population identification cannot be answered on a generalized basis. The needs of each jurisdiction may vary and the program should be modified to meet these needs, after the policy questions have been discussed and resolved.

Some ten years ago, the Public Health Committee of the New York State Bar Association, in a public statement on January 11, 1960, similarly declared:

---

[6]1970 *Washington Univ. L. Q.* 475.

> We have repeatedly drawn attention to the barbarous and futile practice of treating alcoholism as a crime instead of a disease recognized as such by the state, the courts and the principal group health plans. But the state continues to tolerate the dreary cycle of arrest, jail, release, arrest, jail, release over and over again. The waste of public funds, the overcrowding of prisons and the inhumanity of this procedure are indefensible.

The fact of the matter is that New York has done little to solve the problem of public drunkenness.

A clearer picture or portrait of the chronic alcoholic, in public or in private, is found in an article entitled "Alcoholism and Accountability,"[7] by Dr. Cyril B. Courville. Dr. Courville, speaking for insurance carriers generally, declared:

> The problem itself is essentially a paradox, for the initial use of alcohol as a source of pleasurable reaction not infrequently results in untoward, if not tragic, effects insofar as the drinker and those coming into contact with him are concerned. Yet the innumerable object lessons of these ill effects are slow to influence either the drinker or those who are in a position to alter his environment. From the viewpoint of the individual, there are two factors which account for chronic alcoholism, other than the case of recurrent episodes of excessive drinking. The first of these factors is psychological. Alcohol furnishes a means of escape for the immature individual who finds it difficult to cope with his environment. The second factor is concerned with a physiological reaction to its use—an addiction to alcohol as a narcotic.

Dr. Courville then discusses accountability of the chronic alcoholic in these words:

> There is a considerable period of time between alcoholic bouts during which the individual is entirely rational and capable of reasoning from cause to effect. The fact that he is a chronic alcoholic cannot excuse his acts during these intervals, as well as those committed under the influence of alcohol. In such case, three courses may be followed with respect to the ultimate effects of this habituation on the brain. In the first place, the victim of chronic alcoholism may continue to deteriorate with progressive atrophy of the brain until he is no longer reliable as to his responsibility and accountability for his acts. He is not able to enter into contract regarding his own or his family affairs. He should be placed under the care of a guardian.

---

[7] *Insurance Counsel J.*, Jan. 1960, p. 166-8.

A second situation may also develop, particularly in the case of chronic alcoholics who are also chronically undernourished. Such individuals may be stricken with acute psychotic episodes (hemorrhagic encephalopathy). Ordinarily they are delerious and not likely to commit antisocial acts, hence these episodes usually are of no legal significance. On the other hand, true post-alcoholic psychosis of one of three types may occur. Two of these assume the form of a psychosis of a chronic type. One is characterized with physical signs of malnutrition due to lack of vitamin B (alcoholic pellagra). The second type (Korsakoff's psychosis), also due in part to malnutrition, presents a peculiar type of reaction of response to his associates (confabulation). The third form of psychosis is the result of a combination of chronic alcoholism and advanced arteriosclerosis of the cerebral vessels (deteriorated alcoholic). These patients become seriously demented if they survive for any length of time. In cases of fully developed chronic alcoholic psychoses, the individuals are no longer responsible or accountable in the sense of using good judgment in the performance of their regular duties and responsibilities. Therefore, they should have guardians if they are still physically well enough to be kept at home. Many of them should be placed in institutions for care, for they are beyond medical help. They are not likely to commit serious antisocial acts, however.

In many cases of chronic alcoholism, the time comes when a decision on the matter of responsibility and accountability must be reached. This requires the opinion of a competent psychiatrist. Unfortunately some psychiatrists are not fully aware of the damage of the brain (atrophy) as a result of chronic alcoholism, being inclined to interpret the behavior of the individual on a purely functional level. The demonstration of cerebral cortical atrophy and enlarged ventricles of pneumoencephalography (air studies) . . . presents highly significant evidence that chronic alcoholism is a brain destroyer. That this shrinkage of the brain also produces a disordered nervous function, as shown in the electroencephalogram (brain wave) is further evidence of the organic character of this deterioration. Therefore, there is now available objective findings as well as psychiatric evidence to assist in determining the degree of deterioration of the brain in cases of chronic alcoholism. In case of doubt these procedures should be performed in reaching a correct conclusion.

If Dr. Courville is correct, a new approach to the problem of legal responsibility and accountability must be based upon the fact that alcohol acts as a narcotic on the brain and when used in excess for any prolonged period of time will result in atrophy of the brain. Unfortunately, there is some indifference on the part of the public as to the total effects of alcohol, and the reason is economic: the government's hope of increased revenues in taxes; the desire for added income from advertisements on the part of papers and magazines; and the fear of offending certain members of society on the part of jurists who are sometimes inclined to overlook the ill results of drunkenness. These considerations which are economic in origin are nevertheless motivations controlling treatment of the chronic alcoholic. Revenue to run the machinery of government (federal, state and local) is today dependent upon vice, i.e. lotteries, gambling statutes, and even popular acceptance of the liquor industry as an essential cog in the wheel of economic prosperity. No public figure would ever go to bat against the vested liquor interests. At most, efforts to restrict or license distribution of liquor are accepted, and the problems of drunkenness persist. Chronic alcoholism is the price society must pay for the economic prosperity which ignores the adverse and total effects of alcohol in drink.

According to the Midwest Institute of Alcohol Studies at Loyola University in Chicago,[8] it takes from 8 to 15 years for a person to become an alcoholic, based upon a study of 2,000 self-admitted chronic alcoholics in the United States. About 1 out of 13 drinkers becomes an alcoholic, although he may consume less alcohol than the others. The report continued:

> The alcoholic has a peculiar sensitivity to alcohol. According to the newest theory, the alcoholic reacts to alcohol in somehow the same way that the diabetic reacts to sugar. The 13th person's drinking may not differ from the others in its early stages, but after a while something will happen that sets off a chain reaction in him. Although he may not consume more alcohol than some of the other 12, it will become a disease for him. In general, the process begins with increased tolerance as the person becomes able to drink more and more. At this point, the future alcoholic needs about twice as much liquor for a 'lift' as he formerly required. This phase usually

---

[8]New York Times, June 20, 1965.

lasts from six months to five years and ends with the first blackout. The second stage is described as the predromal phase. The subject becomes preoccupied with drinking, begins to sneak drinks but doesn't want to talk about it and takes offense quickly when his habit is mentioned. This lasts from about the fifth to the eighth year. Then comes the acute stage characterized by alibis for drinking to counteract reproof from his employer and family and expressions of remorse. He may go on the "water wagon" or change from hard liquor to beer. This phase usually ends with a long "bender." The last stage is the chronic phase, in which there is a breakdown of ethics and the person will beg, borrow or steal to get alcohol. He develops the "shakes" and has vague, indefinite fears. Oddly, at this point, his physical tolerance for alcohol sometimes reverses. Instead of needing more alcohol than the normal person, he can stay drunk all day on very little.

Dr. Herbert E. Karolus of the Keeley Institute in Dwight, Illinois reported in early 1961 that his two-year study of 442 alcoholics has turned up reasons for believing compulsive drinking is somewhat like the compulsive sneezing of hay fever sufferers, i.e. the latter are allergic to pollens, and once they get pollens in their nostrils they cannot stop sneezing. If some alcoholics are allergic to drink, it could be that their peculiar body chemistry compels them to keep on drinking once the first drink is in them. Dr. Karolus began his scientific exploration of this idea by skin-testing his 442 alcoholics with the individual ingredients of intoxicating beverages. He wanted to see if he could raise the welts or other visible signs of an allergic reaction. The ingredients he tested were apple, barley, blackberry, corn, date, fig, grape, hops, juniper, malt, oats, plum, rice, rye, sugar cane, wheat, yeast, and oak. All 442 alcoholics had an allergic reaction to at least one of these. Two had reactions to 13, and the average for the 442 was 7 of the 18 ingredients. Of the 442, 301 were allergic to rye and 239 reacted to wheat. Dr. Karolus took 20 of the reactors and tested them with a "test meal" of the ingredient to which they were allergic on the surface. This meant they ate very little for three days, and then they consumed a meal composed entirely of corn or rice or wheat. "In some patients there were increased flushing, fidgeting, excitement or unsteadiness of gait. In some a complete change of personality took place. Serenity was replaced by belligerence. A drink was first requested, then demanded." Thus, if alcoholics are truly allergic to one or more ingredients of drink, theoretically it should be possible to "desensitize" at least some of them. Some 200 of the 442 are now taking weekly desensitization treatments from their family physicians.

The American public is today changing its attitude on the treatment of the chronic alcoholic, as evidenced by 1970 findings in the *Quarterly Journal of Studies on Alcohol,* published by the Rutgers University Center on Alcohol. Most lay people who once favored religion, willpower, and legal controls for dealing with alcoholism now often endorse medical and psychological help. As outward signs of this change in public attitudes, the findings cited the sympathetic portrayal of the alcoholic in motion pictures and popular journalism, the accelerated development of clinics and local committees on alcoholism, and the challenges of the constitutionality of imprisoning alcoholics for drunkenness. The Rutgers report also found that each younger age group is more favorable toward social drinking than the next older age group. There was also a progressive increase in acceptance of social drinking, coupled to some extent with contact with the mass media.

A recent step in the right direction towards altering the attitude of the general public with respect to the problem of alcoholism is contained in the Federal Comprehensive Alcohol Abuse and Alcoholism Prevention, Treatment, and Rehabilitation Act, (reproduced at the end of this chapter), enacted into law on December 31, 1970. This new statute, in addition to recognizing the awareness of the federal government of the problems of the alcoholic also provides for the establishment of a National Institute on Alcohol Abuse and Alcoholism to develop and conduct programs for the prevention and treatment of alcohol abuse and the rehabilitation of alcoholics. Even more important, the Act provides for the availability of Federal assistance funds to aid state- and local-supported programs. The allocation of funds amounts to 40 million dollars for 1971, 60 million dollars for 1972, and 80 million dollars for 1973.

One interesting facet of the problem of chronic alcoholism and society at large is the legal responsibility of a seller of intoxicating liquor (dram shops) for injuries caused to others by the intoxication of the purchaser. Tavernkeepers have generally been held liable (in those states having Dram Shop Acts) for negligence in selling liquor to intoxicated persons. In *St. Clair v. Douvas*,[9] a husband, while drunk, stabbed a son of the plaintiff and thereby deprived the dependent plaintiff-wife of support; the defendant tavernkeeper had been sentenced to jail for selling liquor to the intoxicated husband. The trial court dismissed the action against the tavernkeeper, but the Illinois appellate court reversed, holding that "injuries," as used in Illinois Dram Shop Act, does not mean only physical injuries but also that a person entitled to support suffered injury in being deprived of such support. The injury was a violation of legal rights, and the evidence was sufficient to justify recovery for the wife of the decedent on the ground that the wrongful acts of the defendant were the proximate cause of injury to her means of support. And in a New Jersey case, *Rappaport v. Nichols*,[10] the Supreme Court of that state declared:

> Recognition of the plaintiff's claim will afford a fairer measure of justice to innocent third parties whose injuries are brought about by the unlawful and negligent sale of alcoholic beverages to minors and intoxicated persons, will strengthen and give greater force to the enlightened statutory and regulatory precautions against such sales and their frightening consequences and will not place any unjustifiable burdens upon defendants who can always discharge their civil responsibilities by the exercise of due care. It must be borne in mind that the plaintiff's complaint has no relation to service by persons not engaged in the liquor business or to lawful sales and service by liquor licensees, or to sales by reasonably prudent licensees who do not know or have reason to believe that the patron is a minor or is intoxicated when served; the allegations of the complaint are expressly confined to tavern keepers' sales and service which are unlawful and negligent.

An unusual case is delineated in *Waynick v. Chicago's Last Dept. Store*.[11] Here the liquor was purchased in Illinois and quite a bit of it drunk by the inebriates in Illinois; the inebriates

---

[9]158 N.E. 2d 612, 1959.
[10]103 N.J. Super. 445, 247 A2d 495, App. Div., 1968.
[11]CCA7, 1959.

then drove into Michigan where the automobile accident occurred, which injured the plaintiff. (Illinois had a Dram Shop Act, but it had been held to have no extraterritorial effect.) The federal court found the Michigan liquor control act *not* applicable because the sales occurred outside Michigan. Thus a vacuum resulted, which the Court said the law, like nature, abhorred: "Lest we too hastily reject the claim of these plaintiffs for pecuniary redress for death and injuries sustained in what was evidently an appalling automobile accident," the Court continued, "we turn to the common law." So doing, the Court declared that Michigan law, being that of the place where the injury occurred, controlled. But the Court went to an Illinois criminal statute making it a misdemeanor to "sell, give or deliver alcoholic liquor . . . to any intoxicated person" to declare that the tavernkeeper defendants were negligent. As to duty, the Court found that it also flowed from the Illinois statute, which it stated was for the protection of any member of the public injured by the prohibited sale. The Court noted that the common law permitted actions against liquor vendors under some circumstances. In one Illinois case, it was said that there was no liability if the sales were to "strong and able-bodied men." The sales, being in violation of the statute, were not "usual sales to adults or ordinary men," the Court said.

Whether the subject is the liability of a tavernkeeper in selling liquor to an intoxicated person, or whether the topic is the social problem of public drunkenness, chronic alcoholism remains an individual disability that demands from society a solution. It is unfortunate that the judicial system is called upon to resolve the matter when it is the "medical branch" of society that must be called upon to alleviate the problem.

QUESTIONS FOR REVIEW

1. Describe *briefly* why chronic alcoholism is both a social and economic problem.
2. Explain why chronic alcoholism has been labeled by some courts as a "self-inflicted injury" and not the unfortunate disease which it is.

3. Define chronic alcoholism in sociological terms.
4. Are the motivational patterns of drinking important to an understanding of the chronic alcoholic? Explain by reference to "intent."
5. Was Mr. Budd's punishment "cruel and unusual?" Why are chronic alcoholics treated as criminals?
6. How does the *Budd* case differ from the *Easter* Case? Does the latter decision bid well for future understanding of the problem of the chronic alcoholic?
7. What are the provisions of the typical drunkenness statute? Do they simplify or make complex the role of the police?
8. Does awareness of the Skid Row problem generate some understanding of chronic alcoholism as a disease? Can we "cure" public drunkenness?
9. Is a chronic alcoholic *psychiatrically* accountable for his behavior? *Physically* accountable? Explain.
10. Is "temperance" an answer to the problem of alcoholism? What is compulsive drinking?
11. What are the Dram Shop Acts?
12. Can we handle the chronic alcoholic without involvement of the courts? Explain.

ALCOHOL ABUSE ACT

An Act

To provide a comprehensive Federal program for the prevention and treatment of alcohol abuse and alcoholism

Be it enacted by the Senate and House of Representatives of the United States of America in Congress assembled,

Short Title

SEC. 1. This Act may be cited as the "Comprehensive Alcohol Abuse and Alcoholism Prevention, Treatment, and Rehabilitation Act of 1970."

Title I—National Institute On Alcohol Abuse and Alcoholism

Establishment of the Institute

SEC. 101. (a) There is established in the National Institute of Mental Health, the National Institute on Alcohol Abuse and Alcoholism (hereafter in this Act referred to as the "Institute") to administer the programs and authorities assigned to the Secretary of Health, Education, and Welfare (hereafter in this Act referred to as the "Secretary") by this Act and part C of the Community Mental Health Centers Act. The Secretary, acting through the Institute, shall, in carrying out the purposes of section 301 of the Public Health Service Act with respect to alcohol abuse and alcoholism, develop and conduct comprehensive health, education, training, research, and planning programs for the prevention and treatment of alcohol abuse and alcoholism and for the rehabilitation of alcohol abusers and alcoholics.

(b) The Institute shall be under the direction of a Director who shall be appointed by the Secretary.

Reports by the Secretary

SEC. 102. The Secretary shall—

(1) submit an annual report to Congress which shall include a description of the actions taken, services provided, and funds expended under this Act and part C of the Community Mental Health Centers Act, an evaluation of the effectiveness of such actions, services, and expenditures of funds, and such other information as the Secretary considers appropriate;

(2) submit to Congress on or before the expiration of the one-year period beginning on the date of enactment of this Act a report (A) containing current information on the health consequences of using alcoholic beverages, and (B) containing such recommendations for legislation and administrative action as he may deem appropriate;

(3) submit such additional reports as may be re-

quested by the President of the United States or by Congress; and

(4) submit to the President of the United States and to Congress such recommendations as will further the prevention of alcohol abuse and alcoholism.

Title II—Alcoholism Abuse and Alcoholism Prevention, Treatment, and Rehabilitation Programs for Federal Civilian Employees

Alcohol Abuse and Alcoholism Among Federal Civilian Employees

SEC. 201. (a) The Civil Service Commission shall be responsible for developing and maintaining, in cooperation with the Secretary and with other Federal agencies and departments, appropriate prevention, treatment, and rehabilitation programs and services for alcohol abuse and alcoholism among Federal civilian employees, consistent with the purposes of this Act. Such policies and services shall make optimal use of existing governmental facilities, services, and skills.

(b) The Secretary, acting through the Institute, shall be responsible for fostering similar alcohol abuse and alcoholism prevention, treatment, and rehabilitation programs and services in State and local governments and in private industry.

(c) (1) No person may be denied or deprived of Federal civilian employment or a Federal professional or other license or right solely on the ground of prior alcohol abuse or prior alcoholism.

(2) This subsection shall not apply to employment (A) in the Central Intelligence Agency, the Federal Bureau of Investigation, the National Security Agency, or any other department or agency of the Federal Government designated for purposes of national security by the President, or (B) in any position in any department or agency of the Federal Government, not referred to in clause (A), which position is determined pursuant to regulations prescribed by the head of such agency or department to be a sensitive position.

(d) This title shall not be construed to prohibit the dismissal from employment of a Federal civilian employee who cannot properly function in his employment.

Title III—Federal Assistance for State and Local Programs

Part A—Formula Grants

Authorization

Sec. 301. There are authorized to be appropriated $40,000,000 for the fiscal year ending June 30, 1971, $60,000,000 for the fiscal year ending June 30, 1972, $80,000,000 for the fiscal year ending June 30, 1973, for grants to States to assist them in planning, establishing, maintaining, coordinating, and evaluating projects for the development of more effective prevention, treatment, and rehabilitation programs to deal with alcohol abuse and alcoholism. For purposes of this part, the term "State" includes the District of Columbia, the Virgin Islands, the Commonwealth of Puerto Rico, Guam, American Samoa, and the Trust Territory of the Pacific Islands, in addition to the fifty States.

State Allotment

Sec. 302. (a) For each fiscal year the Secretary shall, in accordance with regulations, allot the sums appropriated for such year pursuant to section 301 among the States on the basis of the relative population, financial need, and need for more effective prevention, treatment, and rehabilitation of alcohol abuse and alcoholism; except that no such allotment to any State (other than the Virgin Islands, American Samoa, Guam, and the Trust Territory of the Pacific Islands, for any fiscal year shall be less than $200,000.

(b) Any amount so allotted to a State (other than the Virgin Islands, American Samoa, Guam, and the Trust Territory of the Pacific Islands) and remaining unobligated at the end of such year shall remain available to such State, for the purposes for which made, for the next fiscal year (and for such year only), and any such amount shall be in addition to the amounts allotted to such State for such purpose for such next fiscal year; except that any amount, remaining unobligated at the end of the sixth month following the end of such year for which it was allotted, which the Secretary determines will remain unobligated by the close of such next fiscal year, may be reallotted by the Secretary, to be available for the purposes for which made until the close of such next fiscal year, to other States which have need therefor, on such basis as the Secretary deems equitable and consistent with the purposes of this part, and any amount so reallocated to a State shall be in addition to the amounts allotted and available to the States for the same period. Any amount allotted under subsection (a) to the Virgin Islands, American Samoa, Guam, or the Trust Territory of the Pacific Islands for a fiscal year and remaining unobligated at the end of such year shall remain available to it, for the purposes for which made, for the next two fiscal years (and for such years only), and any such amount shall be in addition to the amounts allotted to it for such purpose for each such next two fiscal years; except that any such amount, remaining unobligated at the end of the first year of such next two years, which the Secretary determines will remain unobligated at the close of the second of such next two years, may be reallotted by the Secretary, to be available for the purposes for which made until the close of the second of such next two years, to any other of such four States which have need therefor, on such basis as the Secretary deems equitable and consistent with the purposes of this part, and any amount so reallotted to a State shall be in addition to the amounts allotted and available to the State for the same period.

(c) At the request of any State, a portion of any allotment or allotments of such State under this part shall be available to pay that portion of the expenditures found necessary by the Secretary for the proper and efficient administration during such year of the State plan approved under this part, except that not more than 10 per centum of the total of the allotments of such State for a year, or $50,000, whichever is the least, shall be available for such purposes for such year.

State Plans

SEC. 303. (a) Any State desiring to participate in this part shall submit a State plan for carrying out its purposes. Such plan must—

(1) designate a single State agency as the sole agency for the administration of the plan, or designate such agency as the sole agency for supervising the administration of the plan;

(2) contain satisfactory evidence that the State agency designated in accordance with paragraph (1) (hereafter in this section referred to as the "State agency") will have authority to carry out such plan in conformity with this part;

(3) provide for the designation of a State advisory council which shall include representatives of nongovernmental organizations or groups, and of public agencies concerned with the prevention and treatment of alcohol abuse and alcoholism, to consult with the State agency in carrying out the plan;

(4) set forth, in accordance with criteria established by the Secretary, a survey of need for the prevention and treatment of alcohol abuse and alcoholism, including a survey of the health facilities needed to provide services for alcohol abuse and alcoholism and a plan for the development and distribution of such facilities and programs throughout the State;

(5) provides such methods of administration of the State plan, including methods relating to the establishment and maintenance of personnel standards on a merit basis (except that the Secretary shall exercise no authority with respect to the selection, tenure of office, or compensation of any individual employed in accordance with such methods), as are found by the Secretary to be necessary for the proper and efficient operation of the plan;

(6) provide that the State agency will make such reports, in such form and containing such information, as the Secretary may from time to time reasonably require, and will keep such records and afford such access thereto

as the Secretary may find necessary to assure the correctness and verification of such reports;

(7) provide that the Comptroller General of the United States or his duly authorized representatives shall have access for the purpose of audit and examination to the records specified in paragraph (6);

(8) provide that the State agency will from time to time, but not less often than annually, review its State plan and submit to the Secretary any modifications thereof which it considers necessary;

(9) provide reasonable assurance that Federal funds made available under this part for any period will be so used as to supplement and increase, to the extent feasible and practical, the level of the State, local, and other non-Federal funds that would in the absence of such Federal funds be made available for the programs described in this part, and will in no event supplant such State, local, and other non-Federal funds; and

(10) contains such additional information and assurance as the Secretary may find necessary to carry out the provisions and purposes of this part.

(b) The Secretary shall approve any State plan and any modification thereof which complies with the provisions of subsection (a).

Part B—Project Grants and Contracts

Grants and Contracts for the Prevention and Treatment of Alcohol Abuse and Alcoholism

Sec. 311. Section 247 of part C of the Community Mental Health Centers Act is amended to read as follows:

Grants and Contracts for the Prevention and Treatment of Alcohol Abuse and Alcoholism

"Sec. 247.(a) The Secretary, acting through the National Institute on Alcohol Abuse and Alcoholism, may make grants to public and private nonprofit agencies, organizations, and institutions and may enter into contracts with public and private agencies, organizations, and institutions, and individuals—

"(1) to conduct demonstration, service, and evaluation projects,

"(2) to provide education and training,

"(3) to provide programs and services in cooperation with schools, courts, penal institutions, and other public agencies, and

"(4) to provied counseling and education activities on an individual or community basis,

for the prevention and treatment of alcohol abuse and alcoholism and for the rehabilitation of alcohol abusers and alcoholics.

"(b) Projects for which grants or contracts are made under this section shall, whenever possible, be community based, provide a comprehensive range of services, and be integrated with, and involve the active participation of, a wide range of public and nongovernmental agencies, organizations, institutions, and individuals.

"(c)(1) In administering the provisions of this section, the Secretary shall require coordination of all applications for programs in a State.

"(2) Each applicant from within a State, upon filing its application with the Secretary for a grant or contract under this section, shall submit a copy of its application for review by the State agency designed under section 303 of the Comprehensive Alcohol Abuse and Alcoholism Prevention, Treatment, and Rehabilitation Act of 1970, if such agency exists. Such State agency shall be given not more than thirty days from the date of receipt of the application to submit to the Secretary, in writing, an evaluation of the project set forth in the application. Such evaluation shall include comments on the relationship of the project to other projects pending and approved and to the State comprehensive plan for treatment and prevention of alcohol abuse and alcoholism under such section 303. The State shall furnish the applicant a copy of any such evaluation.

"(3) Approval of any application for a grant or contract by the Secretary, including the earmarking of financial assistance for a program or project, may be granted only if the application substantially meets a set of criteria established by the Secretary that—

"(A) provide that the activities and services for which assistance under this section is sought will be substantially administered by or under the supervision of the applicant;

"(B) provide for such methods of administration as are necessary for the proper and efficient operation of such programs or projects;

"(C) provide for such fiscal control and fund accounting procedures as may be necessary to assure proper disbursement of and accounting for Federal funds paid to the applicant; and

"(D) provide reasonable assurance that Federal funds made available under this section for any period will be so used as to supplement and increase, to the extent feasible and practical, the level of State, local, and other non-Federal funds that would in the absence of such Federal funds be made available for the programs described in this section, and will in no event supplant such State, local, and other non-Federal funds.

"(d) To carry out the purposes of this section, there are authorized to be appropriated $30,000,000 for the fiscal year ending June 30, 1971, $40,000,000 for the fiscal year ending June 30, 1972, and $50,000,000 for the fiscal year ending June 30, 1973."

Part C—Admission to Hospitals

Admission of Alcohol Abusers and Alcoholics to Private and Public Hospitals

SEC. 321. (a) Alcohol abusers and alcoholics shall be admitted to and treated in private and public general hospitals, which receive Federal funds for alcoholic treatment programs, on the basis of medical need and shall not be discriminated against solely because of their alcoholism. No hospital that violates this section shall receive Federal financial assistance under the provisions of this Act, except that the Secretary shall not terminate any such Federal assistance until the Secretary has advised the appropriate person or persons of the failure to comply with this section, and has provided an opportunity for correction or a hearing.

(b) Any action taken by the Secretary pursuant to this by section shall be subject to such judicial review as is provided by section 44 of the Community Mental Health Centers Act.

PART D—GENERAL

Comprehensive State Health Plans

SEC. 331. Section 314(d)(2) of the Public Health Service Act is amended—

(1) by striking out "and" at the end of subparagraph (J);

(2) by striking out the period at the end of subparagraph (K) and inserting in lieu thereof "; and"; and

(3) by adding after subparagraph (K) the following new subparagraph:

"(L) provide for services for the prevention and treatment of alcohol abuse and alcoholism, commensurate with the extent of the problem."

Specialized Facilities

SEC. 332. Section 243(a) of the Community Mental Health Centers Act is amended (1) by inserting "or leasing" after "construction", and (2) by inserting "facilities for emergency medical services, intermediate care services, or outpatient services, and" immediately before "post-hospitalization treatment of facilities".

Confidentiality of Records

SEC. 333. The Secretary may authorize persons engaged in research on, or treatment with respect to, alcohol abuse and alcoholism to protect the privacy of individuals who are the subject of such research or treatment by withholding from all persons not connected with the conduct of such research or treatment the names or other identifying characteristics of such individuals. Persons so authorized to protect the privacy of such individuals may not be compelled in any Federal, State, or local civil, criminal, administrative, legislative, or other proceeding to indentify such individuals.

Title IV—The National Advisory Council on Alcohol Abuse and Alcoholism

Establishment of Council

SEC. 401. (a) Section 217(a) of the Public Health Service Act is amended—

(1) in the first sentence thereof, by inserting "the National Advisory Council on Alcohol Abuse and Alcoholism," immediately after "the National Advisory Mental Health Council,";

(2) in the second sentence thereof, by (A) inserting "the National Advisory Council on Alcoholic Abuse and Alcoholism," immediately after "the National Advisory Mental Health Council," and (B) inserting "alcohol abuse and alcoholism," immediately after "psychiatric disorders," and

(3) in the fourth sentence, (A) by inserting "(other than the members of the National Advisory Council on Alcohol Abuse and Alcoholism)" after "the terms of the members"; (B) by striking out "and" before "(2)"; and (C) by striking out the period at the end and inserting a semicolon and "and (3) the terms of the members of the National Council on Alcohol Abuse and Alcoholism first taking office after the date of enactment of this clause, shall expire as follows: Three shall expire four years after such date, three shall expire three years after such date, three shall expire two years after such date, and three shall expire one year after such date, as designated by the Secretary at the time of appointment."

(b) Section 217(b) of such Act is amended, in the second sentence thereof, by inserting "alcohol abuse and alcoholism," immediately after "mental health."

(c) Section 217 of such Act is further amended adding at the end thereof the following new subsection:

"(d) The National Advisory Council on Alcohol Abuse and Alcoholism shall advise, consult with, and make recommendations to, the Secretary on matters relating to the activities and functions of the Secretary in the field of alcohol abuse and alcoholism. The Council is authorized (1) to review research projects or programs submitted to or initiated by it in the field of alcohol abuse and alcoholism and recommend to the Secretary any such projects which it believes show promise of making valuable contributions to human knowledge with respect to the cause, prevention, or methods of diagnosis and treatment of alcohol abuse and alcoholism, and (2) to collect information as to studies being carried on in the field of alcohol abuse and alcoholism and, with the approval of the Secretary, make available such information through appropriate publications for the benefit of health and welfare agencies or organizations (public or private) or physicians or any other scientists, and for the information of the general public. The Council is also authorized to recommend to the Secretary, for acceptance pursuant to section 501 of this Act, conditional gifts for work in the field of alcohol abuse and alcoholism; and the Secretary shall recommend acceptance of any such gifts only after consultation with the Council."

Approval by Council of Certain Grants Under Part C of Community Mental Health Centers Act

SEC. 402. Section 266 of the Community Mental Health Centers Act is amended (1) by inserting "(other than part C thereof)" immediately after "this title", and (2) by adding immediately after the period the following: "Grants under part C of this title for such costs may be made only upon recommendation of the National Advisory Council on Alcohol Abuse and Alcholism established by such section.

TITLE V—GENERAL

SEC. 501. If any section, provision, or term of this Act is adjudged invalid for any reason, such judgment shall not affect, impair, or invalidate any other section, provision, or term of this Act, and the remaining sections, provisions, and terms shall be and remain in full force and effect.

SEC. 502. (a) Each recipient of assistance under this Act pursuant to grants or contracts entered into under other than competitive bidding procedures shall keep such records as the Secretary shall prescribe, including records which fully disclose the amount and disposition by such recipient of the proceeds of such grant or contract, the total cost of the project or undertaking in connection with which such grant or contract is given or used, and the amount of that portion of the cost of the project or undertaking supplied by other sources, and such other records as will facilitate an effective audit.

(b) The Secretary and Comptroller General of the United States, or any of their duly authorized representatives, shall have access for the purpose of audit and examination to any books, documents, papers, and records of such recipients that are pertinent to the grants or contracts entered into under the provisions of this Act under other than competitive bidding procedures.

SEC. 503. Payments under this Act may be made in advance or by way of reimbursement and in such installments as the Secretary may determine.

Approved December 31, 1970.

Chapter 9

THE MYTH OF THE NEIGHBORHOOD SCHOOL: A PATH TO SEGREGATION?

PERHAPS THE MOST controversial aspect of American public education today is the validity of the concept of the "neighborhood school." This is a system of education under which

> . . . boundary lines for a school attendance district are established as nearly as possible in the area surrounding the school and it takes into consideration such factors as school capacity, number of students, natural barriers such as rivers and railroad lines, and the possibility of increase or decrease in population. Any student living within the boundaries of that school district may attend the school as a matter of right and ordinarily is required to do so.[1]

This neighborhood school concept has often been called an "inflexible rule of geography," and as a consequence of its inflexibility and inability to be changed with the times and the differing characteristics and circumstances of the neighborhood which it serves, it has often resulted in injustice as well as adventitious racial segregation which were not even considered at the time of its original implementation.

When public education first began to get a foothold in the United States in the early and mid-19th century, school districts were established simply upon a basis of convenience. A child had to walk to school, and if the building was too far away from his home, he would be unable to attend classes. There was little public transportation, and even those horse cars and other modes which did exist were relatively expensive for the type of family

[1]Downs v. Board of Education of Kansas City, 336 F2d 988, CCA10, 1964.

whose children originally attended the public schools.[2] Therefore, the concept of the neighborhood school arose so that every child would be able to study at a place of learning as near and convenient to his home as possible. As the nation moved westward, so did the concept of the neighborhood school; only of necessity, the definition of a neighborhood became somewhat broader than the implication of the term in the East. Often the population of a neighborhood school included children living in an entire county in the sparsely settled western frontier. With the winning of the West, the establishment of urban localities, and the closing of the frontier, however, the West, too, began to adopt the more realistic neighborhood sizes of the East and also accepted the eastern concept of the neighborhood school. The residence of the child, rather than any other factor, determined which neighborhood school he would attend.

Whether he lived in the East or the West, if a child's residence was in a neighborhood which was racially, religiously, ethnically, or socioeconomically homogeneous, then quite naturally the character of the child's neighborhood school, which reflected the character of the neighborhood, would be homogeneous. A situation therefore arose, due to the strict geographical limitations of the neighborhood school concept, where children of a particular race, religion, cultural background, or social and economic strata would be going to a school with other children who also mirrored these same particular characteristics. The explanation for this homogeneity of the children attending a neighborhood school is based almost entirely upon the housing patterns in the community surrounding the school upon which the student population of the neighborhood school itself is superimposed. When the original school district lines were drawn, the neighborhood may have been wealthy with fine, stately

---

[2]Many of the original public schools were specifically for poorer citizens and were called by the somewhat derogatory term "pauper schools." Indeed, prior to the time of Andrew Jackson's Presidency (1824-1832) most children of middle- and upper-class families attended private schools while the public schools were made available for "charity" cases only. Universal free public education for rich and poor alike did not even start to become a vogue in eastern and middle-western cities until approximately 1840.

homes, whereas fifty years later the same buildings could be considered slums. Furthermore, all too frequently these once elite but currently deteriorated neighborhoods were inhabited by Negro families and other poor minority groups, and the unintentional result was a neighborhood school which was predominantly Negro. (This type of inadvertent racial imbalance in the public schools is called *de facto* segregation.)

Even though racial imbalance did result from the neighborhood school system in the northeastern and western United States, it was generally unintentional, and in this respect, it differed from the 17 southern and border states[3] and the District of Columbia which *required* separation of the races in public schools, and the four other states[4] which allowed local communities to determine this question for themsevles. (This system of "separate but equal" public schools which results from design and affirmative state action is called *de jure* segregation.)

In 1954, this southern and border state public school arrangement was summarily ended. The United States Supreme Court, in its most momentous decision of the twentieth century, unequivocally declared "dual" educational systems based upon *de jure* racial segregation to be unconstitutional. Chief Justice Earl Warren, delivering his first judicial opinion in *Brown v. Board of Education of Topeka, Kansas,*[5] stirringly declared, "in the field of public education the doctrine of 'separate but equal' has no place. Separate facilities are inherently unequal." The direct and immediate effect of this decision was not felt in most of the nation which made use of the neighborhood school system and which did not intentionally segregate children upon the basis of the color of their skin, but it did unquestionably affect the South. The entire basis of southern and border state education was destroyed by the outlawing of *de jure* segregation.

---

[3]The 17 states which required segregation in public schools were Alabama, Arkansas, Delaware, Florida, Georgia, Kentucky, Louisiana, Maryland, Mississippi, Missouri, North Carolina, Oklahoma, South Carolina, Tennessee, Texas, Virginia, and West Virginia

[4]The four states which allowed local communities to decide upon racial segregation were Arizona, Kansas, New Mexico, and Wyoming.

[5]347 U.S. 483, 1954.

The question soon arose, however, especially in those areas employing the neighborhood school policy, as to whether or not *Brown v. Board of Education* also outlawed *de facto* unintentional racial segregation. Unquestionably, many neighborhood schools outside of the South were racially imbalanced and in effect were as nearly segregated as those in the South. But a fundamental difference existed in that these schools were segregated inadvertantly as a by-product of segregated and restricted residential housing patterns arising from discrimination in employment which resulted in lower-paying jobs for minorities and thus less desirable housing. In 1971, seventeen years after *Brown,* the controversy is still raging, and the judiciary has as yet not agreed upon a consistent course of action in dealing with the injustice resulting from the neighborhood school program. Some courts have found favor with the neighborhood school and have per se declared them constitutional irrespective of resulting *de facto* segregation. Others have determined that regardless of the good intentions of the school planners in instituting the neighborhood school plan, the mere fact that it results in *de facto* segregation is sufficient to strike it down as unconstitutional.

The classic case in which a federal court ordered school officials to eliminate *de facto* segregation is *Hobsen v. Hansen*[6] involving the public schools of our nation's capital, Washington, D.C. In 1805, the first schools in the District of Columbia opened their doors to white children, followed 57 years later, in 1862, by separate schools for Negro children. For nearly one hundred years, the "separate but equal" school system continued to exist until outlawed by the United States Supreme Court in *Brown v. Board of Education* in 1954. Immediately thereafter, the Washington Board of Education instituted a policy, "with modifications," of neighborhood schools. The adoption of the system, however, did not have the desired effect from an integration standpoint in that it "inevitably impressed the racial patterns within the city on the schools with dramatic consequences." Just as Negroes gradually began to displace whites in the city's residential areas, Negro children displaced white children in the

---

[6]269 F. Supp. 401, DCDC, 1967.

public schools. Furthermore, Washington's increasingly fewer white families became heavily concentrated in one section of the District. As a consequence of the combination of white family exodus and white family insularity, Negroes overwhelmingly predominated in the public schools. From a pre-*Brown* Negro public school enrollment of 56.8 per cent, the number of black pupils in the school system skyrocketed to 79.9 per cent in 1960, 89.4 per cent in 1965, and 90.2 per cent at the time of the *Hobsen* case in 1966. Notwithstanding the enormous percentage of Negro children being educated in Washington schools in 1966 as a result of the neighborhood school policy, 11 of the city's schools in the remaining white residential area were from 85 per cent to 100 per cent white, 4 had a white enrollment of from 67 per cent to 85 per cent and only 1 junior high and 1 high school on the outskirts of the white area were neither predominantly Negro nor white. The remainder of the public schools throughout Washington were predominantly Negro. In place of the *de jure* school segregation existing prior to *Brown,* there arose the unquestionable manifestations of *de facto* segregation.

This trend of *de facto* segregation resulting from the neighborhood school policy was further advanced by the "modifications" to the original 1955 school desegregation plan, to wit: (a) individual whites who were "seriously upset by the prospect of intergration" were allowed to transfer to "white" schools; (b) students registered in one school at the time of the adoption of the new plan did not have to transfer to their neighborhood school but could remain at the school they were attending (this feature ended in 1960 when all the students exercising this perogative had graduated); and (c) certain districts, generally in "fringe" white areas, were put in "optional zones," giving the child a choice of two schools which he could attend, one predominantly white, and one predominantly Negro.

After extensive findings of fact, the federal district Court in *Hobsen v. Hansen,* so as to correct "the racial and economic discrimination found in the operation of the District of Columbia public school system," enjoined racial and economic public school discrimination, abolished the "optional zone," ordered transportation of children volunteering to go to "white" schools from their "Negro" schools, and required the Board of Education to file a plan within four months to eliminate *de facto* segregation resulting from the neighborhood school policy. Circuit Judge Skelly Wright, in writing an opinion exceeding one hundred pages, noted that the affirmative governmental action necessary to a finding of *de jure* segregation and absolute unconstitutionality of the Washington school system attendance plan was not justified, but he did state that the plan clearly developed *de facto* school segregation.

> One of the court's findings of fact is that elements in the school administration, though not necessarily on the Board, are affirmatively satisfied with the segregation which the local neighborhood school policy spawns. . . . But this finding falls somewhat short of showing the kind of actual intent needed if the policy is to be censured under *de jure* principles. Therefore the court approaches the more generalized question of whether the *de facto* or adventitious segregation in Washington is itself unconstitutional. In Washington, as in other Northern cities, this question arises in the context of a neighborhood policy which, superimposed on segregated urban housing, effectively separates white from Negro in the public schools.

Judge Wright then went on to relate the two obvious and vital disadvantages of segregated schools, whether *de jure* or *de facto*: inherent inferiority of education and perpetuation of lack of interracial communication.

> It would be wrong to ignore or belittle the real social values which neighborhood schools doubtlessly promote. But due appreciation of these values must not obscure the fact that the price society pays for neighborhood schools, in Washington and other urban centers, is in racially segregated public education. As the court's Findings indicate, school segregation, whatever its genesis, typically imposes a twofold disadvantage.
>
> One, the Negro schools provide their Negro students with an education inferior to that which others, white and Negro alike, receive in integrated or predominantly white education settings. This the court finds from the evidence adduced at trial. This finding is confirmed by the Supreme Court in *Brown I*, which, besides noting that 'separate' schools are inherently unequal and psychologically harmful to Negro school children, approved the finding entered by

> the lower court explicitly stating that even unmandated segregation has a 'detrimental effect' on Negroes. The court can judicially note that corroborating views can also be found in the conclusions of the federal agency commissioned by Congress to investigate racial questions; in the decisions of federal courts, and of state legislatures and education officers and committees; and in the experienced judgments of American educators and psychologists expert in race relations, who make it clear that the damage segregation causes stems from the sense of confinement it imparts, together with the low esteem which the predominantly Negro school naturally draws from the white as well as the Negro community.
>
> In addition, segregation in the schools precludes the kind of social encounter between Negroes and whites which is an indispensable attribute of education for mature citizenship in an interracial and democratic society. Segregation 'perpetuates the barriers between the races; stereotypes, misunderstandings, hatred, and the inability to communicate are all intensified.' Education, which everyone agrees should include the opportunity for biracial experiences, carries on, of course, in the home and neighborhood as well at school. In this respect residential segregation, by ruling out meaningful experiences of this type outside of school, intensifies, not eliminates, the need for integration within school.

Although the plaintiffs in *Hobsen,* as well as Judge Wright himself by dint of his comprehensive opinion, sought to lay a foundation for an ultimate appeal by Washington school authorities to the United States Supreme Court, no appeal was taken and Washington education officials altered its neighborhood school policy as per the Court's order. Critics of the *Hobsen* decision assert that if true total integration were to be accomplished in the District of Columbia in accordance with Judge Wright's decision, *every* school in the system woud be racially unbalanced, as each would be more than 90 per cent Negro. Thus, *de jure* racial segregation rather than *de facto* would exist and this situation would also be unconstitutional. As a practical matter, most problems involving the neighborhood school concept occur outside of cities which are predominantly or overwhelmingly Negro, such as Washington. Rather, the problems are found in localities which are predominantly white.

One such situation different from that in Washington, D. C., because only a small portion of a community was Negro, arose in the case of *Blocker v. Board of Education*,[7] involving the elite, wealthy Long Island, New York, township of Manhasset. In the 1920's, the sleepy and sparsely populated township started growing as its accessibility to New York City enabled it to become one of that metropolis' suburban "bedroom" communities. One particular section of Manhasset, the Valley area, was in the township's southwest corner, and because of its relative remoteness, when the school board decided to establish a neighborhood school system in 1939, a small neighborhood elementary school was built in the Valley area. Two larger elementary schools were built in the remaining two school districts. In 1939, the year the tridistrict neighborhood school plan was adopted, the Valley area had a Negro population of nearly 50 per cent, while the Negro population of the rest of Manhasset was minimal. By 1962, Negroes in the Valley area accounted for more than 90 per cent of its population. Inasmuch as the neighborhood school reflects the existing residential living pattern, the Valley elementary school was 99.2 per cent Negro and .8 per cent white. The elementary schools of the other two Manhasset districts were 100 per cent white.

In 1964, a group of Black students brought an action in the New York Federal District Court to have the rigid neighborhood school policy of the Manhasset school board revoked because it resulted in *de facto* segregation. The school board, in its defense, claimed that the neighborhood school plan was "color blind" and indeed was "innocent, and harmless in inception." They claimed that the resulting *de facto* segregation of the school population was a consequence of housing segregation and arose from the fact that Negro families moving into Manhasset chose to live with other Negro families in the Valley area, and not from an affirmative plan to segregate Negro children. In discussing the neighborhood school policy, the Federal Court in *Blocker* noted that there was "general agreement among educators" that it was "sound," and that among its several advantages were "easy access and the feasibility of lunch at home." The Court, how-

[7]226 F. Supp. 208, DCNY, 1964.

ever, noted the sagacious statement of former United States Supreme Court Justice Felix Frankfurter that "local customs, however hardened by time, are not decreed in heaven," and the words of Judge Irving Kaufman of the Second Circuit Court of Appeals that "the neighborhood school policy is not sacrosanct. It is valid only insofar as it is operated within the confines established by the Constitution." After remarking that the extent of segregation in Manhasset was almost as bad as that found in Topeka, Kansas, in *Brown v. Board of Education,* albeit *de facto* rather than *de jure,* the Federal Court said:

> The defendants are, and for several years have been, fully aware of the total separation of the entire Negro elementary school population from over 99% of their white contemporaries. With knowledge of this fact, were they to prescribe today the attendance area lines which now exist could such action be justified by the normal criteria supporting the neighborhood school policy? Were the Board to create out of the total District one disproportionately small attendance area, provide a school for a disproportionately small student body composed almost entirely of Negro children and representing 100% of the Negro student population of the District, and couple such action with a rigid no-transfer policy—were the Board to take such action today would it not be reasonable to regard it as a rather ingenuous device to separate the races, protestations to the contrary notwithstanding? Could such attendance lines, if drawn today, be insulated from the Fourteenth Amendment merely because the bylaw or rule of the Board did not mention the word Negro, but, rather, was cast in terms of residence?
>
> The defendants argue that the cause of this racial separation in the District differs from that in Brown; that, here, the Negroes have segregated themselves by moving into the Valley area voluntarily in order to benefit from and enjoy the dual attractions of low-rent housing and a good, conveniently located school for their children. True it is that they have taken up residence in the Valley area under no compulsion of law but, rather, under that of the purse. Considering the disparity in socioeconomic levels within the District, their selection of the Valley was only Hobson's choice.
>
> On the facts of this case, the separation of the Negro elementary school children is segregation. It is segregation by law—the law of the School Board. In the light of the existing facts, the continuance of the defendant Board's impenetrable attendance lines amounts to nothing less than state-imposed segregation.

Thus, notwithstanding the inadvertance of the residential housing patterns that have created the segregated schools and the fact that the neighborhood district lines had been drawn long ago, before the possibility of *de facto* segregation could have been considered, it still contemporaneously exists in violation of the Constitution. The Court continued:

> In a publicly supported, mandatory state educational system, the plaintiffs have the civil right not to be segregated, not to be compelled to attend a school in which all of the Negro children are educated separate and apart from over 99% of their white contemporaries. That they are being so compelled is a fact. . . .
>
> The court does not hold that the neighborhood school policy per se is unconstitutional; it does hold that this policy is not immutable. It does not hold that racial imbalance and segregation are synonymous or that racial imbalance, not tantamount to segregation, is violative of the Constitution. It does hold that, by maintaining and perpetuating a segregated school system, the defendant Board has transgressed the prohibitions of the Equal Protection Clause of the Fourteenth Amendment. The court does not hold that the Constitution requires a compulsive distribution of school children on the basis of race in order to achieve a proportional representation of white and Negro children in each elementary school within a school district. There is no authority to support this claim of the plaintiffs. There is not presented here the question as to whether or not such compulsive distribution, though not required, may be permitted under the Constitution or by state law. . . .
>
> The defendant School Board is hereby directed to present to this court, on or before April 6, 1964, a plan to desegregate the elementary school system of the defendant District, in accordance with this opinion, to begin no later than the opening of the 1964-1965 Fall Term.

Although the Federal Court did not hold the neighborhood school concept unconstitutional, it did hold that a school plan which perpetuates *de facto* segregation, regardless of its original good intentions, may no longer exist.

A case definitely *not* involving good intentions in the creation of a neighborhood school system and one which held unconstitutional the geographical attendance zones of another suburb of New York City, only this time in Westchester County, New York, was *Taylor v. Board of Education of the City School District of New Rochelle.*[8] In the 1930's, the New Rochelle

[8]294 F2d 36, CCA2, 1961.

Board of Education decided to carve two small white residential areas out of the existing predominantly Negro Lincoln School District and assign the children residing in the gerrymandered areas to a school much farther away from their homes but one which was predominantly white. Negro families later moved into these gerrymandered residential areas and the School Board then returned the segments back to the original school district from which they had been taken. Prior to 1949, the Board of Education also had a rule allowing any white child attending a public school in the predominantly Negro Lincoln district to transfer to a white school with the result that by 1949 the Lincoln School was 100 per cent Negro. On January 11, 1949, however, the Board of Education made a decided policy switch and ceased to allow any transfers at all but proceeded upon a rigid neighborhood school policy. This did little to affect the racial population of the Lincoln District and fixed the Lincoln School as a segregated one. In 1960, it was 94 per cent Negro. While acknowledging that the problems of this New Rochelle school district were serious but not "peculiar" to the community, Federal Judge Irving Kaufman noted:

> [The problems] arise when people of a single racial group tend to settle in a particular neighborhood such as the Lincoln District here, and the trend is accelerated by housing developments and real estate transactions increasing the group numbers. Even so, the action of public bodies, of which school boards are most potent because of the importance of public education in American life, must be in accordance with the constitutional standards as expounded by the Supreme Court. The facts recited above showing the Board's acceleration of segregation at Lincoln up to 1949 and its actions since then amounting only to a perpetuation and a freezing in of this condition negate the argument that the present situation in Lincoln School is only the 'chance' or 'inevitable' result of applying a neighborhood school policy to a community where residential patterns show a racial imbalance. Rather they make it appear that the Board considered Lincoln as the 'Negro' school and that district lines were drawn and retained so as to perpetuate this condition. In short, race was made the basis for school districting, with the purpose and effect of producing a substantially segregated school. This conduct clearly violates the Fourteenth Amendment and the Supreme Court decision in Brown v. Board of Education of Topeka.

In essence, Judge Kaufman is saying that the invocation of the strict neighborhood school policy, after the Board of Education had already taken such actions to create the segregated school in the first instance, may not be used as a device to perpetuate this unconstitutional racial segregation. The Federal Appeals Court then went on to approve the decision of the trial court in providing for a transfer system by Negro students in the Lincoln School District to other less segregated school districts.

Another leading case, again involving a suburb of New York City in Long Island, involved the attempt by a group of Negro school children to have the *de facto* racially segregated school system of Hempstead, New York declared unconstitutional. The Board of Education, in its defense, sought to have the lawsuit dismissed before trial upon the basis that it took no affirmative action to create the resultant *de facto* segregation, but in *Branche v. Board of Education of the Town of Hempstead, School District No. 1,*[9] the Federal Court held that the case had to go to trial. The situation arose in 1961 in a Hempstead school district containing approximately 25,000 people and, at the time of the case, a school population that was 47 per cent Negro and 53 per cent white. Prior to 1949, the Board of Education had not adopted official school zoning boundaries, but in that year it instituted a policy of neighborhood schools. As a result, one of the six school zones in the district, comprising the Prospect School, became nearly totally Negro and an appeal of the Prospect neighborhood zone was taken to the State Commissioner of Education who ordered the boundary lines for that school redrawn. The Commissioner approved the new zone because it "encompassed reasonably the area that naturally belongs to the Prospect school as against any charge that it discriminates between Negro and white children." Thereafter, the school boundaries remained unchanged from 1949 until 1961, and the following chart reflects the percentage of Negro children attending the various schools in the district during those two particular years.

---

9 204 F. Supp. 150, DCNY, 1962.

School	*No. of Classrooms*	*Percent of Negro Children 1949*	*1961*
Fulton	16	3.2	1.0
Washington	13	4.7	33.0
Jackson Jackson Annex	21	16.5	67.0
Prospect	11	90.9	86.0
Ludlum	15	6.4	5.0
Franklin Marshall	36	14.3	78.0

As is readily apparent, while only the Prospect school was overwhelmingly Negro in 1949, the Prospect, Franklin, Marshall, Jackson, and Jackson Annex schools were predominantly Negro in 1961. The overwhelmingly white Fulton and Ludlum schools remained thus in the ensuing 12 years, while the Washington School become one-third Negro. Inasmuch as a strict neighborhood school policy was in effect during these years, the changes in the racial character of the public schools was almost solely a consequence of the resultant change in residential living patterns in the Franklin-Marshall, Jackson-Jackson Annex, and Washington neighborhoods, and the continuance of segregated housing in the Prospect, Fulton, and Ludlum neighborhoods. In holding that racial segregation may not be ignored simply because it results accidentally and not from state action, the Federal Court noted:

> The educational system that is thus compulsory and publicly afforded must deal with the inadequacy arising from adventitious segregation; it cannot accept and indurate segregation on the ground that it is not coerced or planned but accepted. . . .
>
> So here it is not enough to show that residence accounts for the fact of segregation and to contend that therefore the segregation is ineluctable. The effort to mitigate the consequent educational inadequacy has not been made and to forego that effort to deal with the inadequacy is to impose it in the absence of a conclusive

> demonstration that no circumstantially possible effort can affect any significant mitigation. What is involved here is not convenience but constitutional interests. It cannot be said at this stage that the 1949 adoption of the geographical rule of school attendance was necessarily free of an unpermitted effect on constitutional interests or that adherence to it in changing circumstances that perhaps increased segregation has not become an infringement of constitutional interests.

The Court thus held that once the existence of *de facto* seggregation is recognized, to avoid making an effort to mitigate the racial imbalance is as reprehensible as creating it in the first place, and unless it is conclusively shown that nothing can be done, something must be done. Just because the Board of Education invoked the neighborhood school policy in 1949 does not mean that the same boundaries must exist forever; neighborhoods change, school population changes, and in order to avoid racial segregation, the neighborhood school lines must change also.

The leading case in support of the absolute validity of the neighborhood school concept, regardless of resulting *de facto* segregation, arose is the City of Gary, Indiana, which has a Negro population of more than 50 per cent. In 1906, when this industrial metropolis was first growing, eight neighborhood school districts were established and a new school built in each district. As the city expanded and more children began attending public schools, the system was forced to build new schools and realign neighborhood attendance patterns as one or another school became too overcrowded. The geographical attendance boundaries were always drawn without regard to race but were conscientiously developed upon the basis of school population density, safety factors (there were a number of major highways and at least nine railroad grade crossings in the city limits), geographic obstacles (Lake Michigan was a boundary on the north and the Calumet River bisected the city from east to west with few bridge crossings), and travel distance to the schools. In 1961, a group of approximately 100 students brought an action in federal court to enjoin the City of Gary from operating a racially segregated public school system. According to the Court in *Bell v. School City of Gary,*[10] the students based their position upon the "fundamental theory that their right to be integrated in school is such an overriding purpose that little, if any, consideration need be given to the safety of the children, convenience of pupils and their parents, and costs of operation of the system." In distinguishing *Brown v. Board of Education* and affirming the decision of the trial court, the Federal Court stated:

> The situation in *Brown* is a far cry from the situation existing in Gary, Indiana. The School District boundaries in Gary were determined without any consideration of race or color. We agree with the argument of the defendants stated as "there is no affirmative U. S. Constitutional duty to change innocently arrived at school attendance districts by the mere fact that shifts in population either increase or decrease the percentage of either Negro or white pupils."
>
> We agree with and the record fully sustains the District Court's finding, "An examination of the school boundary lines in the light of the various factors involved such as density of population, distances that the students have to travel and the safety of the children, particularly in the lower grades, indicates that the areas have been reasonably arrived at and that the lines have not been drawn for the purpose of including or excluding children of certain races."
>
> We approve also of the statement in the District Court's opinion, "Nevertheless, I have seen nothing in the many cases dealing with the segregation problem which leads me to believe that the law requires that a school system developed on the neighborhood school plan, honestly and conscientiously constructed with no intention or purpose to segregate the races, must be destroyed or abandoned because the resulting effect is to have a racial imbalance in certain schools where the district is populated almost entirely by Negroes or whites."
>
> We hold that the constitutional rights of the plaintiffs and others similarly situated, were not violated by the manner in which the defendant School District of Gary, Indiana, maintained and operated its schools, and that the District Court was correct in dismissing the complaint herein.

Thus, the neighborhood school system was upheld even though it lead to *de facto* racial segregation upon the basis that it was fairly arrived at and did not have as its purpose the creation

[10]324 F2d 209, CCA7, 1963.

of segregated schools. This decision is diametrically opposed to those cases which assert that the purity of the motive is no defense to racially segregated schools.

A case closely following the holding in *Bell* was *Webb v. Board of Education of the City of Chicago,*[11] wherein the parents of several Negro children enrolled in Chicago public schools sought an injunction against the Board of Education to require them to cease requiring attendance at racially segregated public schools. These segregated schools were overcrowded, while many schools in white residential areas had empty classrooms. In refusing to grant the injunction, the Federal Court stated:

> This Court is aware of the irreparable harm which could result from segregation under the sanction of Brown v. Board of Education of Topeka . . . . However, this segregation resulting from residential segregation, alone, is not a violation of any right over which this Court can give cognizance. In Bell v. School City of Gary, Indiana, supra, the Court held that there is no Constitutional right to be integrated with persons of other races. The Constitution only forbids States from *actively* pursuing a course of enforced segregation.

In essence, the Federal Court was saying that although it recognizes the evils of segregation, unintentional segregation is not unconstitutional and there is no constitutional right to have integration.

Another situation where the Court has held that unintentional racial segregation cannot be enjoined involved the school district of Pontiac, Michigan, which also included parts of six adjoining townships and a village. In 1867, the State of Michigan passed a statute prohibiting segregation in public schools and relying upon this law and the United States Supreme Court decision in *Brown v. Board of Education,* the parent of a Negro student enrolled in the Pontiac public schools brought an action to enjoin the maintenance of a segregated school system. According to the Court in *Henry v. Godsell,*[12] Mrs. Henry alleged that the school board built a new school in a Negro neighborhood, modified existing school zones to establish segre-

---

[11]223 F. Supp. 466, DC Ill., 1963.

[12]165 F. Supp. 87, DC Mich., 1958.

gated schools, established a new district requiring her child to transfer schools, and refused to permit her child to transfer to another school outside of her neighborhood. The school board countered by admitting that the new school was built in a Negro area, that the attendance districts were altered, that a new school district was established requiring the Henry child to transfer schools and that the student had been refused permission to attend a school of her choice, but denied that any purpose of these actions was to establish or maintain a segregated school system. The Court held in favor of the school board's position on all points, and in respect to the issue of the building of the new school in an exclusively Negro neighborhood, Judge Levin said:

> The school board has a duty to provide educational facilities to all children without regard to their color. If it builds schools in areas where need exists, without arbitrarily fixing attendance areas to exclude any given segment of the school population, it is carrying out that duty. It may consider such factors in selecting sites that it considers relevant and reasonable and, in the absence of a showing that the standards for selection are not relevant and reasonable and that in reality they were adopted as a sham of subterfuge to foster segregation, or for any other illegal purpose, their use is within the administrative discretion of the school board. The fact that in a given area a school is populated almost exclusively by the children of a given race is not of itself evidence of discrimination. The choice of a school site based on density of population and geographical considerations such as distance, accessibility, ease of transportation, and other safety considerations, is a permissible exercise of administrative discretion. The selection of the Lake Street school site was based upon these factors and the standards observed were not adopted as a device to circumvent the law.

Judge Levin also noted that unless it can be shown that the School Board affirmatively acted in such a way so as to create a segregated neighborhood school, its action was constitutional:

> Plaintiff also alleges that some attendance areas in the school district were altered in 1955 to compel or achieve segregation. This allegation is devoid of merit. The Board of Education has altered and modified attendance areas from time to time to accommodate changes in population and as a result of the erection of new schools and additions to existing schools. The changes in attendance areas

> that were made in 1955 were in response to the building construction that was then taking place. In the absence of a showing that attendance areas have been arbitrarily fixed or contoured for the purpose of including or excluding families of a particular race, the Board of Education is free to establish such areas for the best utilization of its educational facilities. . . . . The evidence establishes that the same permissible considerations that served as a basis for selecting new school sites were employed in fixing school attendance areas.
>
> The plaintiff has no constitutionally guaranteed right to attend a public school outside of the attendance area in which she resides. The utter chaos that would prevail if each child were permitted to choose the school that he or she desired to attend without regard to the attendance area in which the child resides is readily apparent. It was a proper exercise of the Board's power to transfer plaintiff and others similarly situated to the Lake Street school when that school was designated to serve the area resided in by these children."

The Court held that the school board could alter the boundaries of a neighborhood school to accommodate changes in population and the building of new schools, and unless it can be shown that the board took such action to include or exclude children upon the basis of race, the board is free to utilize its educational facilities to the best possible advantages. There is no constitutional right not to attend a neighborhood school and a child must attend the school designated by the board of education.

Thus, the controversy remains, more vocal at certain times than at others, but inexorably intertwined in the very substance of American life and the education of American youngsters. Is the neighborhood school system's value as an educational concept valid and worthwhile in light of the unquestioned injustice that it causes? Is the neighborhood school concept a myth or a reality as a path to segregation? Only time and the American legal system can supply an answer.

QUESTIONS FOR REVIEW

1. What is a "neighborhood school?" How and why did it develop in the United States?
2. Differentiate between *de facto* and *de jure* segregation.
3. How did Washington, D. C., meet the requirements of the *Brown* case and what problems were caused as a result?

4. Discuss the disadvantages of segregated schools as noted in the *Hansen* case.
5. What did the court in the *Blocker* case use as its basis for declaring Manhasset's neighborhood school system unconstitutional?
6. How does the *Taylor* case differ from other neighborhood school cases?
7. How do the facts of the *Branche* case demonstrate the traditional concepts of *de facto* segregation, and how did the neighborhood school system create this racial imbalance?
8. How were school boundaries in Gary, Indiana, determined? Why did the court in the *Bell* case hold the Gary neighborhood school plan constitutional?
9. What do the courts in the pro-neighborhood-school case differ from the courts in the anti-neighborhood-school case with respect to their approach to the law?

Chapter 10

THE EXTREMIST IN AMERICA: NECESSITY FOR A SPOTLIGHT OF PUBLIC AWARENESS

If America is today sitting on a powder keg, it is the political extremists, black and white, of both the Radical Right and the Radical Left, who are attempting to explode it, by fanning the flames of discontent, religious prejudice, and race hatred. Ostensibly opposed to each other, they somehow make common cause in their hatred of democracy and their contempt for responsive government. Political extremism does not grow in a vacuum. It reflects real needs, economic and psychological. We are a nation which has not solved the problem of poverty in the midst of plenty. We have not found the route to peace. We are ill at ease in our relations with the world. It is difficult to assess the numerical strength of the varied extremist groups and their lunatic fringes; but the last Presidential campaign, when nearly 10 million people—13.6% of the total electorate—voted for George Wallace, disclosed the reach of at least the Far Right and its growing respectability. The continuing influence of the John Birch Society (JBS), the most potent of the Radical Right organizations, remains ominous. Although JBS membership seems to have peaked at 60,000, its professionalism, its well-oiled propaganda machine, its publishing operations, chain of book stores, and imposing network of front groups enable the John Birch Society to manipulate millions of Americans for undemocratic and reactionary purposes. The best antidote to all extremism is maximum exposure, spotlighting publicly these Far Right, Far Left, and Black Separatist groups *et al.*, their programs, secret activities, memberships, sources of income, propaganda, and front operations, as well as their relationships with each other and with foreign agents. Only by the spotlight of publicity and of public awareness can the threat they represent to democratic institutions be effectively repulsed.

The Wallace movement in 1968 wrapped up in plausible language such incredible ideas as these: (a) the Civil Rights movement is a Communist front; (b) we must repeal open housing laws; (c) we must use force to squash dissent especially as to our Vietnam policy ("Who needs free speech?"); (d) we must remove *civilian* control over the Nation's military; (e) we must "Get the U.S. out of the U.N., and the U.N. out of the U.S."; (f) we should sever diplomatic relations with Russia and all Communist countries; (g) we must return to a "Confederation of States"; (h) bureaucracy and Washington itself is the "enemy"; (i) Rhodesia is a "true Christian anti-Communist Nation" with "law and order" and "good race relations"; and (j) members of the United States Supreme Court are "sick and insane." Other *Wallace-ite* ideas, apparently bought by millions of Americans yearning for nice easy answers to our terribly complex problems, included the following: (a) Communists are calling the shots for both major political parties; (b) treason had been rampant in the Eisenhower, Kennedy, and Johnson Administrations; (c) the real purpose of the War on Poverty is to finance subversion; and (d) we are deliberately not winning the war in Vietnam in order to help Communism along.

Extremism, whether from the Left or from the Right, has certain basic, common characteristics which delineate their movements: (a) *extremists live in "closed rooms,"* in the sense that they read their own books, listen to their own leaders, refuse to listen to the outside world, and blindly believe in the "justice" of their extremist cause; (b) *extremists take orders gratefully* and do not insist upon democratic procedures for arriving at the will of the majority; (c) *the outside world has "conspired" against them,* and it is this "conspiracy" from which all evil flows; (d) they are obsessed with the fact that "problems" only fit their particular patterns for "solution," but they have no "solutions"; (e) *they are fighting a "holy war,"* in the sense that they are convinced that their ends justify their sinister means; (f) *they rewrite history* (and even today's news) to fit into their patterns; the news media, radio, and TV are always corrupt; (g) *they must "control"* or they must "discredit" the opposition; no outside group is allowed to produce evidence which refutes their "facts" or stimulates "incorrect" attitudes; (h) *they are haters,* not lovers, because they are really not "for" anything; but they "know" where to assign blame and how to vent their spleen; (i) *they feed on "whipping boys,"* e.g., Negroes, Jews, Catholics, Mexican-Americans, and Puerto Ricans, the poor or the rich; they must feel superior, and subtle racism and character assasination are their weapons; (j) *they must work behind camouflage* as they set up "front groups" to keep their membership secret and their motives obscured; and (k) *their movement yearns for power,* and self-interest is their total motivation.

The Institute for American Democracy, Inc., (I.A.D.) of Washington, D. C. has for many years "charted" extremist movements in a publication, "Homefront," edited by I.A.D.'s resourceful Executive Director, Mr. Charles R. Baker. In the July-August, 1970, issue is the chart (pages 220 and 221) of extremism in the United States today.

The length and breadth of involvement by both the Far Right and the Far Left is evident, especially by reference to the estimated circulation of their various publications, their radio programs of national coverage, and even their television programs. Extremism in the United States is a force to be reckoned with, in the sense that such evil powers cannot be lightly dismissed.

The Radical Left today consists of extremists of varying colors of skin, modes of dress, and "hang-ups" embracing every social, economic, political, and religious persuasion. Resistance to American policy in Indochina is probably the chief matrix which enables Marxists and other left extremists, including black nationalists and even radical peace groups, to make common cause. Generally all these groups have a surprising degree of intercommunication; and yet they are badly splintered for a variety of reasons, including lack of funds. Lacking the capacity to achieve power through established channels, the Radical Left looks for some vague *confrontation* which will produce a brave, new world—i.e. perhaps striking a match in a tinder box situation!

The Radical Right, in contrast to the Radical Left, is visibly

FAR LEFT

Organization	Ideology	Estimated Membership	Chief Publication	Estimated Circulation
Communist Party of U.S.A.	Soviet	13,000[1]	*Daily World* *People's World*	14,000 5,000
W.E.B. DuBois Clubs	Soviet	defunct	*Insurgent*	defunct
†Young Workers Liberation League	Soviet	500		
Progressive Labor Party	Maoist	(2,000)[2]	None	
Worker-Student Alliance	Maoist	1,000	*Progressive Labor Chal.*	(8,000)
Revolutionary Action Movement	Maoist	may be defunct	*Black America*	
Socialist Labor Party	Marxist	(2,000)[3]	*Weekly People*	(12,000)
Socialist Workers Party	Trotskyite	(1,000)[4]	*Militant*	(8,000)
Young Socialist Alliance	Trotskyite	7,500[5]	*Young Socialist*[6]	30,000[7]
Spartacist League	Trotskyite	minimal	*Spartacist*	?[8]
Student National Cord. Comm.	Nationalist	350[9]	*SNCC Newsletter*	minimal
Students for Democratic Soc.	Independent	7,000	*New Left Notes*	defunct[10]
Weekly Guardian Association	Independent	none	*Guardian*	27,000
Workers World Party	Maoist		*Workers World*	minimal
Youth Against War and Fascism	Maoist	300 activists*	*The Partisan*	(1,000)
Liberation News Service	Independent	none	250 Underground Papers	(1,000,000)

[1] FBI appropriations report, 1968. No change in '69.
[2] Placed at 1,200 by *NYT*, 4/25/65.
[3] Received 52,111 votes in 13 states in 1968.
[4] Received 41,300 votes in 19 states in 1968.
[5] Estimated at between 5,000 to 10,000, *CSM*, 1/9/70.
[6] To be discontinued in 1970, *Minneapolis Star*, 12/31/69.
[7] *Minneapolis Star*, 12/31/69.
[8] May have discontinued publication or gone underground.
[9] Placed at 470 by *NYT*, 10/7/68.
[10] *NYT Magazine*, 6/15/69 placed circulation at 7,000.
Undocumented estimates in ( ).
* Nonmembership organization.
† Justice Dep't press release 7/14/70

( ) Estimate only.

Organization	Ideology	Estimated Membership	Chief Publication	Estimated Circulation
RACIAL NATIONALISTS:				
Black Panther Party	Independent	1,000[1]	*Black Panther*	130,000[5]
Black Muslims	Independent	7,000	*Muhammad Speaks* 29 Radio, 1 TV Outlet[2]	300,000[5]
Deacons for Defense & Justice	Independent	(500)	None	
Black Man's Volunteer Army of Liberation	Independent	(2,000)	None	
Republic of New Africa	Independent	(1,000)[3]	None	
Jewish Defense League	Independent	7,000[4]	None	

[1] *NYT*, 12/14/69 placed total at 2,500. Panthers have purged ranks, however.
[2] *Muhammad Speaks*, 6/13/69.
[3] Organization claimed 17,000 Justice Department estimates at less than 1,000, *Washington Post*, 4/1/68.
[4] *NYT*, 5/25/70.
[5] Muslins and Panthers carry on aggressive street sale campaign.

FAR RIGHT

Organization	Chief Publications	Circulation	Compared to '68	Estimated Radio-TV Outlet	Estimated '69 Income
JOHN BIRCH SOCIETY	*JBS Bulletin*	(120,000)			
	American Opinion	39,352**	+14%	Spots only	($4,225,000*)
(Dean) Manion Forum	*Manion Forum News*	n.a.		71 R, 45TV	(817,600[1])
Dan Smoot	*Dan Smoot Reports*	28,000[1]		64 R, 25TV	(350,000[1])
Hargis' Christian Crusade	*Christian Crusade*	119,500**	+41%	(115[1])	(1,521,000*)
America's Future (Scott)	*America's Future*	(7,500[1])		(200[1])	(200,000[1])
Cons. Society of America					
Kent & Phoebe Courtney	*Independent American*	not avail.		—	—
Voice of America (McBirnie)	*Documentation*	n.a.		64[1]	—
(White) Citizens Councils	*The Citizen*	25,089**	+8%	—	—
	The Councilor	defunct			
20th CENT. REFORM. (McIntire)	*Christian Beacon*	108,900**	+9%	(275)	(1,750,000*)
Bundy's Church League of Am.	*News & Views*	(10,000)			(350,000[2])
LIBERTY LOBBY (Carto)	*Liberty Letter*	221,546**	+12%	None	(925,000[6])
Noontide Press (Carto)	*American Mercury*	9,918**	+50%	—	—
Richard Cotten	*Conservative Viewpoint*	n.a.		(20[1])	—
Frank Capell	*Herald of Freedom*	(5,000)		—	—
Nat'l Youth Alliance	*NYA News*	(4,000)		—	—
Christ. Nat'l Crusade (Gerald L. K. Smith)	*Cross and the Flag*	28,890**	−3%	—	—
H. L. HUNT	*Life Lines*	7,100**	−12%	660[5]	(1,400,000*)
BIBLE INST. OF AIR (Burpo)	*Bible Inst. News*	35,000[3]		30[3]	(461,840[4])
HARDING COLLEGE (NEP)	*Nat'l Program Letter*	(50,000)[8]			(175,660*)
AMERICAN SECURITY COUNCIL	*Washington Report*	10,000[9]	n.a.	350[9]	n.a.
YOUNG AMERICANS for FREEDOM	*New Guard*	17,492**	+70%	—	(725,000*)
TWIN CIRCLE (Fr. Lyons)	*Twin Circle*	66,218**	+45%	200 R, 3 TV	n.a.
NAT'L REVIEW (Buckley)	*National Review*	123,351**[7]	+20%	30 TV	n.a.
HUMAN EVENTS	*Human Events*	97,383**	−3%	—	n.a.

The underground Minuteman publication *Crosshairs,* the KKK's *Fiery Cross* and the National States Rights Party's *Thunderbolt* have limited circulation.

Estimates only in ( ).
* Estimates only. Projection based on best available but incomplete data
** Post Office Reports, 2nd Class mailing statements.
[1] No 1969 data available. Same report as for '68.
[2] Projected from 1967 IRS 990-A form.
[3] April, 1968 listing.
[4] Projected from Arizona Corp. Commission Report, 1968.
[5] *Life Lines,* April, 1969.
[6] Projected from Liberty Lobby reports to Clerk of House.
[7] Apparently up from 110,000 figures supplied from standard rate service.
[8] Free distribution.
[9] From ASC promotional material.

wealthy and has access to the unlimited funds of business tycoons of right-wing persuasion. Furthermore, their ties with top-level government are alarming; the American Security Council, for example, has an open door to officials at the White House and at the Pentagon and plunged itself into politics during the 1970 election campaign, attacking incumbents and candidates whom they deemed not to be concerned with the alleged Communist threat! The right-wing forces in the United States continue to spawn many front groups. Their aggregate income is at the 50 million dollar level; they crave power and promote a frightening brand of fascism, super-patriotism, anti-Semitism, and racism. Their major weakness is their apparent inability to produce a youth movement of any substance.

A survey of selected, specific 1970 extremist activities on many fronts is in order:

1. *Rev. Carl McIntire* is a deposed minister of the United Presbyterian Church, who had in the past few years (a) lost control of the American Council of Christian Churches which he had founded, (b) been requested by the State of New Jersey to relinquish control of his tiny Shelton College after it developed that the Dean's academic degrees were all bogus, and (c) became the first head of a radio broadcasting station told by the Federal Communications Commission to stop broadcasting because of its failure to meet the FCC "Fairness Doctrine" obligations. In the spring of 1970, with an introductory letter from the late Representative Mendel Rivers (Chairman of the House Armed Services Committee), Rev. McIntire got an interview with the Commander of United States forces in Vietnam, General Creighton Abrams, in Saigon, and with South Vietnamese Vice-President Nguyen Cao Ky. It was Rev. McIntire who invited Ky to participate in a "Victory March" in Washington, D. C., only to find that the Nixon Administration had changed its mind about the rally. In the meantime, Rev. McIntire continues his right-wing activity on many fronts.

2. The *American Security Council* can be best described in these words: "If you took the most conservative executives from major corporations and mixed them with hardline retired generals and admirals for your basic ingredient; added an assortment of

intellectuals preoccupied with Soviet military strength to provide dogma; put in a dash of similarly inclined notables for political flair and worked in an overpowering sense of mission and bitterness toward the liberal establishment, you'd have an explosive combination . . . The American Security Council." The ASC represents the ultraconservative and the military-industrial complex, advances its cause under the guise of "patriotism" and "nationalism," and is aligned with such right-wing organizations as the John Birch Society, Liberty Lobby, the National Right to Work Committee, the American Farm Bureau Federation, and the White Citizens Council. Its objectives include expanding America's military might, alarmistically publicizing the Soviet Union's growing military threat, and perhaps preparing the way for a military takeover of the federal civilian government. The American Security Council has been financed in part by the Schick-Eversharp Company which employs retired General Thomas Power, who is a member of the ASC Board along with Dr. Robert Morris, former counsel for the Senate Internal Security Committee, Father Daniel Lyons, Dean Clarence Manion, retired Generals Mark Clark, Albert Wedemeyer, Curtis LeMay, and Bernard Schriever; Admirals Ben Morrell and Chester Ward; intellectuals Dr. Edward Teller and Professor Stefan Possony; and politicians Strom Thurmond and the late Mendel Rivers. In October, 1970, the ASC issued its ratings on senators and congressmen (based upon voting records on six key military issues selected by the ASC) in an envelope with a White House return address (inside was a signed note from Charles W. Colson, special counsel to President Nixon). This technique is indicative of the excessive "military-official pressure" placed upon elected representatives. Three of the selected Senate issues involved the controversial ABM, the C-5A, and the AMSA bomber, so that voting for weaponry whose effectiveness has been questioned accounted for half the Senate total. (The ASC position was in support of all the issues). Indicative of the ASC's overall posture regarding the "military-industrial complex" include its positions *against* cutting military aid to South Korea; *against* the Cooper-Church bill to curtail our activities in Cambodia; *for* the Byrd-Griffin amendment which would have softened the impact of Cooper-Church, and *against* the McGovern-Hatfield bill which would have had the effect of cutting off funds for Vietnam at the end of 1971. Four of the issues chosen for the House ratings involved internal security matters: the ASC was *for* retaining the House Un-American Activities Committee (1969) and *for* a 1970 measure (passed) to set up a House Committee on Internal Security; *for* the 1970 Defense Facilities and Industrial Security Act (passed); and *for* a measure which prohibited picketing at the Pentagon. Although support or opposition to the above-noted measures does not, of itself, strike a chord of extremism, it does demonstrate the singlemindedness of the ASC with respect to their overall objectives. Two other ASC issues, *for* aid to Nationalist China and in *opposition* to trade with Communist nations (in opposition to the position of the Nixon administration), were squarely foreign policy matters. The ASC "positions," while expressive of their ultraconservative bent, are important only in terms of their polarizing exertion upon elected representatives. Indeed, the role of the American Security Council must be carefully scrutinized as it prepares to take the *lead* at the head of right-wing organizations because of its semi-official support.

3. The *Jewish Defense League,* which was created in the spring of 1968, is a right-wing extremist vigilante organization playing upon the fears of some American Jewish citizens. It labels itself as the self-appointed savior of Jews and militantly practices violence and paramilitary skills to accomplish its ends, which they describe as the "defense of Jews." The JDL has several thousand Jewish members in New York City, Philadelphia, Cleveland, Boston, and Hartford, as it practices its business of hysteria, erratic sensationalism, and attacks upon public and private authorities (including synagogues and all major Jewish organizations) who do not respond to JDL demands. JDL members are taught to harass, to challenge all who dispute them, even the police; and to use rifles and karate against their "enemies." The Jewish Defense League came into being largely because of Rabbi Meir Kahane's incredibly horrific view of "the alternatives" —his gross distortion of the position of Jews in America. The United States is a violent country, claims Kahane, and American

Jews, he insists, are living in a fiercely hostile society, facing much the same dangers as the Jews in Nazi Germany and those in Israel who are surrounded by 80 million Arab enemies. And so the JDL units, exhibiting paranoia as readily as proficiency in paramilitary tactics, strut with blue berets and brass insignia under the slogan, "Never Again"—never again the Nazi death camps. One night, 40 JDL members with clubs and chains and baseball bats gathered in the street outside New York's Temple Emanu-El, against the wishes of the Rabbi and the congregation, drawn by the *rumored* appearance of a Black militant; but the "invader" (according to the JDL) did not appear, so the Temple's shocked Rabbi and the New York City police (summoned in advance by JDL) were confronted only with the problem of the armed JDL vigilantes! On another day six unidentified young men burst into the offices of two Arab propaganda agencies in New York and severely beat three Arab men with wooden clubs. They wrecked desks and filing cabinets and left the offices in shambles. All three of the attack victims required hospital treatment. The JDL took credit for this fiendish attack! And there are sometimes arrests: JDL's Queens County, New York, coordinator was charged with unlawful possession of a blackjack! Nine JDL members were accused of criminal trespass of a blackjack! Nine JDL members were accused of criminal trespass at the New York Board of Education! Twenty-seven JDL members were arrested outside the Soviet United Nations Mission, including their leader, Meir Kahane, and the charges ranged from harassment to felonious assault. (After publicly warning of possible violence in their protest against Soviet anti-Semitism, the JDL stormed police barricades at the building!) Kahane and thirteen others were taken into custody after two Soviet offices in Manhattan and a Soviet airliner at Kennedy Airport had been smeared with slogans in red paint! A B'nai B'rith Lodge president in Brooklyn, the author of an article in the Lodge newspaper that implied criticism of the JDL received a *midnight* telephone call from an anonymous person: "If you don't want to be found laying next to your car in the parking lot, lay off the Jewish Defense League." The caller may not necessarily be connected with JDL, but the JDL has made its clear contribution to the electrified atmosphere in which people can think that way. The "vigilante" atmosphere has grown even more noxious: on May 18, 1970, some 50 JDL members "took over" New York City's Orthodox Park East Synagogue opposite the Soviet United Nations Mission. Stationing themselves on the roof and on temporary scaffolding that surrounded the building, as well as in the sanctuary itself, young JDL "toughs" unfurled huge banners bearing slogans about Soviet Jewry. Those on the roof shouted demands and played martial music through a high-powered loudspeaker turned toward the Soviet headquarters across the way. The congregation's spiritual leader, Rabbi Arthur Schneier, told the JDL they were *not* welcome and pleaded with them to leave. Meir Kahane told the Rabbi that as far as he was concerned there was "nothing to talk about." JDL members, aware that the congregation officials were hesitant to aggravate the incident by asking the police to act, continued their forced occupation of the building for nine hours. "This synagogue has long been known for its concern for Soviet Jewry," said Rabbi Schneier, who had seen the plight of Soviet Jews at first hand during his recent trips to the Soviet Union: "This JDL kind of tactic . . . is harmful and counter-productive." The greater harm, he added, is to the position of the Soviet Jews themselves!

Recent harassment of Soviet citizens in the United States by this lunatic fringe is indeed the action of an unrepresentative notoriety-seeking group of hoodlums that endangers the cause of Soviet Jewry and is condemned by the Israeli Government as well as by all American citizens. It is morally reprehensible and politically self-defeating. Although the Soviet campaign of harassment of American officials and visitors cannot be justified nor condoned, it is obvious that the Soviets have seized upon the practices of the Jewish Defense League as a pretext for their own misdemeanors.

Indeed, the JDL has become the kind of counterproductive phenomenon in the Jewish community that the Black Panthers have been in the black community, the kind of liability that the Ku Klux Klan has been to the Protestants, and the old "Christian Mobilizers" to the Catholics. The *New York Times,* on January 25, 1971, carried a story that more than 30 policemen were on duty on Sunday at the Port Authority Bus Terminal in New York City. It seems that four extremist organizations, the JDL, the neo-Nazi National Renaissance Party, the Black Panthers, and the Young Lords were soliciting funds and distributing literature. Violent political expression makes strange bedfellows! Every major Jewish organization in the United States, as well as the Israeli Government itself, has repudiated the Jewish Defense League.

4. The *Black Panthers* have in recent years launched upon violent confrontations with police. This New Left "gang" produces a constant stream of vitriolic propaganda against the police, openly calling upon ghetto residents to arm "in self-defense" against the "Fascist pigs." "The Black Panther" weekly newspaper for the supermilitant group continuously reports on a barrage of incidents of alleged police brutality. The growing body of research by various Presidential Commissions and the literature of the Black Panthers provide considerable evidence that many young blacks have a deep-seated *fear* of the police. The same research documents a deep-seated police *fear* of the Black Panthers and allied groups. On both sides, the fears seem justified. (Police raids on Black Panther headquarters are not exactly new, but the near-simultaneous swoops on Black Panther offices in Los Angeles and Chicago have brought eight official investigations into charges that the nation's police are involved in a conspiracy to break up the Black Panthers.) Whether the arms seized by police in the raids were legally held by the Black Panthers and whether individual rights were violated, is a matter for the courts to decide. But involved here are both facts and soul-searching! What is overt is the Black Panthers' propaganda which the police see in black neighborhoods: these placards and publications threaten death to "pigs" and at the same time provide the reader with information on how to prepare and use explosives against the police. It is easy for police to become convinced, rightly or wrongly in a given instance, that the Black Panthers were responsible for a law violation and that Black Panthers would kill any policeman who sought to investigate. This does not make for *calm* police inquiry! A year ago, while he was on parole, Eldridge Cleaver, author of the best-selling

book, *Soul on Ice,* made a series of speeches in which he taunted the police who, he told the crowds, were looking for possible parole-violation charges. (Subsequently he fled the country rather than go back to prison.)

The Black Panther party sprang up in Oakland, California, in mid-1966 as a magnet for Negroes who completely distrusted "whitey." Among the Black Panther demands *then and now* are the following: reparations, the cash equivalent of "forty acres and two mules" promised at the end of the Civil War; full employment and decent housing for all blacks; black control of education, police and jury procedures where blacks are affected; and a United Nations plebiscite "to be held throughout the Black colony in which only Black colonial subjects will be allowed to participate, for the purpose of determining the will of Black people as to their national destiny." Members of the Black Panthers swear to uphold its 26 rules, some of which are admittedly commendable, i.e. "No party member can have narcotics or weed in his possession while doing party work." (Rule No. 1) Rule No. 8 forbids members to "commit any crimes against other party members or Black people at all!" Black Panthers are also under orders to avoid maltreating any hostage they may be obliged to take. Indeed, the 26 Rules paint the image of a kind of Black Robin Hood band, in which members are told to "pay for anything you damage" and told not to "damage property or crops of the poor, oppressed masses." But the "band" does not have any Friar Tucks: the rank and file members are "up-tight"; they tend to be young, often high-school dropouts. Before Eldridge Cleaver went into exile, he conceded that the Party's attraction for criminal types created problems. Any organization as militantly "anti-cop" as the Black Panthers had to be hard-pressed for allies. (Some police officials privately concede, however, that the Black Panthers do sometimes purge hard-core criminals from their ranks.) The fear of infiltrators and "stool pigeons" puts loyalty to the Party on virtually a life-and-death basis. There is no surface of joviality about Black Panthers efforts to tear down what they view as "capitalist-racist institutions" or the liberal establishment, in order to secure what they view as "justice." Instead of forest green, such members as can afford them wear black leather jackets, often topped by a black beret.

A polished machine gun bullet is sometimes worn as a good luck charm. Their alliance with Al Fatah and the Palestine guerrillas insures an anti-Israel stance with anti-Semitic overtones. Their violence and use of force to accomplish their ends marks the Black Panthers as an important extremist organization.

5. The *Underground Press Syndicate* (U.P.S.) and its Intertribal News Service is a small "collective" phenomenon of the New Left wholly destructive of the Establishment and wholly without any constructive program to replace it. The U.P.S. is responsible for the publication of perhaps 400 underground extremist newspapers whose combined circulation is perhaps one million. The papers exist in many major cities and on nearly every college campus; they range in size from the *New Prairie Primer* of Cedar Falls, Iowa (circ. 2,000) to the famed *Berkeley Barb* of Berkeley, California and New York's *East Village Other* (circ. over 50,000). Distribution of the news is, however, the assignment of the 15-member staff of the Liberation News Service in New York City. Marxist-oriented, the movement press also takes up the cudgels for migrant labor, the farm workers and other minority groups which society likes to ignore, in a distorted manner and outside the law. It promoted coffee house dissent within the military, for its major concern remains the Indochina war. The movement press is ever replete with "stories" of police brutality, frequently accompanied with advice to the readers on self-defense and "first aid for street fighters."

The Underground Press Syndicate and the Liberation News Service, it should be noted, are just as concerned with achieving universal justice as the John Birch Society is with universally enforcing law. Like the Birchers, they are quite convinced their ends justify the means. Like the Birch-right, they have their own movement sources for distortion of news. Like the Birch-right, hot targets include the Presidency and university administrations. While the Birch-right "Supports Your Local Police" and hopes they will legally clobber the protestors (as at Kent State), thus relying on law to get around the clamor for social justice, the movement heroes preach that their concern for social justice justifies working outside the law, which serves only the privileged few.

6. *White Citizens Councils* (WCC), comprising 100,000 dues-

paying members, still fights for segregation throughout the country. The WCC has active units in 30 states. What started as a purely southern phenomenon in Indianola, Mississippi, 15 or 16 years ago has grown into an enormously powerful combine. A shift of but 156,000 votes in two states in the 1968 presidential sweepstakes would have deadlocked the election, and the balance of power would have then switched to the five southern states which George Wallace carried. (In all but Alabama, the electors were as beholden to the White Citizens Councils as they were to Wallace.) Thus, a plausible case can be made that a microscopic switch in the vote would have placed the American destiny in White Citizens Councils' hands. While the relatively obscure hold the top posts in the White Citizens Councils groups in the bordering northern and western states, it is in the Deep South that the offices are held by men accustomed to power with access to wealth and the machinery of government. To the WCC, the superiority of the white Christian race is an article of faith, and the battle against school integration is a matter of sacred honor. They readily ascribe to the John Birch Society principle that the civil rights movement is a part of the Communist conspiracy.

In 1970, the WCC claimed to be operating more than 150 private schools, with a total enrollment of 9,000. The White Citizens Council's Schools Foundation operated three schools in Jackson, Mississippi, with about 3,000 students and anticipated opening at least one more school each fall. The total number of schools in 1970 in Louisiana is between 60 and 70, with 54 in Mississippi, 24 in South Carolina and others scattered around the South. The WCC supplies technical advice, but the financing and curriculum are handled locally. While the White Citizens Councils shun any open association with the Ku Klux Klan, George Thayer in his book, *The Farther Shores of Politics* (New York, Simon & Shuster, 1968), described the WCC movement as having the same aims but appealing to a better-educated segregationist: "If the mark of a Klansman is cracking skulls, then the mark of a member of the White Citizens Councils is twisting arms." For the silent, so-called "forgotten American," worried about "non-American" control, property values, and street crime, the White Citizens Councils offer a kind of bogus status and a scapegoat to rally against. In Cairo, Illinois, for example, the issues were spelled out bigger than life, and there is some of Cairo spirit in every town; and while the fears and frustrations may not take the form of an ongoing organization in most communities, there is much of the spirit of White Citizens Councils in a good many hearts! By joining the WCC (incidentally, the "White" is not an official part of the name), the citizen gets a vehicle to advance his self-interest, but he may not notice the price for the hidden extras. The motor is the John Birch Society ideology and the fuel is the dissipation of the very energies which America will need if America is to make democracy work.

There are perhaps another 50 extremist organizations on the American scene, and their activities also must be continuously disclosed by the alert media and by public-spirited organizations. For example, the speech which the President of the United States was to deliver in Dallas, Texas, on November 22, 1963, was based almost entirely upon materials on extremism made available to him by the ADL of B'nai B'rith. Perhaps the assasination of President John F. Kennedy will be a constant reminder of the danger of extremism in our midst. We must keep the public aware and we must be concerned. We must give a damn!

QUESTIONS FOR REVIEW

1. Why should we be concerned about extremist organizations in the United States? Is their "potential" or their real power the "hang-up?" Explain.
2. Did the 1968 national presidential election raise the spectre of the Radical Right or the Radical Left? How plausible were their programs and their ideas?
3. List at least six characteristics of all extremist organizations.
4. Distinguish between the Far Right and the Far Left in terms of income, circulation of newspapers and pamphlets, and radio and TV outlets, as evident from the I.A.D. chart.
5. What is the chief matrix today of the Far Left? What is the major weakness of the Far Right?
6. Why is Rev. McIntire an important example of the Radical Right?

7. Does the American Security Council represent the military-industrial complex?
8. As an extremist organization does the Jewish Defense League have the backing of the Jewish community? How does it resemble the Black Panthers?
9. Why is hatred of the police the dominant theme of the Black Panthers? Is this extremist organization paramilitary? Is it a political party?
10. Explain the origins of the "underground press" and its extremist positions.
11. Why are White Citizens Councils a dominant Radical Right organization in the north? Are private, segregated schools legal?
12. Why is exposure of extremist activities the best safeguard for American democracy?

Chapter 11

NOISE POLLUTION: METHODS AND PROCEDURES OF ABATEMENT

THE ENGLISH WORD NOISE is derived from the Latin noun *nausea,* and if the devastating effects of NOISE are as yet incapable of producing a universal "nauseousness," NOISE has been found to cause acute physiological pain[1] as well as extreme psychological neuroses.[2] Of the trio of environmental pollutions, i.e. noise, air, and water, NOISE is the pollutant most universally ignored and denigrated, the one least easily remedied by the processes of law, and yet, the one most easily abated by private

[1]The most severe and noticeable effect of exposure to excessive noise is loss or impairment of hearing. In the United States alone, 11 million adults and 3 million children suffer some form of hearing loss. . . . On the adult level, physicians have reported a causal relationship between exposure to excessive noise over a period of time and the incidence of heart disease and cardiovascular dysfunction, migraine headaches, gastrointestinal disorders, and allergies, as well as endocrine and metabolic effects. A recent report by the Federal Council for Science and Technology has stated that "[i]ncreasing numbers of competent investigators believe that [prolonged exposure to intense noise] may adversely affect other organic, sensory and physiologic functions of the human body."

This statement was made by James L. Hildebrand, in "Noise Pollution: An Introduction to the Problem and an Outline for Future Legal Research, 70 *Colum. L. Rev.* 652, 656, 1970."

[2]Psychiatrists and psychologists have recently noted the connection between excessive undesired noise and mental disorders. Drs. [Samuel J.] Rosen [Professor of Otology at Mount Sinai School of Medicine, New York City] and [Vern O.] Knudsen [founder of the Acoustical Society of America and former Chancellor of the University of California] suggest that loss of hearing may in fact be the *least* serious impairment to the human organism caused by noise pollution. Both of these doctors point out that one no longer has to work in a boiler factory to suffer noise-induced psychological and physiological damage. Day and night most of us are exposed to a general racket. These noises are now being recognized as a major factor in the celebrated "tensions" of modern living; they contribute and aggravate all of the tension-related diseases—from stomach ulcers, neuroses, and mental illness to allergies and cardiovascular and circulatory diseases (*Id.* at 661).

efforts as opposed to governmental restraints. NOISE is also the pollutant most likely to make the Earth uninhabitable by man.

The former chancellor of the University of California at Los Angeles and a renowned physicist, who has studied sound for 40 years, has expressed the view that "if the noise level we live with today continues to increase at the same rate for the next 30 years as it has for the last 30, it could become *lethal*"[3] (emphasis added.) Background NOISE is increasing at the rate of one decibel[4] (dB) per year, and all too frequently, NOISE exceeds what experts consider the danger level of 80 dB (sports car and truck engines reach 90 dB, subways, motorcycles, and electric blenders achieve a 100 dB rating, and power lawn mowers and amplified rock music are measured at 110 dB.), and often even exceeds the level of the threshold of pain, 120 dB (pneumatic hammers and sirens are at the 130 dB level and low-flying jets can exceed 150 dB). Indeed, even short exposure to sounds at the 150 dB level can result in permanent hearing damage. Scientists believe that NOISE of 180 dB would prove fatal to man. Unquestionably, the situation is becoming serious, and often the victim of NOISE pollution (the pollutee) looks to the law to offer some protection and some opportunity for redress or remedy. However, private law is presently inadequate to deal with NOISE pollution, in that the law reflects older and less-sophisticated technology and simply has not kept pace with fast-progressing science. In rhetorical response to his own question, "How did we get into such a situation?", attorney James L. Hildebrand in his 1970 article "Noise Pollution: An Introduction to the Problem and an Outline for Future Legal Research,"[5] stated:

> The primary reason is the same as in other areas of environmental pollution—social and legal measures were not taken to

---

[3]"Noise Takes Toll, Says Experts," *Today's Health,* October, 1967, alluding to a contention of Dr. Vern O. Knudsen.

[4]NOISE is measured by the decibel, a unit which represents the intensity of a sound from the threshold of hearing, zero decibels, and the lowest point of audibility to humans, one decibel, to infinity. Each decibel is ten times greater in sound intensity than the prior decibel.

[5]70 *Colum. L. Rev.* 652.

> prevent it, and for the failure to act in time the public authorities bear the major responsibility. The increase in noise has been accepted as a natural process, as a price to be paid for our technological progress. Law, justice, and public authorities all have capitulated to technology.

Yet even giving credence to this "capitulation," environmental legal specialists and legal scholars are nevertheless today scurrying about to solve the problems created by NOISE's "sister" pollutants. But so very little has yet been done to find remedies and solace for the bombarded eardrum! The only sensible answer for this failure to attack NOISE pollution is public apathy. NOISE pollution is taken for granted by everybody—by the state legislatures, Congress, the courts, environmental agencies, private ecology groups, and until recently, by the President of the United States. How often have you yourself been made uncomfortable or been caused pain or experienced unreasoning anger because of unwanted and unnecessary NOISE? And how often have you simply shrugged and accepted NOISE as an unavoidable consequence of living in the Space Age? What is far worse is that you are not the only one who is experiencing and has experienced the intolerable pain of NOISE. The very men whose machines create loathesome noises likewise shrug their shoulders, pointing out that if you want progress you must pay for it and one of the not-so-hidden costs is blaring NOISE.

Examples of the monumental neglect of the problem of NOISE pollution are overwhelmingly evident. In 1969, Congress passed the historic Environmental Protection Act, which contained a provision for the establishment of a Federal Environmental Protection Agency to combat air and water pollution but completely failed to mention NOISE. In President Nixon's 1969, 1970, and 1971 State of the Union messages, the only pollutant of the ecological trio which he failed to delineate was NOISE. (It was not until the 1971 environmental message that NOISE was given any emphasis at all.) Furthermore, the Federal budget for fiscal 1970 allotted only 32 million dollars for NOISE control programs, of which 29 million dollars was earmarked to combat aircraft noises. Even more indicative of the inconsequentiality with which NOISE pollution is treated, is a leading ecological article in the January, 1971, issue of the *American Bar Association Journal.* Of the 139 column inches devoted to pollution, only four inches, or 3.6 percent of the text, dealt with NOISE! And even then, it was noted in the next-to-the-last paragraph. A universal awareness and vigilance regarding NOISE pollution cannot begin soon enough, although such emphasis is not to demean the equally serious threats of air and water pollution.

On October 9, 1969, Senator Mark O. Hatfield of Oregon sounded the alarm in a speech before the Noise Abatement Council of America.

> The effects of noise, although long a problem, have only begun to receive the well-founded concerns of government, health, industrial and commercial organizations. We are already far behind the rest of the world in appreciating the scope of the problem. For our backwardness in the field of noise abatement, the United States is now the noisiest country on this planet, and frankly, I hate to think that we are now carrying this lack of respect for civilized standards to other planetary bodies. Basically, noise pollution is reaching crisis proportions in the United States and I think that it is time that all of us wake up to this fact."

Senator Hatfield unfortunately did not take the bull by its horns and demand specific legislation. He did, however, open the door toward recognition of this treacherous ecological destroyer on a national scale. Other environmental advocates must take up the cry of NOISE pollution with the same fervor with which they swing the cudgel in behalf of air and water pollution. Until local and state governments give ear to their plea, our cities can become as uninhabitable as Arctic ice floes and our farms as devastated as the vast wastes of forgotten equatorial deserts. Indeed, NOISE pollution is not by any means a strictly urban problem, for neither rural nor suburban areas are immune. Automobiles, trucks, and motorcycles are as evident on sleepy country roads as on a city's commercial thoroughfares and as easily disturb the sleep, the tranquility, and the peace of mind of an apartment dweller as well as that of a dairy farmer. The housewife in the mountains of Vermont has as many noisy kitchen appliances as her counterpart in Dallas, Texas; and since the grass in the north of Utah does not grow any slower than the grass in Richmond, Virginia, the home gardener in Utah and Virginia is just as likely to use his jarring power mower early Saturday morning and disturb the serenity of his community. Large jet aircraft are landing at almost every one of the 140 major air terminals in the United States, most of which are situated at the fringes of metropolitan complexes. Residents adjoining these airports are literally "blasted" from their homes. With the advent of the smaller, noncommercial jet, even people who dwell near smaller local and private airports are beginning to understand the meaning and frightening import of "flyby" and "sideline" NOISE. Furthermore, if in the future the supersonic transport (SST) is allowed to fly across our nation, even though in 1971 Congress declined to authorize additional funds for its development, then sonic booms may do immeasurable damage to the nation's eardrums, not to mention the property damage to plaster, window glass, and entire structures.

In a 1964 series of tests conducted in the skies above Oklahoma City, the 1,254 supersonic flights resulted in more than 15,000 complaints, including nearly 5,000 property damage claims amounting to more than 100,000 dollars. Personal injury claims were not tabulated, but it cannot be doubted that ruptured eardrums were probably present.

NOISE is omnipresent. If drastic legislative controls are not forthcoming, NOISE may also become omnipotent and control our very lives. Our legal system is perhaps the most effiicacious means to counteract this problem and current legal solutions with respect to this pollutant proceed down two separate paths towards the same ultimate goal—elimination of unwanted and unnecessary NOISE. This can be done by means of (a) *private* law, whereby an individual (or a group of individuals) can seek to effectuate the ancient maxim that "silence is golden" by suing for damages caused by the NOISE, or seeking an injunction against the creator of the NOISE, or both and (b) *public* law, which involves the promulgation by legislative and executive authorities and regulatory bodies of appropriate, enforceable laws, ordinances, and regulations. But inasmuch as governmental activity in bringing about this NOISE abatement is still, for all practical purposes, just a wishful dream, the area of *private* law today offers the only reasonable remedy. As in every area of the Anglo-American legal system, private law remedies derive either from the Common Law of England or from statute, including the federal and state constitutions. What is somewhat unusual, however, is the theory upon which the relief is sought, for it is entirely dependent upon whether or not the identifiable creator of the NOISE is a government (state, local, or federal) or is a private person or agency. If the NOISE emanates from a *public* source, in the absence of any enabling legislation (and generally it is absent), a pollutee or victim of the pollution must rely upon elaborate and highly technical language, i.e. the "taking of property without due process," or upon the United States Constitution's "domestic tranquility" clause and "general welfare" clause, or perhaps upon a state constitution's equivalent in order to obtain relief. Where the NOISE pollution emanates from a *private* source, however, the pollutee may sue either under a theory of a private nuisance at common law, or under general public nuisance statutes (note that "due process" and other Constitutional arguments can only be used against governmental and quasigovernmental organizations and bodies). Neither of these remedies, however, were developed with the security of a victim's eardrums as the basic deterrent. But inasmuch as nuisance presupposes redress, it is the nuisance form of legal action that provides the remedy for the environmental havoc caused by NOISE. Prior to defining "nuisance," however, the following explanation of this tort by Dean William Prosser in his *Law of Torts* [3rd ed., 1964], is in order:

> There is perhaps no more impenetrable jungle in the entire law than that which surrounds the word "nuisance." It has meant all things to all men, and has been applied indiscriminately to everything from an alarming advertisement to a cockerroach baked in a pie. There is general agreement that it is incapable of any exact or comprehensive definitions.

Prosser's "warning" notwithstanding, for our purposes, *nuisance* may be defined as tortious or wrongful conduct which results in either the intentional, negligent (nonintentional), or abnormal invasion of the victim's enjoyment and use of his property. An intentional invasion delineates, for example, the situation where an individual fires his target rifle at glass bottles in a residential neighborhood and thus intentionally creates offensive NOISE. Negligent invasion would occur, for instance, when an individual inadvertently loses the muffler of his car, causing it to sound more like a Sherman tank, and thereby carelessly causing irritating NOISE. An abnormal invasion of another's property would encompass either or both negligent and intentional conduct. For example, if a violin teacher builds a house in an industrial area, perhaps next door to a factory which tests police sirens, the maestro cannot complain that his factory neighbor is creating a nuisance, because it is his studio and not the factory which is "*out of place*" in the clearly industrial locality; therefore the NOISE of the sirens was expected as a normal occurrence. It is the inept bowing screeches of the students of the maestro and not the police siren shrieks that are abnormal intrusions under this set of facts. If the reverse were true, and the siren-testing plant moved into a relatively quiet residential neighborhood inhabited by violin teachers, the siren noises would be unusual and would constitute the abnormal invasion. It is this requirement that the nuisance which is caused be an abnormal invasion that is the first hurdle a NOISE pollutee must overcome before he can proceed to abate the nuisance in a court of law. To illustrate further, in the 1905 Massachusetts case of *Wade v. Miller*,[6] Mr. Miller kept a chicken farm next to his house in a small rural community. A nearby neighbor, Mr. Wade, was unable to sleep late because of the constant clucking and cockadoodledooing of the poultry, and when Mr. Miller refused Mr. Wade's demand to get rid of his chickens, Mr. Wade sued him. The highest court of Massachusetts held that Mr. Wade could *not* recover damages for the nuisance and could *not* enjoin the existence of the chicken coops because the customs of the community where the victim resided were taken into account, and the chicken noises were not offensive to the ordinary citizen of that hamlet. Mr. Wade accordingly had no cause to complain. Thus, the intrusion upon Mr. Wade's proprietary interest and his eardrums was *not* an abnormal one and not a nuisance, so that Mr. Wade could not find relief in a court of law.

[6] 73 N.E. 849, Mass., 1905.

Another situation involving unreasonable NOISE arose in a small Georgia city, where the victim sued to enjoin the blowing of a factory whistle. In *Hill v. McBurney Oil & Fertilizer Co.*,[7] a Georgia court declared that whistle blowing was both an abnormal and intentional invasion of the peaceful enjoyment of surrounding property, noting that although many persons living nearby worked at the factory and that the community was populous, the loud and harsh whistling occurred at unreasonable hours and for unduly long periods of time. Accordingly, the Court affirmed the issuance of the injunction in favor of Mr. Hill. In contrast to the *Wade* case, above, where the chicken coop owner had no control over the volume, ferocity, duration, or starting time of the clucking, the factory here could use its whistle at a more reasonable time and in a more moderate manner. The principle of the *Wade* case was discussed as long ago as 1876 by Judge Earl of the New York Court of Appeals in *Campbell v. Seaman.*[8]

> Persons living in organized communities must suffer some damage, annoyance and inconvenience from each other. For these they are compensated by all the advantages of civilized society. If one lives in the city he must expect to suffer the dirt, smoke, noisome odors, noise and confusion incident to city life. As Lord Justice James beautifully said, in *Salvin v. Northbrancepeth Coal Co.* . . . :"If some picturesque haven opens its arms to invite the commerce of the world, it is not for this court to forbid the embrace, although the fruit of it should be the sights and sounds and smells of a common seaport and ship-building town which would drive the Dryads and their masters from their ancient solitudes."

However, Judge Earl then opined:

> But every person is bound to make a reasonable use of his property so as to occasion no unnecessary damage or annoyance to his neighbor. If he make an unreasonable, unwarrantable or unlawful use of it, so as to produce material annoyance, inconvenience, discomfort or hurt to his neighbor, he will be guilty of a nuisance to his neighbor. And the law will hold him responsible for the consequent damage. What is a reasonable use of one's own property cannot be defined by any certain general rules, but must depend

[7] 38 S.E. 42, Ga., 1901.
[8] 63 N.Y. 568, 577, 1876.

upon the circumstances of each case. A use of property in one locality and under some circumstances may be lawful and reasonable, which, under other circumstances, would be unlawful, unreasonable and a nuisance. To constitute a nuisance, the use must be such as to produce a tangible and appreciable injury to neighboring property, or such as to render its enjoyment specially uncomfortable or inconvenient.

Thus, whether or not an invasion is abnormal would also depend upon the atmosphere and environment in which the NOISE is heard. A recent case in New York involved a large middle-income apartment development which was situated next to a highway paralleling New York City's East River. On the far side of the highway, and directly abutting on the water, was a concrete plant which mixed its product, often on a semiemergency basis, early in the morning and late at night. Although the plant used the most modern equipment, kept it in good repair, and did all that was possible to eliminate NOISE, 74 residents of the apartments instituted a private nuisance suit claiming that the NOISE was a nuisance which should be abated. In holding that an injunction would *not* lie and that the cement plant, which had been in its location *prior* to the construction of the apartment houses, was not creating a nuisance, the New York court refused plaintiff's request for relief. In *Pelletier v. Transit-Mix Corp.*,[9] the Court declared:

While the law will not permit a person to be driven from his home or to be compelled to live in it in positive distress or discomfort because of the use to which other property nearby has been put, it is not every annoyance connected with business which will be enjoined. Many a loss arises from acts or conditions which do not create a ground for legal redress. *Damnum absque injuria* is a familiar maxim. Factories, stores and mercantile establishments are essential to the prosperity of the nation. They necessarily invade our cities, and interfere more or less with the peace and tranquility of the neighborhood in which they are located.

One who chooses to live in the large centers of population cannot expect the quiet of the country. Congested centers are seldom free from smoke, odors and other pollution from houses, shops and factories, and one who moves into such a region cannot

---

[9]11 Misc. 2d 617, Sup. N.Y., 1958.

> hope to find the pure air of the village or outlying district. A person who prefers the advantages of community life must expect to experience some of the resulting inconveniences. Residents of industrial centers must endure without redress a certain amount of annoyance and discomfiture which is incident to life in such a locality. Such inconvenience is of minor importance compared with the general good of the community.

The New York Court, in essence, stated that an abnormal NOISE invasion is more difficult to establish in a citified environment because it is to be more likely expected there than in the country.

Professors Harper and James, in their three-volume *Law of Torts* (1956, p. 74), make an apt analogy between the elasticity of what the courts will enjoin as nuisance under given circumstances as an abnormal invasion and an informal common law system of zoning which the courts will not enjoin.

> When a neighborhood becomes dominantly impressed with a particular use—such as a residential community, a business district or an industrial area—intrusions by inconsistent activities adversely affecting such use may produce liability as nuisance. On the other hand, the law recognizes changes in suitability for particular uses. Merely because a community originated as a residential area does not mean that it forever must remain such regardless of growth in population and the accompanying need for expanded business and service establishments. Every large and growing American city has witnessed the gradual encroachment of such activities as shops, funeral parlors, professional and other offices on what, in earlier years, were the "best" residential streets. Sometimes this encroachment increases property values, as where large old mansions become desirable for office space. Sometimes it decreases values, as when such buildings become usable only as tenement and low-price rooming houses. In any event, the law does not attempt to stay the tide of change beyond reasonable limits.
>
> Similarly, business or industrial activities will not be permitted to characterize an area beyond possibility of change. A factory, for example, cannot limit for all time the uses to which adjoining landowners may commit their property. Urban development may be such that, in time, the factory must close down or change its site. Again, the gravity of the harm weighed against the utility of the activity in the light of the suitability of the area for the respective competing uses, cost of change of location and other conditions will be the criteria to guide the courts' judgment."

Thus, in contrasting the above statement with the opinion in the

Pelletier case, above, it must be observed that if the apartment dwellers argued that the construction of their buildings had so altered the nature of the neghborhood that the unwanted NOISE emanating from the cement plant was in fact abnormal and a nuisance, the complainants would have won. However, more often than not, the urban antinoise action fails because it is *not* an abnormal invasion of the victim's property rights.

A second requirement of the *private* nuisance action is that the NOISES and destructive sounds must be deemed by the court as offensive by the "average and reasonable man." If the susceptibility of the victim to the NOISE in question is acute, and if a person of ordinary NOISE sensibilities would be unduly disturbed, then there is a cause of action. In contrast, the Supreme Judicial Court of Massachusetts in *Rogers v. Elliott,*[10] refused to consider the ringing of a church bell to be a NOISE sufficiently acute and unduly offensive to be a nuisance, simply because a sick person was annoyed by the sound. Nuisance was not to be determined by the individual's reaction to the bell ringing if that individual was a nervous, ailing person with unusual sensitivities. As the same Court noted in a later case, *Stevens v. Rockport-Granite Co.,*[11]

> In order that a noise may amount to a nuisance, it must be harmful to the health and comfort of ordinary people. It is not enough that a person of peculiar temperament, unusual sensibilities or weakened physical condition may be affected. Nor is it protected if those of exceptional strength and robustness or whose faculties have become benumbed by close business or other experience with it are not disturbed. The pertinent inquiry is whether the noise materially interfered with the physical comfort or existence, not according to exceptionally refined, uncommon or luxurious habits of living, but according to the simple tastes and unaffected notions generally prevailing among plain people. The standard is what ordinary people, acting reasonably, have a right to demand in the way of health and comfort under all the circumstances. The number of people concerned by the noise and the magnitude of the industry complained of are both elements entitled to consideration in reaching a conclusion as to the facts.

---

[10] 15 N.E. 768, 1888.
[11] 104 N.E. 371, 1914.

To quote Dean Prosser in his *Law of Torts* again, "the law does not concern itself with trifles, or seek to remedy all of the petty annoyances and disturbances of everyday life in a civilized country." The law of nuisance will not remedy a mere squeak! In the words of Professor Lloyd in his 1934 article "Noise as a Nuisance,"[12] "Exceptionally nervous persons, or those whose refinement exceeds the standards of the 'American people in their present state of enlightenment', . . . must seek refuge in sound proof rooms, if they can afford them, or take their chances of the padded cell."

If the prerequisites for an action to abate a private nuisance, i.e. NOISE pollution, meet all of the above criteria, there is still another absolutely essential but quite perplexing element that in many situations is simply unsurmountable, to wit: the pollutee must find somebody to sue! The sounds which are bothering the victim frequently come from a vast conglomeration of sources, which sounds, if taken singly, would be of little consequence. For example, in an urban apartment, a dweller cannot sue his neighbor across the courtyard because the latter's air conditioner is too noisy, or the lady upstairs for using her vacuum cleaner during the Johnny Carson Show on television, or the pizzeria downstairs because the jukebox is too loud, or even the small canning factory down the street that has a noisy late shift. Each of these sounds, taken singly would be bearable, but together, they sound to the listener like a cavalry charge. There is no remedy for this private nuisance because the total sound is not that readily identifiable in terms of individual wrongs.

As a final requirement for the private suit to abate the nuisance, the abnormal invasion of the victim's interest must ostensibly involve interference with his rights in his use of land. This does not mean that the pollutee must own the land but that he merely have some recognizable legal right with respect to the land. Therefore, apartment renters, house trailer owners who lease plots, and even those who *adversely* possess the land (as opposed to the individual who in truth holds title) have a right to bring an action in private nuisance. What they are suing for

---

[12] 82 U. Penna. L. R., 567, 582.

is not necessarily the audible assault upon their eardrums, or peace of mind, or disruption of life style, but the interference with their quiet use and enjoyment of their property right. This "nicety," which is a carryover from English Common Law of the 13th century, is generally disregarded by the courts so long as the victim is an owner, renter, or lessee of "real property" or land and there is a violation of that right of "ownership." In 1914, in the case of *Barnard v. Finkbeiner*,[13] George Barnard was the lessee of a building in which he and his family lived and used as a theatre. The Finkbeiners, who lived in an apartment in the next house, constantly "indulged in loud and profane swearing and vile and obscene talk; such profane swearing and obscene language could at times be clearly heard in plaintiff's theatre." The New York Court held that Mr. Barnard had a good cause of action in private nuisance, but ruled that it was not because of the nature of the NOISE which was interfering with the morality, personal dignity, and even business of Mr. Barnard and his family, but instead: "The frequent use of loud, profane, vile, and obscene language that can be heard in plaintiff's building may be said to render *it* [the building] 'unfit for comfortable or respectable occupation, and unfit for the purposes *it* was intended for.'" (Emphasis added.) Thus, the "damage" was to the use of the building and not to the personal health or morality of the occupants. This ruling with respect to the requirement that the NOISE intrude upon an interest in land rather than upon the victim becomes more acute when the pollutee who seeks to sue is neither an owner, renter or lessee, but simply an employee. If the employer, for whatever reason, refuses to sue to abate the nuisance, the employee has no course of action except to quit his job! Similarly, a licensee, who is on property with the permission of the owner or possessor, such as a painter who has received a farmer's permission to paint a barn over a period of weeks, has no right to sue. A lodger or hotel guest, although he pays for his room, cannot bring an action. Even members of the family of the person who hold the interest in the land may not commence suit under private nuisance. (For

---

[13] 162 App. Div. 319, N.Y., 1914.

example, old Aunt Tillie, who owns the family homestead and is hard of hearing, may decide she is too old to go to court and sue the newly built foundry next door. Her young nephew, who lives with Tillie and wants to enjoin the NOISE is barred from suing, even though he tests tuning forks for a living. The nephew holds no interest in the land.)

The secondary course to abate NOISE under a *public* nuisance statute involves a civil complaint, although the statute is primarily penal in nature. In the words of Professor Stephen in his *General View of the Criminal Law of England* of 1890, a *public* nuisance is an act or omission "which obstructs or causes inconvenience or damage to the public in the exercise of rights common to *all Her Majesty's* subjects." (If the word "citizens" is substituted for "Her Majesty's subjects," the definition of a public nuisance is perfectly applicable to twentieth century America. Furthermore, the statutes on the books of most states fit far better the anglicized rather than the Americanized terminology.) As of 1971, almost all of the public nuisance laws ignore the realities of the modern age and present-day technology because they fail to define the "crime" and are construed to include only those instances that would have been *public* nuisances at English Common Law. Furthermore, this remedy appears applicable only to employee-lodger-licensee situations where the private nuisance remedy is not available. These laws, of course, can be amended, but, it is still more difficult to curb NOISE pollution through use of the public statute than the private remedy. In order to avail oneself of the civil remedy under the *public* nuisance statute, the victim must first have experienced "special damage," i.e. different in kind, rather than different in degree, from other members of the public. For example, if a man has a dog which barks constantly from midnight to 5 A.M. and causes his neighbors for three square blocks to remain awake, a "crime" may have been committed and a criminal prosecution is possible, but if a Mrs. Smith lost three hours of sleep and everybody else lost only two hours, Mrs. Smith could not bring a civil suit under the public nuisance statute because her damage was merely *different in degree* than that of her neighbors. If, however, Mrs. Smith had a dog which went amuck and wrecked her furniture every time another dog barked during the night, and no one else had a dog, Mrs. Smith's damages would be *different in kind*, and she would have a cause of action under the statute. (The only reason, of course, for her to sue under the public law is if she is otherwise disqualified from using the *private* nuisance remedy in her particular state.)

New York, for example, has a penal public nuisance statute, enforceable by peace officers of the state but which may be used by others as the basis of a civil suit. It states, in part:

> §240.45 Criminal nuisance. A person is guilty of criminal nuisance when: (1) By conduct either unlawful in itself or unreasonable under all the circumstances, he knowingly or recklessly creates or maintains a condition which endangers the safety or health of a considerable number of persons; . . . Criminal nuisance is a class B misdemeanor. [Punishable by up to three months imprisonment and/or a fine of up to $500.]

Few civil suits are brought under §240.45 because the requirement that the nuisance affect "a considerable number of people" is not met. Also, district and county attorneys and other prosecuting officials are reluctant to indict except for the most serious "criminal" NOISE pollution. However, a number of cases were serious enough to reach the highest court of New York. In the *Rubenfeld* case[14] (which is just as applicable to civil suits as to criminal ones brought under the statute), the accused ran a catering establishment in upper Manhattan where dances, weddings, and other entertainments began in the early evening and often continued until dawn. Frequently, the guests danced to the music of three large bands, and in the glib words of Judge Benjamin Cardozo, "the sounds of revelry by night, to the accompaniment of drums and brasses, assail the quiet of the vicinage." In upholding the conviction of Rubenfeld, it was shown that the NOISE which he created affected enough people to be delineated a "considerable number." The renowned and witty jurist remarked in these words:

> Long ago it was adjudged that one dwelling in a city who with the aid of a speaking trumpet made great noises in the night time to the disturbance of the neighborhood, must answer to the King . . .

[14]People v. Rubenfeld, 254, N.Y. 245, 1930.

> The precedent is not one to be hastily renounced in days when trumpets have a power unknown to a simpler age. . . .
>
> We have gone back to early days, but not for dearth of modern instances. . . .
>
> The organs of smell and hearing, assailed by sounds and odors too pungent to be borne, have been ever favored of the law, . . . more conspicuously, it seems, than sight, which perhaps is more inured to what is ugly or disfigured . . . . Even so, the test for all the senses, for sight as well as smell and hearing, has been the effect of the offensive practice upon the reasonable man or woman of average sensibilities. . . . One of the unsettled questions of the law is the extent to which the concept of nuisance may be enlarged by legislation so as to give protection to sensibilities that are merely cultural or aesthetic. The question need not be answered to decide the case at hand.
>
> We think the area of this tumult, the range of its disturbing power, is wide enough to bring it within the category of an offense to the community, or so the triers of the facts might find. Here is something more than an interference with a single dwelling or even two or three. Here is tumult so great, if the witnesses are to be credited, as to be a plague to a whole neighborhood.

This requirement under a *public* nuisance statute of a "considerable number" of individuals being effected by the NOISE is unnecessary in a *private* nuisance action. Most states have public nuisance statutes which are similar to New York's, and the probability of success in a civil suit is equally remote. One Brooklynite, in an attempt to circumvent the requirement of the New York State law, found a New York City anti-noise ordinance which referred only to the conduct of an individual. The victim relied upon governmental officials to bring the lawsuit, to wit, the District Attorney of Brooklyn. In *People v. Arknow,*[15] the victim, a neighbor of Sam Arknow, became so enraged at the NOISE made by the three-quarter ton air-conditioner installed in a window of the Arknow home that he convinced the Brooklyn District Attorney's office to charge Arknow with violation of a section of the New York City Administrative Code entitled "Unnecessary noises prohibited." The air-conditioner, which was a nationally known residential type, was in good working order and its sound similar to that made by countless thousands of

[15]204 Misc. 635, Magistrate's Co., Brooklyn, N.Y. 1953.

similar air conditioners. The applicable part of the New York City Code stated: "The creation of any unreasonably loud, disturbing and unnecessary noise is prohibited. Noise of such character, intensity and duration as to be detrimental to the life or health of any individual is prohibited." But the New York Court, held that Arknow did *not* violate the statute and dismissed the indictment.

> A person who resides in the centre of a large city must not expect to be surrounded by the stillness which prevails in a rural district." . . . "No one is entitled to absolute quiet in the enjoyment of his property; he may only insist upon a degree of quietness consistent with the standard of comfort prevailing in the locality in which he dwells."
>
> The air-conditioning machine is a product of man's constant search for the improvement of his own comfort and enjoyment of life. That its use may cause some annoyance to others does not justify denouncing its use as criminal. It is an unfortunate truth that virtually every scientific invention has carried with it not only advantages but burdens. The airplane, invented for the purpose of speeding transportation, has become the principal weapon of inflicting death in war. The automobile, designed for man's pleasure, has become the most destructive peacetime weapon. And so it is with many other inventions.
>
> Unfortunately, progress is not marked by a straight line in a constant forward direction, but rather by a zig-zag course, only the ultimate direction of which is clearly marked. A conviction in this case would not only ignore the way pointed out by firmly established principles in the law of nuisance, but would constitute a vain attempt to arrest scientific progress.
>
> No doubt the manufacturers of air-conditioning units are aware of the desirability and necessity of producing their machines in such manner as to render them as noiseless as is consistently possible with their efficient operation. No doubt the course of time will result in progress in that direction.
>
> The present case involves the operation of a properly functioning air-conditioning unit. Another question would be presented if, due to defective construction or disrepair, the unit were to be excessively noisy.
>
> The court finds that the operation of the defendant's air-conditioning unit did not create an 'unreasonably loud' noise within the meaning of section 435-5.0 of the Administrative Code, and does not constitute a public nuisance. The complaint is accordingly dismissed.

The Magistrate wrongly equated the requirements of the public nuisance statute with the elements necessary in a private nuisance action. Specifically, the unusual sensitivity of the victim and the requirement of an abnormal invasion are necessary, although in this case, unlike the *Rubenfeld* decision, there was no problem in respect to the number of people affected. It is quite possible that if the victim had been complaining about a more serious type of NOISE pollution, one which would most probably have been heard and been annoying to many people, the result may have been different.

Thus, the remedy of a private action nuisance, whether through the common law or public statute, is at best an unpredictable course of action, replete with the complexities and nuances of "judge-made law" and lack of substantial statutory guidance. If NOISE pollution is to be affirmatively abated and the "din" merchants and other purveyors of unwanted and unnecessary sounds be stilled, the law of nuisance must be expanded and updated so that it may become an effective weapon in the arsenal of our fight to save our environment.

QUESTIONS FOR REVIEW

1. Why has the problem of NOISE pollution drawn so little commentary from scholars, politicians, public interest groups, and other generally concerned individuals and organizations? Give examples of the neglect of the problem of NOISE pollution.
2. What are the two methods whereby NOISE pollution may be eliminated or abated, and what does proceeding by each of these two methods entail?
3. What is the definition of "nuisance?" Give examples of NOISE as a nuisance.
4. What criteria do the courts use in differentiating abnormal from normal NOISE invasions? Give examples of abnormal and normal invasions.
5. Why must NOISE be considered offensive to the "average and reasonable man" to constitute a nuisance? Give examples of such NOISE.

6. What is the most difficult problem a pollutee must overcome to succeed in a private nuisance suit?
7. Discuss the necessity of an "interest in the use of the land" as a requirement for a private nuisance suit.
8. What is the definition of a "public nuisance?" Give examples of NOISES which may constitute public nuisances.
9. What is the "special damage" that must be present for a NOISE victim to recover by means of a civil suit under a public nuisance statute?
10. Differentiate civil suits under public nuisance statutes and under Common Law private nuisance.

Chapter 12

THE PRAYER AMENDMENT: PRESERVATION AND PROTECTION OF RELIGIOUS FREEDOM AND FREEDOM FROM RELIGION

IN OUR MULTISECTARIAN American Society, there is a need to preserve and protect religious freedom as well as freedom from religion. There is a recurring danger when state institutions exercise their power in behalf of any religious sect or in behalf of religious sects generally, or to the detriment of those who espouse no religion. Religious commitment and religious training must remain free from government influence or coercion. Prayer and/or devotional Bible reading in public schools is but one aspect of this threat to religious freedom and freedom from religion guaranteed by the First Amendment.

In 1963, the United States Supreme Court stated unequivocally that the First Amendment, to wit, "Congress shall make no law respecting the establishment of religion nor the free exercise thereof," must be interpreted as prohibiting the state or government from establishing prayer and Bible reading in the public schools. According to the court in *Arlington School Board v. Schempp,*[1] which outlawed a Pennsylvania law requiring the reading of at least ten lines from the Bible daily, religious proceedings of any kind in public schools were unconstitutional because they tended to "coerce" students to take part and thus violated the First Amendment's prohibition against "an establishment of religion" by an agency of the government. (This business of public schools arranging sectarian religious ceremonies is not new. There were riots leading to the burning of two churches and a convent in Pennsylvania in 1843

[1]374 U.S. 203, 1963.

when Bishop Francis Kendrick of Philadelphia asked the school board of that city to allow Catholic children to read from the Catholic rather than the King James version of the Bible where Bible reading was required.) No sooner than the ink was dry on that court opinion, the late Senator Everett Dirksen of Illinois proposed an amendment to the United States Constitution which would permit "voluntary" prayer in the public schools. In 1966, the Subcommittee on Constitutional Amendments of the Senate Judiciary Committee held hearings which were bitterly monopolized by small but highly vocal groups seeking to impose their religious practices upon others through the media of the public school. In essence, their proposal read as follows:

> Nothing in this Constitution shall be deemed to prohibit the offering of prayers or Biblical scriptures if participation therein is on a *voluntary* basis in governmental or public school institutions, etc., etc.
>
> Nothing in this Constitution shall be deemed to prohibit reference to reliance upon belief in or invocation of the aid of God, or a supreme being in any governmental or public document, proceeding, activity, ceremony, school, etc.
>
> Nothing in this article shall constitute an establishment of religion.

Advocates of the "amendment" argued: What is wrong with the Commandment to pray to God daily—collectively—in a major area of daily assembly for children *if* the parents of children *voluntarily* desire that they do so? They ask: How does this act do violence to the historic and valuable concept of separation of church and state? Was not this concept related to control of organized religion over state? Or vice versa? All this "amendment" asks for is permission to pray at the beginning of the school day if one desires. These groups point out that no one can seriously believe that the presence of children reciting a nondenominational prayer—or at least one acceptable to all religions—does damage to those children who desire not to pray? Affirmatively, these "prayer" advocates delineate the long history of prayer in the public schools attended by persons who did not join in the prayer. They point to the lack of any record of undesirable results arising from this practice. As a matter of fact, they contend, the public school system came into existence after the First Amendment was enacted; and today practically all schools have had a measure of religious ceremonials and practice. Furthermore, what can damage us as a people is prohibition—prohibition *against* prayer! The public school system is more than an apparatus which provides organized lessons. It is a window on the world for the young; it is the beginning of life's experiences. Is it right to obliterate at this early impressionable stage of life a reminder of and the importance of a Supreme Being, they ask. In a real sense, this issue is not legal but moral. It is not whether we believe prayer in the schools is legal but whether we believe that religion is a force for good in our world. If religion is contaminating, let us by all means abolish it. But since the majority believe that men are helped, *not* corrupted, by religion, it seems incongruous, they contend, that we should consent to sweep God out of our children's daily lives by relegating Him to places that do not pertain to our public business.

Opponents of the "prayer amendment" base their arguments upon the following grounds:

1. Opposition to tampering with the Bill of Rights.
2. Recognition that our public schools must remain neutral and unifying, not divisive because of any religious practices.
3. Not accentuating the "differences" in children when any do not conform with others due to religious commitments.
4. The fact that there is no "nonobjectionable" or "universally acceptable" prayers because prayers are deeply sectarian. It would be interesting to see how prayer can be "nondenominational," for people are still taught their faith, religious observances, and religious rituals through the disciplines of churches, temples and synagogues. Indeed, respect for the mutual differences in the various religions must also include respect for the views of those who profess no religion whatsoever. The place for "denominational prayer" is in the church, the temple, and the synagogue.

Separation of Church and State has been guaranteed under the

Bill of Rights, and tampering with that revered document can only lead to a breakdown of that guarantee of religious freedom and freedom from religion. Our founding fathers created this Nation as an escape from persecution that can result from a State religion. Too much blood has been shed by zealots in every religious group whenever a State became allied with this or that religion. In the 1970's the back-to-the-Bible movement calling for prayers in the public schools is perhaps but a visible symptom of a desire to stop talking and start acting in fundamentalistic terms; it is a reaction to the youth rebellion, crime in the streets, permissive courts, the new self-awareness of minority groups, taxes, welfare, and all other problems or ills of our society. Prayer in the public schools is not a panacea even for one of these problems or ills!

Defiance of the 1963 United States Supreme Court ruling against prayers in public schools has become the order of the day in many communities. In Netcong, New Jersey, for example, the Board of Educataion adopted a resolution in September 1969 providing "that the Superintendent be instructed by the Board of Education to institute prayers in the Netcong schools, forcing no student to pray if unwilling but denying no student the right to pray, details to be worked out by the Board of Education." It was further resolved that: "Members of the clergy from the communities of Netcong and Stanhope be invited to meet with representatives of the Board of Education and compose a suitable prayer for the Board's consideration. In the interim, the Superintendent is instructed to institute 30 seconds of silent meditation until the Board takes further action." On September 10, 1969, the Board rescinded its prior resolution and adopted a new one making available to teachers and students up to five minutes before classes begin for any "who may wish to participate voluntarily in the free exercise of religion as guaranteed by the United States Constitution." The claimed purpose of the new resolution was "not to favor one religion over another nor to favor religion over non-religion but rather to promote love of neighbor, brotherhood . . . and to preserve the values that constitute our American heritage." In a supplementary resolution adopted six days later, the Board authorized the Superintendent of Schools to implement the September 10 resolution by whatever means he considered best. The Superintendent chose to do so only at Netcong High School. Under the procedure he set up, the "voluntary" exercises were conducted in the high school gymnasium five minutes before the start of classes each day. A student volunteer read from the *Congressional Record,* first citing the particular issue being read, and then repeating verbatim the remarks of the Chaplain of the House or the Senate. Such remarks usually included a brief quotation from the Scriptures and a prayer, beginning "In the Redeemer's name we pray." The Attorney General of the State of New Jersey thereafter ruled that the Netcong resolution and the practices under it violated the "establishment clause" of the First Amendment to the United States Constitution, in that, first, reading a prayer from the Congressional Record was clearly a religious observance, i.e. even the Congressional Record referred to the Chaplain's remarks as a "prayer period." Certainly, since the United States Supreme Court found in the *Arlington* case, *above,* that the reading of Bible verses, even without comment, constitutes a religious exercise, Biblical quotations followed by ministers' prayers would clearly fall under that category. (The Attorney General also found that the use of the *Congressional Record* as the source for the readings does not insulate the practice from the constitutional ban. "It is the reading of the prayer and Bible passages that is proscribed, not the source books from which they are taken.") Second, the voluntary nature of the religious observance is no defense, i.e. the real issue "is not whether the child is compelled to attend the service but whether the service exists with the official sanction of school authorities. Third, the Netcong resolution did not satisfy the criterion laid down by the United States Supreme Court, since its "primary purpose was to circumvent the Supreme Court's school prayer decisions and to aid religion generally." The New Jersey Attorney General distinguished the practice at issue from certain state action which has been held constitutional because its primary purpose is child benefit rather than aid to religion. Furthermore, he disposed of the argument that the challenged practice could be considered primarily for the benefit of children since it presumably instills "non-religious moral values". This suggestion, he pointed out, was rejected by the Supreme Court, in the *Arlington* case, "which indicated that if that were truly the purpose, the exercises would not be voluntary."

Obviously the conflict here was between an agency of the state, the Netcong School Board, and individual citizens—perhaps a minority—who believed that the Board's action violated constitutional guarantees designed to protect the rights of religious minorities. It was the Netcong School Board, not private individuals, which, by formal resolution, started the prayer procedure. Consequently, any call for action by "the people" to resist the tyranny of the state is misplaced. The passion for prayer in the public schools in New Jersey did not subside. In 1970, Governor Richard Hughes vetoed a bill authorizing individual teachers and boards of education to conduct a daily "brief period of silent prayer or meditation with the participation of all the pupils therein assembled." (The bill was identical to one he vetoed in 1968). The Governor stated that at best the bill would be a meaningless gesture; at worst it could be construed as another unconstitutional attempt at legislative usurpation of the legitimate function of the courts. The Governor also repeated his prior criticism of requiring the participation of all pupils in the exercise, which adds an objectionable element of religious compulsion.

In 1970, the Attorney General of Massachusetts rendered an opinion declaring unconstitutional the programs of opening prayer instituted by a local school board. A motion passed by the Leyden School Committee provided for a period of up to five minutes to be made available before class instruction begins each school day "to those teachers and students who may wish to participate voluntarily in the free exercise of religion as guaranteed by our United States Constitution." The practice was administered by having the Bible read by a teacher in the Leyden Elementary School, or by a volunteer chosen by her, or by having the Lord's Prayer recited under the teacher's supervision. Students were advised that they could choose whether or not to participate in these exercises. According to the Massachusetts Attorney General, the "purpose" of these practices was "the advancement or inhibition of religion," and therefore the acts were unconstitutional.

In Oregon, the State Department of Education prepared a set of guidelines on religious matters for the public schools. These guidelines encouraged factual and objective teaching about, rather than of, religion. "Instruction in morality, ethics and values" is advocated, and teachers are told not to "resort to partisan religious sanctions." Although "Bible reading for historical or literary instructional purposes is encouraged," the guidelines forbade requiring prayers in classes or assemblies. In general, Oregon schools may in no way promote or encourage either religion or nonreligion. The "devotional display of religous symbols" is not permitted on public school property. Religious baccalaureate services cannot be made required activities, but students may attend them voluntarily outside of school, on their own time. Although members of religious orders may be hired as teachers, they are not allowed to wear distinctive religious garb while teaching. It would appear that these Oregon guidelines may comply with the mandate of the United States Supreme Court, but until the court decides the issue, the guidelines are but guidelines.

Basic to the issue here is the question Who is to say what is "voluntary?" Are children in public schools the equal of their teachers in terms of decision-making? When schools permit prayers as a school function (official or unofficial), is not the effect on children one of compulsion? As Mr. Justice Felix Frankfurter stated in the *McCollum* case: "Non-conformity is not a virtue of little children." Indeed, how can any school sanctioning a prayer be neutral among and between different religions or to those opposed to religion? Freedom of religion is a *guaranteed* individual freedom, which is to be protected against interference by the state. It is, therefore, not a question of majority view, however overwhelming, verus minority. If a single person's religious freedom or even freedom from religion is denied, everyone's religious freedom is in danger. The First Amendment protects all children from being induced to participate—or embarrassed by not participating—in religious ceremonies alien to their beliefs or those of their parents. It protects them from being nonconformists, which is a highly sensitive emotional element in an impressionable child. While theoretically pupils may be excused from officially scheduled religious exercises, it does not obscure the tacit obligation of attendance and the initiative necessary for the sensitive, immature child to say "no"—to stand at times in the corridor while others participate. Voluntary prayer simply does not exist in this kind of environment for children of public school age.

Essentially, prayer needs an atmosphere of solemnity and reverence; to make prayer a classroom exercise is to demean it and render it meaningless. Many of those who oppose this amendment are truly religious people, but they have a deep feeling that religious belief *should not* be external, mechanical, or official. Indeed, the ancient prophets taught that religion of this nature is sheer idolatry. An official prayer is a contradiction in terms; it might be a religious expression of a sort, but it certainly cannot be one of true devotion. In summary, we must recognize that religion can flourish only so long as it remains purely a matter of *free voluntary* choice and is never subjected to controls or pressures by the State. To every devoutly religious person, an *official* prayer, even one which purports to be voluntary, is a contradiction in terms. Voluntary school prayers sponsored by the State or government coerce and injure children of minority religious groups. In no country in the world is religion as vibrant and dynamic a force for truth and good as it is in the United States. This is due to the fact that the religious clauses of the First Amendment have enjoined neutrality with respect to *all matters* of religion.

Religious instructions and devotions belong in the church, the synagogue, the mosque, and the home, and not in the public school. Prayer must come from the heart and not from the deliberations of any school board. The late President Kennedy correctly saw the United States Supreme Court's decision in *Arlington, above,* as a challenge to all of us within the realm of religion to strengthen prayer and religious education in our homes and places of worship. The worst thing that could happen to the houses of worship in this land would be to undermine their sacred role and their integrity by developing in the public schools an American "public school religion," which would not be identical with any of the three major faiths in America and which would constitute inevitably a set of meaningless, watered-down, nonsectarian platitudes. As the great philosopher and writer George Santayana has said, "religion in general is nothing. What America needs is authentic religious belief and action, which can be transmitted wholly and meaningfully only by each respective religious group in its own unique way." To be meaningful, religion must be taught in its full integrity, with all the emotional and spiritual context of a particular background, tradition, and faith, and with its own regimen of ceremonies and practices. This cannot be done in the public schools without violation to one another of the great religions which constitute the spiritual heritage of this country.

QUESTIONS FOR REVIEW

1. Is there a constitutional ban against recital of prayers in the public schools? Is there a constitutional right of freedom *from* religion?
2. State the substance of the First Amendment in terms of freedom of religion.
3. Can a *private* school legally impose upon its students the recitation of a prayer? Why?
4. State the substance of the so-called Dirksen Prayer Amendment. Is there a definition of "voluntary prayer"?
5. Is there a "nonobjectionable" or "universally acceptable" prayer, according to the courts?
6. What was the thrust of the Netcong, New Jersey "defiance" of the United States Supreme Court. Was it successful?
7. Can the reading of Bible verses in a public school be constitutionally acceptable? Explain.
8. Does the United States Supreme Court find a place for prayer in the home and the church or synagogue?
9. Is there here a price for nonconformity which a child in the public school must pay?
10. How can freedom of prayer best be maintained outside the restraints of government?

Chapter 13

"SEVEN DAYS TO LIFE": LEGAL PENALTIES FOR THE FIRST-TIME POSSESSION OF MARIHUANA[1] IN THE UNITED STATES

"THAT WHICH WE CALL a rose/ By any other name would smell as sweet," and so does *Cannabis*, whether it is called marihuana, hemp, "pot," "grass," "hay," "mary jane," "reefer," "tea," or its related substances or derivatives such as *hashish, kif, ganja, charas,* or *bhang.*[2] It is obvious that the drug marihuana has a universal reputation, but regardless of the name the drug user gives it, everywhere in the United States, the *possession* of marihuana[3] is illegal and punishable by law. In some states, posses-

1Although both "mari*j*uana" and "mari*h*uana" are proper spellings of the word, the orthographers have not as yet universally agreed upon one or the other as the preferred spelling. Therefore, the authors have adopted the orthographic spelling, "marihuana," which is also used by the Federal Government, most state governments, and many of the courts and scholarly authorities cited in the text.

2Other terminology used in the United States to designate marihuana includes: "bo," "boo," "bu," "dooby," "dubie," "duby," "charge," "gage," "gauge," "gangster," "green," "jay," "mezz," "mota," "muta," and "snop." Words and phrases denoting marihuana outside of the United States includes: *anascha, banj, blang, canamo, chanvre, charras, churrus, ciemba, dagga, diamba, djamba, numo, haium, heigum, hjemu, kaal, keif, las tres, l'herbe, liamba, machoma, maconha, ma jen, manteca, mata kwane, ma-yo, mbangi, mbanzhe, mota, moto, moto kwano, mo-tul, njagd, rongony, setol, shira, snstanga, ssruma, takouri, vongony, yamba, yerba,* and *yerba santa.* For other terms, see the Appendix to John Rosevear's *Pot, A Handbook of Marihuana,* New Hyde Park, N.Y. University Books, Inc., 1967), a work cited by the United States Supreme Court in *Leary* v. *U.S.* [395 U.S. 6, 1969].

3Goodman and Gilman *The Pharmacological Basis of Therapeutics,* 3rd ed., New York, Macmillan, 1969, define marihuana as a form of common hemp and a herbaceous annual plant of which *Cannabis sativa* (L.) is the sole species and *Cannabis indica* and *Cannabis americana* are varieties: "The resinous exudate of the tips of the female plant contain most of the active ingredients," the most active of which is *tetrahydrocannabinol.*

sion of marihuana is punishable with far greater severity than in other states, e.g. Nebraska declares a first conviction for the possession of less than one-twentieth of an ounce of marihuana to be punishable by incarceration in the county jail for seven days, in contrast with Texas, where the hapless criminal, convicted for the identical offense, can be imprisoned in a state penitentiary for LIFE!

Since the 1930's, the possession of marihuana has been illegal, notwithstanding that from earliest colonial times not only had hemp been legal but its cultivation as a cash crop for use in the manufacture of rope and other products was encouraged in the United States. In the diary of George Washington, there is an entry dated August, 1765, concerning the separation of the male and female hemp plants, thus attesting to our first President's knowledge or familiarity with marihuana in its cultivated form. Marihuana's history, however, is ancient, extending back nearly fifty centuries to 2737 B.C. when the pharmacopoeia of the legendary Chinese Emperor Shen Nung was written. This oriental potentate described *Cannabis* as a medicine for treating "female weaknesses, gout, rheumatism, malaria, beri-beri, constipation, and absentmindedness," diseases and conditions for which *Cannabis* was not again prescribed until thousands of years later. Other authenticated antediluvian references to hemp either as a medicine, a fiber, or an intoxicant appear in Sanskrit, Egyptian, Assyrian, Greek, Scythian, and Thracian documents and artifacts. Some scholars even claim that King Solomon referred to hemp in the "Song of Songs" and that the blind poet Homer sang of it in his epic "The Odyssey." Throughout the Roman Empire (both before and after the start of the Christian era), hemp was widely known and widely used as a fiber for making clothing, sails, and rope. Latin writers such as Lucilius and Pliny wrote of the plant's medicinal as well as its commercial properties. Arab physicians used hemp for curing various and sundry ills that beset their patients, and the Italian explorer and adventurer, Marco Polo, wrote of the use of hemp by Hasan-ibn-Sabah, the infamous "Old Man of the Mountains," and the leader of the equally infamous "Assassins." (Marco Polo claimed that Hasan-ibn-Sabah used the plant as an intoxicant to imbue his followers with undying devotion by conjuring up visions of paradise with potions made from the substance.)

The Spanish conquistadores found hemp growing in the New World, particularly in Mexico and Chile, and English boatwrights of the same era used hemp to make ropes for the riggings of the British ships that eventually defeated the Spaniards and "ruled the waves." Furthermore, England's King James I in the early 17th century instructed settlers in the American colonies to raise hemp along with other production such as "iron, cordage, flax, silkgrass, pitch, tar, potash, soap, ashes, timber, salt, and wine," so as to increase the commercial value of these settlements for the Crown. It was also the British who, in 1893, made the first significant scholarly study of the hemp plant when it created the India Hemp Commission to examine the scientific properties, preparation, cultivation, and uses of the plant, as well as effective methods for its control. In an exhaustive two-year project, this Commission gathered evidence from 1,193 witnesses including 335 physicians, peasants, tax collectors, yogis, army officers, fakirs, hemp dealers, and clergymen; it also gleaned data from court proceedings and from every mental hospital in British India. The India Hemp Commission's findings, which were published in a report with six volumes of appendices, included the following excerpt from its recommendations:

I. Total prohibition of the cultivation of the hemp plant for narcotics, and of the manufacture, sale, or use of the drugs derived from it, is neither necessary nor expedient in consideration of their ascertained effects, of the prevalence of the habit of using them, of the social and religious feeling on the subject, and of the possibility of its driving the consumers to have recourse to other stimulants or narcotics which may be more deleterious.

II. The policy advocated is one of control and restriction, aimed at suppressing the excessive use and restraining the moderate use within due limits.

III. The means to be adopted for the attainment of these objects are:
(a) adequate taxation;
(b) prohibiting cultivation, except under license, and centralizing cultivation;
(c) limiting the number of shops;

(d) limiting the extent of legal possession;

IV. The method adopted should be systematic and as far as possible uniform for the whole of British India, and it is advisable that this method should be suggested for adoption by certain of the Native States.

V. A Government monopoly of production and sale is not recommended for practical reasons, though there is no theoretical objection to it.

VI. For the purpose of adequately taxing consumption, the combination of a direct duty with the auction of the privilege of vend is ordinarily the best method.

VII. When sufficient provision has been made for restricting consumption of the drugs by the means above detailed, there should be as little interference as possible on the part of the Government with their distribution.

These recommendations essentially stated that it was imprudent to criminalize the manufacture, sale, or use of hemp but called upon the government to control its excessive use by taxing, licensing, and limiting its sale and the amount of legal possession. The Commission also found no evidence that hemp or *Cannabis* caused mental or moral injuries or disease if used in moderation as an intoxicant, the drug's principal use in British India.

In the United States, however, the utilization of *Cannabis* for its intoxicating effects had little impact until the first two decades of the 20th century. During this time, Mexican laborers in large numbers crossed into the Southwest[4] and their use of marihuana to get "high" soon spread and became a growing fad in the bustling city of New Orleans. According to John Rosevear in *Pot, A Handbook of Marihuana,* the city in 1926

> was 'soaked' with the weed, from the criminal set to the social elite. Clumps of marihuana began appearing as a weed in many parts of the southwest. The habit of smoking the stuff went up the Mississippi River via steamboats, and in 1930 there was hardly a major city in the United States that did not have a few smokers.

Within three years, when the Depression hit the United States, many out-of-work, disheartened, and deprived Americans (es-

[4]Many authorities believe that the term "marihuana" in fact derives from the Mexican and Spanish names for "Mary and Jane," Maria y Juana.

pecially those of the lower classes living in ghettoes) learned about this easily cultivated, intoxicating plant which was far cheaper than alcohol. At the same time, the Federal Government learned about marihuana and decided to embark upon a campaign to ban the drug. Perhaps it was the newly revived liquor lobby, fearful of losing customers to the new euphoriant that prompted the Government to act;[5] or it may have been more personal, and prohibitory activties were begun at the behest of the Chief of the Federal Narcotics Bureau, as well as disappointed "drys" who lamented "repeal," but for whatever reason, a campaign was launched to ban marihuana. Marihuana was headlined by the press as a new and dreaded "menace" to society. Not only did it cause crime, murder, insanity, depravity, and every imaginable disease, but marihuana also was deemed to be detrimental to the existence and morality of the middle-class family who typified the American society of that day. Yet few members of the middle class had ever seen or heard of marihuana until these lurid stories began appearing in newspapers and magazines. David Solomon wrote in his "Editor's Forward" to *The Marijuana Papers* (New York, Bobbs-Merrill, 1966) that "Americans were sold a mythological bill of goods" because they were:

> deprived of the facts and primed on hysteria-provoking, apocryphal horror stories given to the press by the Federal Bureau of Narcotics. . . . They were told that marihuana was a 'killer drug' that triggered crimes of violence and acts of sexual excess; a toxic agent capable of driving normal persons into fits of madness and depraved behavior; a destroyer of the will; a satanically destructive drug which, employing lures of euphoria and heightened sensuality, visited physical degeneration and chronic psychosis upon the habitual user.
>
> The most unprincipled aspect of this yellow journalism played upon the public's concern for the health and safety of their children: front-page headlines and feature articles in popular magazines such as the now defunct *Literary Digest* depicted insidious pushers selling marihuana everywhere, including in high schools throughout

[5]The Eighteenth Amendment to the Constitution, called the Volstead Act, which ushered in the era of Prohibition in 1919, was repealed by the Twenty-first Amendment in 1933.

> the nation, thus precipitating wild orgies and outbursts of crime and violence.

The Federal Narcotics Bureau then proposed to Congress the enactment of an anti-marihuana law to stop the spread of the "drug." This bill, which finally reached the House of Representatives' Ways and Means Committee, was labeled the Marihuana Tax Act of 1937. Curiously, it did not ban the possession or use of the plant outright but taxed its possession and sale. The statutory scheme involved (a) a tax on the transfer of the plant and (b) an occupational use tax (similar to a liquor license tax) upon those who dealt with the plant. Thus an individual transferee who failed to pay the applicable tax violated the law and was liable for the same penalties as someone violating the Harrison Narcotic Act (which outlawed the use and possession of "hard" drugs); to wit: five years imprisonment, a fine of 2,000 dollars, or both. The purpose of the new legislation, according to Clinton M. Hester, the Assistant General Counsel for the Department of the Treasury, in his statement before the House Committee, was:

> to employ the Federal taxing power not only to raise revenue from the marihuana traffic, but also to discourage the current and widespread undesirable use of marihuana by smokers and drug addicts and thus drive the traffic into channels where the plant will be put to valuable industrial, medical, and scientific uses. In accomplishing this general purpose, two objectives should dictate the form of the proposed legislation; first, the development of a scheme of taxation which would raise revenue and which would also render virtually impossible the acquisition of marihuana by persons who would put it to illicit uses without unduly interfering with the use of the plant for industrial, medical, and scientific purposes; and, second, the development of an adequate means of publicizing dealings in marihuana in order that the traffic may be effectively taxed and controlled.

Similarly, the Senate Subcommittee, in a more concise statement, regarded the purpose of the new legislation to be the employment of "the Federal taxing power to raise revenue by imposing occupational and transfer taxes upon dealers in marihuana and to discourage the widespread use of the drug by smokers and drug addicts." The taxing and revenue-raising purposes of the Act were a "smoke screen" to bring marihuana under the same laws as "hard" narcotics (such as heroin, cocaine, and morphine) and absolutely prohibit its possession and use. But the Congressmen had heard little first-hand factual evidence as to the nature of and abuses caused by the marihuana plant. They relied, for the most part, on the often unsupported and sometimes dubious statements of major proponents of the law. Commissioner Harry J. Anslinger of the Federal Narcotics Bureau, for example, in his testimony before the House Ways and Means Committee, became involved in the following repartee:[6]

MR. ANSLINGER. It is only in the last 2 years that we had a report of seizures anywhere but in the Southwest. Last year (1936) New York State reported 195 tons seized, whereas before that I do not believe that New York could have reported 1 ton seized.

Let me quote from this report to the League of Nations:

"The discussion disclosed that from the medical point of view in some countries the use of Indian hemp in its various forms is regarded as in no way indispensable and that it is therefore possible that little objection would be raised to drafting limitations upon medical use of derivatives."

That is only last year.

Here is what Dr. J. Bouquet, hospital pharmacist at Tunis, and inspector of pharmacists at Tunis, says. He is the outstanding expert on *Cannabis* in the world. He says:

"To sum up, Indian hemp, like many other medicaments, had enjoyed for a time a vogue which is not justified by the results obtained. Therapeutics would not lose much if it were removed from the list of medicaments."

That comes from the greatest authority on cannabis in the world today.

MR. McCORMACK. What are its first manifestations, a feeling of grandeur and self-exaltation, and things of that sort?

MR. ANSLINGER. It affects different individuals in different ways. Some individuals have a complete loss of a sense of time or a sense of value. They lose the sense of place. They have an increased feeling of physical strength and power.

Some people will fly into a delirious rage, and they are temporarily irresponsible and may commit violent crimes. Other people will laugh uncontrollably. It is impossible to say what the

[6]Messrs. McCormack, Reed, and Lewis, were Congressmen and members of the House Ways and Means Committee.

effect will be on any individual. Those research men who have tried it have always been under control. They have always insisted upon that.

MR. McCORMACK. Is it used by the criminal class?

MR. ANSLINGER. Yes, it is. It is dangerous to the mind and body and particularly dangerous to the criminal type because it releases all of the inhibitions.

I have here statements by the foremost expert in the world talking on this subject and by Dr. Cutter, a noted and distinguished medical man in this country.

The statements referred to are as follows, from the report by Dr. J. Bouquet, Tunis, to League of Nations

"Does Indian hemp (*Cannabis sativa*) in its various forms give rise to drug addiction?

The use of cannabis, whether smoked or ingested in its various forms, undoubtedly gives rise to a form of addiction, which has serious social consequences—abandonment of work, propensity to theft and crime, disappearance of reproductive power . . .

MR. REED. The testimony before the committee of which I was formerly chairman in reference to heroin said in reference to the effect of it that it made men feel fearless and that a great majority of the crimes of great violence that were committed were committed by addicts, and one man stated that it would make a rabbit fight a bulldog. Does this drug have a similar effect?

MR. ANSLINGER. Here is a gang of seven young men, all seven of them young men under 21 years of age. They terrorized central Ohio for more than two months, and they were responsible for 38 stick-ups. They all boast they did those crimes while under the influence of marihuana.

MR. LEWIS. Was that as an excuse, or a defense?

MR. ANSLINGER. No, sir.

MR. LEWIS. Does it strengthen the criminal will; does it operate as whiskey might, to provoke recklessness?

MR. ANSLINGER. I think it makes them irresponsible. A man does not know what he is doing. It has not been recognized as a defense by the courts, although it has been used as a defense.

MR. LEWIS. Probably the word 'excuse' or 'mitigation' would be better than defense, I think.

MR. ANSLINGER. Here is one of the worst cases I have seen. The district attorney told me the defendant in this case pleaded that he was under the influence of marihuana when he committed that crime, but that has not been recognized.

We have several cases of that kind. There was one town in Ohio where a young man went into a hotel and held up the clerk and killed him, and his defense was that he had been affected by the use of marihuana.

The Senate Subcommittee, during its hasty consideration of the anti-marihuana legislation, also faced up to substantially unsupported material, such as the following statement addressed to the Subcommittee:

> Marihuana is also used illicitly by smoking it in crudely prepared cigarettes, which are readily procurable in almost all parts of the country at prices ranging from 10 to 25 cents each. Under the influence of this drug the will is destroyed and all power of directing and controlling thought is lost. Inhibitions are released. As a result of these effects, many violent crimes have been and are being committed by persons under the influence of this drug. Not only is marihuana used by hardened criminals to steel them to commit violent crimes but it is also being placed in the hands of high-school children in the form of marihuana cigarettes by unscrupulous peddlers. Its continued use results many times in impotency and insanity.

Incredible as it seems, the lawmakers in 1937 simply had no grasp of the realities of the situation.

The only witness before either the House or Senate seriously opposing the Act, other than a group of manufacturers who used hemp in their industries, was Dr. William C. Woodward of the American Medical Association. As a physician and as an attorney, Dr. Woodward strongly attacked Commissioner Anslinger's hearsay statements, only to meet derision and antagonism from the House Ways and Means Committee. Dr. Woodward stated that the legislation was too hastily conceived and that scientifically supportable studies were needed before Congress should pass such a law. He also observed:

> That there is a certain amount of narcotic addiction of an objectionable character no one will deny. The newspapers have called attention to it so prominently that there must be some grounds for their statements. It has surprised me, however, that the facts on which these statements have been based have not been brought before this committee by competent primary evidence. We are referred to newspaper publications concerning the prevalence of marihuana addiction. We are told that the use of marihuana causes crime.
>
> But yet no one has been produced from the Bureau of Prisons

to show the number of prisoners who have been found addicted to the marihuana habit. An informal inquiry shows that the Bureau of Prisons has no evidence on that point.

You have been told that school children are great users of marihuana cigarettes. No one has been summoned from the Children's Bureau to show the nature and extent of the habit among children.

Inquiry of the Children's Bureau shows that they have had no occasion to investigate it and know nothing particularly of it.

Inquiry of the Office of Education—and they certainly should know something of the prevalence of the habit among the school children of the country, if there is a prevalent habit—indicates that they have had no occasion to investigate and know nothing of it.

Moreover, there is in the Treasury Department itself, the Public Health Service, with its Division of Mental Hygiene. The Division of Mental Hygiene was, in the first place, the Division of Narcotics. It was converted into the Division of Mental Hygiene, I think, about 1930. That particular Bureau has control at the present time of the narcotics farms that were created about 1929 or 1930 and came into operation a few years later. No one has been summoned from that Bureau to give evidence on that point.

Informal inquiry by me indicates that they have had no record of any marihuana or *Cannabis* addicts who have ever been committed to those farms.

The Bureau of the Public Health Service has also a division of pharmacology. If you desire evidence as to the pharmacology of *Cannabis,* that obviously is the place where you can get direct and primary evidence, rather than the indirect hearsay evidence.

Notwithstanding Dr. Woodward's logic and reason and his disclosures of the precise information that Congress should consider prior to passage of this law, the House Committee completely ignored him. The hysteria of the press and the public outcry was too demanding for a leisurely study of marihuana. Both Houses of Congress passed the Marihuana Tax Act and President Franklin D. Roosevelt signed the bill into law on August 2, 1937.

As ill-conceived as the new law was, and as unremittingly harsh as the penalty was for violation, the heinous "Regulations No. 1 Relating to the Importation, Manufacture, Production, Compounding, Sale, Dealing in, Dispensing, Prescribing, Administering, and Giving Away of Marihuana Under the Act of August 2, 1937" went far beyond logic and reason. These Treasury

Regulations, promulgated under Section 14 of the Marihuana Tax Act, contained more than 60 pages of administrative and enforcement procedures by the Bureau of Narcotics. If there had been any question concerning the prohibition of the possession of marihuana, "Regulations No. 1" answered the question in a manner that labeled the substance as being as dangerous and illegal as heroin, cocaine, and morphine!

Although the Marihuana Tax Act of 1937 had an observable impact upon the public, it was not the first law passed in the United States which outlawed the possession and use of marihuana. Between 1932 and 1937, 46 states had passed a piece of legislation called the Uniform Drug Act; and Pennsylvania and California passed drug laws which were substantially similar. This Uniform Drug Act, which referred to narcotics in general, also included the following definition of *Cannabis*:

> "*Cannabis*" includes all parts of the plant *Cannabis sativa l.*, whether growing or not; the seeds thereof; the resin extracted from any part of such plant; and every compound, manufacture, salt, derivative, mixture, or preparation of such plant, its seeds, or resin; but shall not include the mature stalks of such plant, fiber produced from such stalks, oil or cake made from the seeds of such plant, any other compound, manufacture, salt, derivative, mixture or preparation of such mature stalks (except the resin extracted therefrom), fiber, oil, or cake, or the sterilized seed of such plant which is incapable of germination.

The Uniform Drug Act defined "Narcotic Drugs" as including:

> Coca leaves, opium, *Cannabis,* and every other substance neither chemically nor physically distinguishable from them; any other drugs to which the Federal Narcotic Laws may now apply; and any drug found by the (State Commissioner of Health or other competent state officer), after reasonable notice and opportunity for hearing, to have an addiction-forming or addiction-sustaining liability similar to morphine or cocaine, from the effective date of determination of such finding by said (State Commissioner of Health or other competent state officer). (Emphasis added).

Thus, marihuana, which for 5,000 years had been known and used in varying ways by civilized man, was summarily classified as a narcotic drug along with other substances which for centuries had been known to the world as "killer drugs."

But the Uniform Drug Act did not provide a specific penalty provision for violation of the statute because "punishments were left to the individual states, so that each might better fit the Act to meet its laws and constitution." There naturally arose an enormous disparity in the punishment meted out to offenders in the various states. While the federal law, to wit, the Marihuana Tax Act of 1937, required the *same* punishment throughout the United States, i.e. a minimum of five years imprisonment and a 2,000 dollar fine, or both, state penalties ran the gamut from misdemeanors punishable by penal servitude of less than one year to sentences of life imprisonment.

During the next forty years, i.e. 1932 to 1971, penalties for possession of marihuana not only continued to vary greatly from state to state but also varied greatly from year to year within a given state. After World War II, due to the exposure of our Armed Forces to drugs, as well as to foreign cultures which had accepted narcotics for the alleviation of pain or for intoxication, penalties for possession of drugs were increased. Since marihuana was treated like morphine, cocaine, or heroin under the Uniform Drug Act, its possession also become subject to harsher penalties. The vacillating trend continued into the early and mid-1950's. Indeed, the few federal figures available concerning arrests for possession of marihuana most strikingly demonstrate the seesaw tendency of marihuana law enforcement. In 1952, there were 1,300 marihuana arrests made by federal authorities, while this number dipped to 169 in 1960. In the 1960's, however, the birth of the so-called "hippie" and "drug" cultures prompted heavier penalties for possession of drugs and more stringent enforcement. Arrests for possession of marihuana rose to 7,000 in 1964 and 15,000 in 1966, thus attesting to the increased federal vigilance.

Perhaps Nebraska is the state with the most lenient law, calling for seven-day punishment of a first offender possessing less than eight ounces of marihuana (or less than 25 marihuana cigarettes). Chapter 197, Section 3(1) of the Nebraska Session Laws of 1969 states:

> A person knowingly and unlawfully possessing cannabis . . . shall upon conviction thereof, be imprisoned in the county jail

> for seven days separate and apart from other prisoners for the first offense; and upon conviction of a second or subsequent offense shall be imprisoned in the Nebraska Penal and Correctional Complex not less than one year nor more than five years; *Provided,* it shall not be unlawful for an owner or lessee of land to possess *Cannabis* growing thereon in its natural state and not cultivated or harvested.

Nebraska's 1943 law, repealed in 1969, had provided that the first offender who possessed marihuana would be imprisoned for no less than two nor more than five years or fined any amount up to 3,000 dollars, or both. The 1969 statute is more enlightened, especially with respect to the requirements that the marihuana offender be segregated from other criminals. In this respect, the new law is probably indicative of the direction in which modern jurisprudence is going, howsoever slowly, in terms of the punishment for minor violations of marihuana laws.

The most severe penalty imposed upon the marihuana offender is found in the law of the Lone Star State, Texas. A first offender convicted of possession of *any* amount of marihuana under Vernon's Annotated Penal Code, Article 725b, Section 23, is guilty:

> . . . of a felony, and upon a first conviction is punishable by imprisonment in the penitentiary for not less than two years nor more than life; and upon a second or subsequent conviction, he is punishable by imprisonment in the penitentiary for not less than ten years nor more than life. Suspended sentence or probation under the Adult Probation and Parole Law is not available to a person upon a second or subsequent conviction.

Thus, a Texas criminal convicted of violation of the marihuana law of Texas must be sentenced to a minimum of two years in prison and can even be sentenced to life imprisonment. As a practical matter, possession of a small amount of marihuana will generally not result in the invocation of the maximum penalty, although under Texas law, there is no restriction if the jury so desires to impose the maximum penalty. In the case of *Garcia v. State,*[6] Anastacio Garcia was convicted of illegal possession of marihuana. Two San Antonio narcotics detectives gave testi-

---

[6]316 SW2d 735, 1958.

mony that they found a paper bag under his shirt containing 111 gm of marihuana (less than four ounces). The lower Texas court found Garcia guilty and sentenced him to life imprisonment, and the Court of Criminal Appeals of Texas affirmed, holding that the jury had acted properly:

> Their [defendant and his attorneys] principal grounds for reversal grow out of the alleged excessiveness of the punishment. The Legislature of this State, by Article 725b, Section 23, which became effective April 24, 1957, Vernon's Ann.P.C., provided a punishment of not less than two (2) nor more than life for a first offender of the narcotics law. This Court has presently reaffirmed the rule which has long existed in this State to the effect that if the punishment is within that prescribed by the statute it is beyond the province of this Court to pass on the question as to whether the evidence is sufficient to support a punishment greater than the minimum. These matters we must necessarily leave to the wisdom of the Legislature and the jury which tried the case.

Similarly, in *Martinez v. State,*[7] Raymond Benjie Martinez was convicted of dropping a partially smoked marihuana cigarette into a paper cup. He was sentenced to 25 years' imprisonment. In upholding the constitutionality of the Texas statute, the same Court said, "The cases cited [by defendant's attorney] furnish no authority for striking down the statute which provides life as the maximum punishment for the unlawful possession of a narcotic drug." In another case involving the same crime of possession of marihuana, *Trevino v. State,*[8] the Texas Court of Criminal Appeals again stated: "The offense is the unlawful possession of marihuana; the punishment [is] 90 years. . . . The punishment assessed, being within the limits authorized by the statute, was for the jury [to decide]."

Draconian laws of this sort notwithstanding, the President's Commission on Law Enforcement in 1967 published a comprehensive survey of federal criminal laws, *The Challenge of Crime in a Free Society—A Report by the President's Commission On Law Enforcement and Administration of Justice.*

7373 SW2d 246, 1963.
8380 SW2d 118, 1963.

In Chapter 8, entitled "Narcotics and Drug Abuse," there is a reference to a previous Presidential Commission which had recommended that the sentencing judge should have full discretion as to all marihuana offenses. The 1967 President's Commission, approved the prior recommendation, also recommended that "state and Federal drug laws should give a large enough measure of discretion to the courts and correctional authorities to enable them to deal flexibly with violators, taking account of the nature and seriousness of the offense, the prior record of the offender and other relevant circumstances." In fulfillment of the Commission's suggestions, President Nixon signed into law, on October 26, 1970, a new "Comprehensive Drug Abuse Prevention and Control Act," which completely revised the federal narcotic and drug laws. The new law is more flexible and has less severe penalties than the Marihuana Tax Act of 1937, which has been repealed. Section 404, for example, which deals with marihuana possession, along with possession of other "controlled substances" states:

PENALTY FOR SIMPLE POSSESSION; CONDITIONAL DISCHARGE AND EXPUNGING OF RECORDS FOR FIRST OFFENSE

Sec. 404. (a) It shall be unlawful for any person knowingly or intentionally to possess a controlled substance unless such substance was obtained directly, or pursuant to a valid prescription or order, from a practitioner, while acting in the course of his professional practice, or except as otherwise authorized by this title or title III. Any person who violates this subsection shall be sentenced to a term of imprisonment of not more than one year, a fine of not more than $5,000 or both, except that if he commits such offense after a prior conviction or convictions under this subsection have become final, he shall be sentenced to a term of imprisonment of not more than 2 years, a fine of not more than $10,000, or both.

(b) (1) If any person who has not previously been convicted of violating subsection (a) of this section, any other provision of this title or title III, or any other law of the United States relating to narcotic drugs, marihuana, or depressant or stimulant substances, is found guilty of a violation of subsection (a) of this section after trial or upon a plea of guilty, the court may, without entering a judgment of guilty and with the consent of such person, defer further proceedings and place him on probation upon such reasonable conditions as it may require and for such period, not to exceed one year, as the court may prescribe. Upon violation of a condition of the probation, the court may enter an adjudication of guilt and proceed as otherwise provided. The court may, in its discretion, dismiss the proceedings against such person and discharge him from probation before the expiration of the maximum period prescribed for such person's probation. If during the period of his probation such person does not violate any of the conditions of the probation, then upon expiration of such period the court shall discharge such person and dismiss the proceedings against him. Discharge and dismissal under this subsection shall be without court adjudication of guilt, but a nonpublic record thereof shall be retained by the Department of Justice solely for the purpose of use by the courts in determining whether or not, in subsequent proceedings, such person qualifies under this subsection. Such discharge or dismissal shall not be deemed a conviction for purposes of disqualifications or disabilities imposed by law upon conviction of a crime (including the penalties prescribed under this part for second or subsequent convictions) or for any other purpose. Discharge and dismissal under this section may occur only once with respect to any person.

(2) Upon dismissal of such person and discharge of the proceedings against him under paragraph (1) of this subsection, such person, if he was not over twenty-one years of age at the time of the offense, may apply to the court for an order to expunge from all official records (other than the nonpublic records to be retained by the Department of Justice under paragraph (1)) all recordation relating to his arrest, indictment or information, trial, finding of guilty, and dismissal and discharge pursuant to this section. If the court determines, after hearing, that such person was dismissed and the proceedings against him discharged and that he was not over twenty-one years of age at the time of the offense, it shall enter such order. The effect of such order shall be to restore such person, in the contemplation of the law, to the status he occupied before such arrest or indictment or information. No person as to whom such order has been entered shall be held thereafter under any provision of any law to be guilty of perjury or otherwise giving a false statement by reason of his failures to recite or acknowledge such arrest, or indictment or information, or trial in response to any inquiry made of him for any purpose.

Subsection (a) provides that a first offender who is convicted of possession of marihuana will be subject to a penalty of not more than one year in jail or a fine not to exceed 3,000 dollars, or both. In contrast with the two-year minimum and five-year maximum prison sentences expressly required by the Marihuana Tax Act, of 1937, (and subsequent amendments thereto which provide for imprisonment of from two to ten years), the new law is convincingly liberal. Subsection (b)(1) is also exceedingly liberal in authorizing a federal district court to place on probation for not more than one year on such reasonable conditions as the court may prescribe, any individual found guilty of possessing marihuana who has never before been convicted of any narcotic, drug, or marihuana offense. If the period of probation is successfully completed, the court has the authority to dismiss the charges against the person without adjudication of his guilt. An individual found guilty of violating the Act may be extended the "privileges" of subsection (b)(1) only ONCE. A court may also expunge all records of arrest, indictment, trial, guilt, and dismissal or discharge, with respect to someone under 21 years of age, according to subsection (b)(2), except that the records of the United States Department of Justice will reflect the fact in its nonpublic files. Furthermore, this person under 21 will be considered in the eyes of the law to have been restored to the position he was in prior to his arrest. His failure to acknowledge his involvement with the marihuana laws may in no way be used as a basis for a perjury indictment for purposes of testimonial impeachment or for any other reason in a court of law.

Although most state laws have not yet kept pace with the farsightedness of this Federal statute, some states have made decided progress from the original limitations of the Uniform Drug Act of 1932. The highest court of the State of New Jersey, for example, recently had an opportunity to adjudicate with respect to penalties for first offenders convicted of violation of the state's anti-marihuana possession law. In *State v. Ward,*[9] the New Jersey police search (pursuant to a warrant) of Stephen Douglas Ward's bureau drawer in his mother's home, led to the discovery of a small package of marihuana. The police

---

[9]270 A2d 1, N.J., 1970.

also found a pipe stem containing marihuana in his desk drawer and the remnant of a marihuana cigarette in an adjoining room. Ward, an 18-year old, was found guilty of violating the New Jersey anti-marihuana possession statute, and was sentenced to from two to three years in state prison and fined 100 dollars. [The applicable law provided for imprisonment of from 2 to 15 years at hard labor and a fine not exceeding 2,000 dollars, for a first offense.] The highest New Jersey court overturned and suspended Ward's sentence, asserting that a two- to three-year prison term for a first offender whose possession of marihuana was incidental to his own use was far too severe. The court was desirous of establishing guidelines:

> for the sentencing of first offenders who were found guilty of possessing marihuana for their own use. We cannot escape the unhappy fact that our youth have been involved with marihuana in disturbing numbers. That this is so does not palliate the wrong. Nor should we be thought to encourage or condone such conduct. The statute should and will be enforced. But it remains the policy of the law to reform the youthful offender. Sentencing judges should direct the punishments they impose to the goal of reformation. Too severe a punishment will do little toward advancing this goal. Incarceration is a traumatic experience for anyone. The effect must be particularly devastating upon young persons such as the defendant here. A sentence of two to three years in State Prison in a case like this will probably be more detrimental to both the offender and society than some other discipline. Even a sentence to a reformatory as suggested by the Appellate Division may be more punitive than is required. We think that generally a suspended sentence with an appropriate term of probation is sufficient penalty for a person who is convicted for the first time of possessing marihuana for his own use. Probation is designed to aid both society and the offender by affording opportunity for correction under suitable supervision. It is hoped that during the probation the offender will establish himself as a law-abiding member of the public and thus avoid the need for confinement with its possibly adverse consequences.

Judge Proctor, who wrote the majority opinion in this case, held that the primary purpose of such punishment should be the reformation of the criminal and that a prison term for a person possessing a small amount of marihuana is detrimental both to that person as well as to society as a whole because such a minor criminal should more promptly be returned to society. He therefore recommended that suspended sentences be given to all youthful offenders, so that they may sooner become "law-abiding members of the community. In addition, the Court noted that a new law providing milder penalties for a first conviction of the possession of marihuana had recently been signed into law by New Jersey Governor William Cahill. The Court expressed the opinion that the new law would be followed, especially with respect to penalties, notwithstanding the fact that it was not as yet in force:

> Since the argument in this case, a new statute has been enacted which deals comprehensively with the problems of drugs, L.1970, c.226, approved by Governor Cahill October 19, 1970. The statute lowers the penalties for possessing a small quantity of marihuana and reduces the category of the offense to that of a disorderly person. The statute under which the defendant was tried will be repealed 90 days from the date of the enactment of the statute (§ 48), but the repealer does not abate past or pending prosecutions (§ 40). *We expect that any sentences imposed within the 90-day interim will be in conformance with this opinion.*[10] (Emphasis added.)

Another state where change is definitely in the wind with respect to punishment for possession of marihuana is New York, where no less than six bills were filed in the 1971 State Legislature. Currently in New York, any person convicted of possession of a small amount of marihuana for the first time is guilty only of a misdemeanor and is subject to not more than one year in prison. Most of these proposed statutes provide that a first conviction for possession of a small amount of marihuana will be considered merely a "violation" and not a misdemeanor and therefore punishable only by a fine of not more than 100 dollars. Still another bill declares that the cultivation of marihuana and the manufacture of marihuana cigarettes are legal! Obviously

---

[10]This most unusual judicial mandate, i.e. that the lower courts disregard the law actually in effect, is unprecedented and of doubtful constitutionality, but nevertheless demonstrates the uncomplimentary view of one court with respect to harsh penalties for violation of the marihuana possession laws.

the enactment of these measures is highly questionable, but these bills do portend the wave of the future.[11]

Most states today have ignored this liberalizing trend and continue to punish violators of their marihuana laws as if the statutes were like "the law of the Medes and the Persians." On February 6, 1971, the *New York Times* reported that a sharply divided Minnesota Supreme Court had ruled that Robert Sirila, a Minneapolis "hippie," could be sentenced to 20 years in prison for the possession of "a microscopic" amount of marihuana. According to Associate Justice James Otis in his dissent to the majority opinion, "It is inconceivable to me that the Legislature intended 20 years imprisonment for possessing an unusable amount of marihuana which could neither be sold, consumed or in any other way pose a threat to society . . . [the defendant] faces 20 years in prison for having in the lining of his jacket traces of marihuana so minute they could not be chemically tested but had to be identified miscroscopically." The *New York Times* also reported that the Minneapolis police had "vacuumed Sirila's jacket in a futile search for marihuana" at the time when he was arrested for obstructing a sidewalk one week prior to his arrest on the marihuana charge. The majority of the Court noted that, "his jacket was used as a vehicle for transportation of marihuana" between the time of the vacuuming and the second arrest.

Other states where unusually harsh sentences have been handed down to first-time offenders of anti-marihuana possession laws include Virginia, where an 18-year-old Richmond high school student was sentenced to 20 years; Wisconsin, where a young man was sentenced to 4 years for possessing one small marihuana cigarette; and Michigan, where a poet and political activist was given 9½ years in jail, without possibility of parole, for being found with two marihuana cigarettes in his possession.

---

[11]On April 29, 1971, the *New York Times* reported one of the more liberal bills to lower penalties for marihuana offenses was killed by the New York State Assembly Codes Committee. Assemblyman Dominick L. DiCarlo, of Brooklyn, the Committee Chairman, stated that a majority of the Committee members felt studies concerning the physical and mental effects of marihuana were incomplete and that "it wasn't the time to make a change."

Twenty-one states continue to require *minimum* sentences varying from six months in Utah to five years in Alabama and Minnesota, for first offenders convicted of possessing this outlawed plant; in Texas there is the possibility of life imprisonment. Alabama, Minnesota, and Missouri provide *maximum* penalties of twenty years, while Colorado, Ohio, and Rhode Island have maximum prison terms of fifteen years. On the other side of the scale, Nebraska imposes but seven days in the county jail, and Iowa, New Jersey, Washington, and Wyoming provide for maximum prison terms of but six months. More than a dozen other states have maximum penalties of one year.

While the determination of the legalization of marihuana must await incontrovertable scientific evidence, the trend is clear. The states are beginning to follow the lead of the Federal Government in overturning outdated laws providing for stringent punishment of the first-time marihuana possessor. In order to develop a nation of law-abiding citizens, the law by which the citizens abide must be reasonable and reflective of the mores of the citizenry themselves. Reasonable punishment for the violation of a law is a first and vital step.

QUESTIONS FOR REVIEW

1. Trace the history of marihuana from 2737 B.C. through the 1930's.
2. What was the India Hemp Commission and what were its recommendations with respect to marihuana?
3. How did the "menace" of marihuana first come to the attention of the American public and what were the reasons for its use, possession, and sale being outlawed?
4. What were the ostensible and actual purposes of the Marihuana Tax Act of 1937? What were its terms and circumstances of its enactment into law?
5. What was the Uniform Drug Act and what were its provisions with respect to marihuana?
6. What provision did the Uniform Drug Act make with respect to marihuana's offenses, as opposed to the punishment provided for by the Tax Act of 1937?
7. What was the trend with respect to punishment for viola-

tion of the possesion laws from the 1930's to the present? What were the reasons for these trends?

8. What state has the most lenient law for the possession of marihuana and what is the nature of the law?
9. What state has the most severe law with respect to possession of marihuana and what is the nature of this law?
10. What were the recommendations with respect to marihuana made by the Presidential Commission of 1967?
11. What is the substance of the provisions of the Comprehensive Drug Abuse Prevention and Control Act of 1970 with respect to punishment for marihuana possession offenses?
12. What principles did the court assert in the *Ward* case with respect to punishment for the possession of marihuana?
13. What is the current trend with respect to laws providing for the punishment of marihuana possession offenses?

Appendix I

TITLE VII OF THE CIVIL RIGHTS ACT OF 1964[1]

SEC. 701. DEFINITIONS

FOR THE PURPOSES of this title—

(a) The term "person" includes one or more individuals, labor unions, partnerships, associations, corporations, legal representatives, mutual companies, joint-stock companies, trusts, unincorporated organizations, trustees in bankruptcy, or receivers.

(b) The term "employer" means a person engaged in an industry affecting commerce who has twenty-five or more employees for each working day in each of twenty or more calendar weeks in the current or preceding calendar year, and any agent of such a person, but such term does not include (1) the United States, a corporation wholly owned by the Government of the United States, an Indian tribe, or a State or political subdivision thereof, (2) a bona fide private membership club (other than a labor organization) which is exempt from taxation under section 501(c) of the Internal Revenue Code of 1954: *Provided,* That during the first year after the effective date prescribed in subsection (a) of session 716, persons having fewer than one hundred employees (and their agents) shall not be considered employers, and, during the second year after such date, persons having fewer than seventy-five employees (and their agents) shall not be considered employers, and, during the third year after such date, persons having fewer than fifty employees (and their agents) shall not be considered employers: *Provided fur-*

[1]78 Stat. 253.42 U.S.C. § 2000e et seq. (1961).

ther, That it shall be the policy of the United States to insure equal employment opportunities for Federal employees without discrimination because of race, color, religion, sex or national origin and the President shall utilize his existing authority to effectuate this policy.

(c) The term "employment agency" means any person regularly undertaking with or without compensation to procure employees for an employer or to procure for employment opportunities to work for an employer and includes an agent of such a person; but shall not include an agency of the United States, or an agency of a State or political subdivision of a State, except that such terms shall include the United States Employment Service and the system of State and local employment services receiving Federal assistance.

(d) The term "labor organization" means a labor organization engaged in an industry affecting commerce, and any agent of such an organization, and includes any organization of any kind, any agency, or employee representation committee, group, association, or plan so engaged in which employees participate and which exists for the purpose, in whole or in part, of dealing with employers concerning grievances, labor disputes, wages, rates of pay, hours, or other terms or conditions of employment, and any conference, general committee, joint or system board, or joint council so engaged which is subordinate to a national or international labor organization.

(e) A labor organization shall be deemed to be engaged in an industry affecting commerce if (1) it maintains or operates a hiring hall or hiring office which procures employees for an employer or procures for employees opportunities to work for an employer, or (2) the number of its members (or, where it is a labor organization composed of other labor organizations or their representatives, if the aggregate number of the members of such other labor organization) is (A) one hundred or more during the first year after the effective date prescribed in subsection (a) of section 716, (B) seventy-five or more during the second year after such date or fifty or more during the third year, or (C) twenty-five or more thereafter, and such labor organization—

(1) is the certified representative of employees under the provisions of the National Labor Relations Act, as amended, or the Railway Labor Act, as amended:

(2) although not certified, is a national or international labor organization or a local labor organization recognized or acting as the representative of employees of an employer or employers engaged in an industry affecting commerce; or

(3) has chartered a local labor organization or subsidiary body which is representing or actively seeking to represent employees of employers within the meaning of paragraph (1) or (2); or

(4) has been chartered by a labor organization representing or actively seeking to represent employees within the meaning of paragraph (1) or (2) as the local or subordinate body through which such employees may enjoy membership or become affiliated with such labor organization; or

(5) is a conference, general committee, joint or system board, or joint council subordinate to a national or international labor organization, which includes a labor organization engaged in an industry affecting commerce within the meaning of any of the preceding paragraphs of this subsection.

(f) The term "employee" means an individual employed by an employer.

(g) The term "commerce" means trade, traffic, commerce, transportation, transmission, or communication among the several States; or between a State and any place outside thereof; or within the District of Columbia, or a possession of the United States; or between points in the same State but through a point outside thereof.

(h) The term "industry affecting commerce" means any activity, business, or industry in commerce or in which a labor dispute would hinder or obstruct commerce or the free flow of commerce and includes any activity or industry "affecting commerce" within the meaning of the Labor-Management Reporting and Disclosure Act of 1959.

(i) The term "state" includes a State of the United States, the District of Columbia, Puerto Rico, the Virgin Islands, American Samoa, Guam, Wake Island, the Canal Zone, and Outer

Continental Shelf lands defined in the Outer Continental Shelf Lands Act.

SEC. 702. EXEMPTION

This title shall not apply to an employer with respect to the employment of aliens outside any State, or to a religious corporation, association, or society with respect to the employment of individuals of a peculiar religion to perform work connected with the carrying on by such corporation, association, or society of its religious activities or to an educational institution with respect to the employment of indivduals to perform work connected wth the educational activities of such institution.

SEC. 703. DISCRIMINATION BECAUSE OF RACE, COLOR, RELIGION, SEX, OR NATIONAL ORIGIN

(a) It shall be an unlawful employment practice for an employer—

(1) to fail or refuse to hire or to discharge any individual, or otherwise to discriminate against any individual with respect to his compensation, terms, conditions, or privileges of employment, because of such individual's race, color, religion, sex, or national origin; or

(2) to limit, segregate, or classify his employees in any way which would deprive or tend to deprive any individual of employment opportunities or otherwise adversely affect his status as an employee, because of such individual's race, color, religion, sex, or national origin.

(b) It shall be an unlawful employment practice for an employment agency to fail or refuse to refer for employment, or otherwise to discriminate against, any individual because of his race, color, religion, sex, or national origin, or to classify or refer for employment any individual on the basis of his race, color, religion, sex, or national origin.

(c) It shall be an unlawful employment practice for a labor organization—

(1) to exclude or to expel from its membership, or otherwise to discriminate against, any individual because of his race, color, religion, sex, or national origin;

(2) to limit, segregate, or classify its membership, or to classify or fail or refuse to refer for employment any individual, in any way which would deprive or tend to deprive any individual of employment opportunities, or would limit such employment opportunities or otherwise adversely affect his status as an employee or as an applicant for employment, because of such individual's race, color, religion, sex, or national origin; or

(3) to cause or attempt to cause an employer to discriminate against an individual in violation of this section.

(d) It shall be an unlawful employment practice for any employer, labor organization, or joint labor-management committee controlling apprenticeship or other training or retraining, including on-the-job training programs to discriminate against any individual because of race, color, religion, sex, or national origin in admission to, or employment in, any program established to provide apprenticeship or other training.

(e) Notwithstanding any other provision of this title, (1) it shall not be an unlawful employment practice for an employer to hire and employ employees, for an employment agency to classify, or refer for employment any individual, for a labor organization to classify its membership or to classify or refer for employment any individual, or for an employer, labor organization, or joint labor-management committee controlling apprenticeship or other training or retraining programs to admit or employ any individual in any such program, on the basis of his religion, sex, or national origin in those certain instances where religion, sex, or national origin is a bona fide occupational qualification reasonably necessary to the normal operation of that particular business or enterprise, and (2) it shall not be an unlawful employment practice for a school, college, university, or other educational institution or institution of learning to hire and employ employees of a particular religion if such school, college, university, or other educational institution or institution of learning is, in whole or in substantial part, owned, supported, controlled, or managed by a particular religion or by a particular religious corporation, association, or society, of if the curriculum of such school, college, university, or other educational institution or institution of learning is directed toward the propagation of a particular religion.

(f) As used in this title, the phrase "unlawful employment practice" shall not be deemed to include any action or measure taken by an employer, labor organization, joint labor-management committee, or employment agency with respect to an individual who is a member of the Communist Party of the United States or of any other organization required to register as a Communist-action or Communist-front organization by final order of the Subversive Activities Control Board pursuant to the Subversive Activities Control Act of 1950.

(g) Notwithstanding any other provision of this title, it shall not be an unlawful employment practice for an employer to fail or refuse to hire and employ any individual for any position, for an employer to discharge any individual from any position, or for an employment agency to fail or refuse to refer any individual for employment in any position, or for a labor organization to fail or refuse to refer any individual for employment in any position, if—

(1) the occupancy of such position, or access to the premises in or upon which any part of the duties of such position is performed or is to be performed, is subject to any requirement imposed in the interest of the national security of the United States under any security program in effect pursuant to or administered under any statute of the United States or any Executive order of the President; and

(2) such individual has not fulfilled or has ceased to fulfill that requirement.

(h) Notwithstanding any other provision of this title, it shall not be an unlawful employment practice for an employer to apply different standards of compensation, or different terms, conditions, or privileges of employment pursuant to a bona fide seniority or merit system, or a system which measures earnings by quantity or quality of production or to employees who work in different locations, provided that such differences are not the result of an intention to discriminate because of race, color, religion, sex, or national origin, nor shall it be an unlawful employment practice for an employer to give and to act upon the results of any professionally developed ability test provided that such test, its administration or action upon the results is not designed, intended or used to discriminate because of race, color, religion, sex, or national origin. It shall not be an unlawful employment practice under this title for any employer to differentiate upon the basis of sex in determining the amount of the wages or compensation paid or to be paid to employees of such employer if such differentiation is authorized by the provisions of section 6(d) of the Fair Labor Standards Act of 1938 as amended (29 U.S.C. 206(d)).

(i) Nothing contained in this title shall apply to any business or enterprise on or near an Indian reservation with respect to any publicly announced employment practice of such business or enterprise under which a preferential treatment is given to any individual because he is an Indian living on or near a reservation.

(j) Nothing contained in this title shall be interpreted to require any employer, employment agency, labor organization, or joint labor-management committee subject to this title to grant preferential treatment to any individual or to any group because of the race, color, religion, sex, or national origin of such individual or group on account of an imbalance which may exist with respect to the total number or percentage of persons of any race, color, religion, sex, or national origin employed by any employer, referred or classified for employment by any employment agency or labor organization, admitted to membership or classified by any labor organization, or admitted to, or employed in, any apprenticeship or other training program, in comparison with the total number or percentage of persons of such race, color, religion, sex, or national origin in any community, State, section, or other area, or in the available work force in any community, State, section, or other area.

SEC. 704. OTHER UNLAWFUL EMPLOYMENT PRACTICES

(a) It shall be an unlawful employment practice for an employer to discriminate against any of his employers or applicants for employment, for an employment agency to discriminate against any individual, or for a labor organization to discriminate against any member thereof or applicant for membership, because he has opposed any practice made an unlawful employment practice by this title, because he has made a charge, testified, assisted, or participated in any manner in an investigation, proceeding, or hearing under this title.

(b) It shall be an unlawful employment practice for an employer, labor organization, or employment agency to print or publish or cause to be printed or published any notice or advertisement relating to employment by such an employer or membership in or any classification or referral for employment by such a labor organization, or relating to any classification or referral for employment by such an employment agency, indicating any preference, limitation, specification, or discrimination, based on race, color, religion, sex, or national origin, except that such a notice or advertisement may indicate a preference, limitation, specification, or discrimination based on religion, sex, or national origin when religion, sex, or national origin is a bona fide occupational qualification for employment.

SEC. 705. EQUAL EMPLOYMENT OPPORTUNITY COMMISSION

(a) There is hereby created a Commission to be known as the Equal Employment Opportunity Commission, which shall be composed of five members, not more than three of whom shall be members of the same political party, who shall be appointed by the President by and with the advice and consent of the Senate. One of the original members shall be appointed for a term of one year, one for a term of two years, one for a term of three years, one for a term of four years, and one for a term of five years, beginning from the date of enactment of this title, but their successors shall be appointed for terms of five years each, except that any individual chosen to fill a vacancy shall be appointed only for the unexpired term of the member whom he shall succeed. The President shall designate one member to serve as Chairman of the Commission, and one member to serve as Vice Chairman. The Chairman shall be responsible on behalf of the Commission for the administrative operations of the Commission, and shall appoint, in accordance with the civil service laws, such officers, agents, attorneys, and employees as it deems necessary to assist it in the performance of its functions and to fix their compensation in accordance with the Classification Act of 1949, as amended. The Vice Chairman shall act as Chairman in the absence or disability of the Chairman or in the event of a vacancy in that office.

(b) A vacancy in the Commission shall not impair the right of the remaining members to exercise all the powers of the Commission and three members thereof shall constitute a quorum.

(c) The Commission shall have an official seal which shall be judicially noticed.

(d) The Commission shall at the close of each fiscal year report to the Congress and to the President concerning the action it has taken; the names, salaries, and duties of all individuals in its employ and the moneys it has disbursed; and shall make such further reports on the cause of and means of eliminating discrimination and such recommendations for further legislation as may appear desirable.

(e) The Federal Executive Pay Act of 1956, as amended (5 U.S.C. 2201-2209), is further amended—

(1) by adding to section 105 thereof (5 U.S.C. 2204) the following clause: "(32) Chairman, Equal Employment Opportunity Commission"; and

(2) by adding to clause (45) of section 106(a) thereof (5 U.S.C. 2205 (a)) the following: "Equal Employment Opportunity Commission (4)."

(f) The principal office of the Commission shall be in or near the District of Columbia, but it may meet or exercise any or all its powers at any other place. The Commission may establish such regional or State offices as it deems necessary to accomplish the purpose of this title.

(g) The Commission shall have power—

(1) to cooperate with and, with their consent, utilize regional, State, local, and other agencies, both public and private, and individuals;

(2) to pay to witnesses whose depositions are taken or who are summoned before the Commission or any of its agents

the same witness and mileage fees as are paid to witnesses in the courts of the United States;

(3) to furnish to persons subject to this title such technical assistance as they may request to further their compliance with this title or an order issued thereunder;

(4) upon the request of (i) any employer, whose employees or some of them, or (ii) any labor organization, whose members or some of them, refuse or threaten to refuse to cooperate in effectuating the provisions of this title, to assist in such effectuation by conciliation or such other remedial action as is provided by this title;

(5) to make such technical studies as are appropriate to effectuate the purposes and policies of this title and to make the results of such studies available to the public;

(6) to refer matters to the Attorney General with recommendations for intervention in a civil action brought by an aggrieved party under section 706, or for the institution of a civil action by the Attorney General under section 707, and to advise, consult, and assist the Attorney General on such matters.

(h) Attorneys appointed under this section may, at the direction of the Commission, appear for and represent the Commission in any case in court.

(i) The Commission shall, in any of its educational or promotional activities, cooperate with other departments and agencies in the performance of such educational and promotional activities.

(j)All officers, agents, attorneys, and employees of the Commission shall be subject to the provisions of section 9 of the Act of August 2, 1939, as amended (the Hatch Act), notwithstanding any exemption contained in such section.

SEC. 706. PREVENTION OF UNLAWFUL EMPLOYMENT PRACTICES

(a) Whenever it is charged in writing under oath by a person claiming to be aggrieved, or a written charge has been filed by a member of the Commission where he has reasonable cause to believe a violation of this title has occurred (and such charge sets forth the facts upon which it is based) that an employer, employment agency, or labor organization has engaged in an unlawful employment practice, the Commission shall furnish such employer, employment agency, or labor organization (herein-after referred to as the "respondent") with a copy of such charge and shall make an investigation of such charge, provided that such charge shall not be made public by the Commission. If the Commission shall determine, after such investigation, that there is reasonable cause to believe that the charge is true, the Commission shall endeavor to eliminate any such alleged unlawful employment practice by informal methods of conference, conciliation, and persuasion. Nothing said or done during and as a part of such endeavors may be made public by the Commission without the written consent of the parties, or used as evidence in a subsequent proceeding. Any officer or employee of the Commission, who shall make public in any manner whatever any information in violation of this subsection shall be deemed guilty of a misdemeanor and upon conviction thereof shall be fined not more than $1,000 or imprisoned not more than one year.

(b) In the case of an alleged unlawful employment practice occurring in a State, or political subdivision of a State, which has a State or local law prohibiting the unlawful employment practice alleged and establishing or authorizing a State or local authority to grant or seek relief from such practice or to institute criminal proceedings with respect thereto upon receiving notice thereof, no charge may be filed under subsection (a) by the person aggrieved before the expiration of sixty days after proceedings have been commenced under the State or local law, unless proceedings have been earlier terminated, provided that such sixty-day period shall be extended to one hundred and twenty days during the first year after the effective date of such State or local law. If any requirement for the commencement of such proceedings is imposed by a State or local authority other than a requirement of the filing of a written and signed statement of the facts upon which the proceeding is based, the proceeding shall be deemed to have been commenced for the purposes of this subsection at the time such statement is sent by registered mail to the appropriate State or local authority.

(c) In the case of any charge filed by a member of the Commission alleging an unlawful employment practice occurring in a State or political subdivision of a State, which has a State or local law prohibiting the practice alleged and establishing or authorizing a State or local authority to grant or seek relief from such practice or to institute criminal proceedings with respect thereto upon receiving notice thereof, the Commission shall, before taking any action with respect to such charge, notify the appropriate State or local officials and, upon request, afford them a reasonable time, but not less than sixty days (provided that such sixty-day period shall be extended to one hundred and twenty days during the first year after the effective day of such State or local law), unless a shorter period is requested, to act under such State or local law to remedy the practice alleged.

(d) A charge under subsection (a) shall be filed within ninety days after the alleged unlawful employment practice occurred, except that in the case of an unlawful practice with respect to which the person aggrieved has followed the procedure set out in subsection (b), such charge shall be filed by the person aggrieved within two hundred and ten days after the alleged unlawful employment practice occurred, or within thirty days after receiving notice that the State or local agency has terminated the proceedings under the State or local law, whichever is earlier, and a copy of such charge shall be filed by the Commission with the State or local agency.

(e) If within thirty days after a charge is filed with the Commission or within thirty days after expiration of any period of reference under subsection (c) except that in either case such period may be extended to not more than sixty days upon a determination by the Commission that further efforts to secure voluntary compliance are warranted), the Commission has been unable to obtain voluntary compliance with this title, the Commission shall so notify the person aggrieved and a civil action may, within 30 days thereafter, be brought against the respondent named in the charge (1) by the person claiming to be aggrieved, or (2) if such charge was filed by a member of the Commission, by any person whom the charge alleges was aggrieved by the alleged unlawful employment practice. Upon application by the complainant and in such circumstances as the court may deem just, the court may appoint an attorney for such complainant and may authorize the commencement of the action without the payment of fees, costs, or security. Upon timely application, the court may, in its discretion, permit the Attorney General to intervene in such civil action if he certifies that the case is of general public importance. Upon request, the court may, in its discretion, stay further proceedings for not more than sixty days pending the termination of State or local proceedings described in subsection (b) or the efforts of the Commission to obtain voluntary compliance.

(f) Each United States district court and each United States court of a place subject to the jurisdiction of the United States shall have jurisdiction of actions brought under this title. Such an action may be brought in any judicial district in the State in which the unlawful employment practice is alleged to have been committed, in the judicial district in which the employment records relevant to such practice are maintained and administered, or in the judicial district in which the plaintiff would have worked but for the alleged unlawful employment practice, but if the respondent is not found within any such district, such an action may be brought within the judicial district in which the respondent has his principal office. For purposes of sections 1404 and 1406 of title 28 of the United States Code, the judicial district in which the respondent has his principal office shall in all cases be considered a district in which the action might have been brought.

(g) If the court finds that the respondent has intentionally engaged in or is intentionally engaging in an unlawful employment practice charged in the complaint, the court may enjoin the respondent from engaging in such unlawful employment practice, and order such affirmative action as may be appropriate, which may include reinstatement or hiring of employees, with or without back pay (payable by the employer, employment agency, or labor organization, as the case may be, responsible for the unlawful employment practice). Interim earnings or amounts earnable with reasonable diligence by the person or persons discriminated against shall operate to reduce the back pay otherwise allowable. No order of the court shall require the admission or reinstatement of an individual as a member of a union or the hiring, reinstatement, or promotion of an individual as an employee, or the payment to him of any back pay, if such individual was refused admission, suspended, or expelled or was refused employment or advancement or was suspended or discharged for any reason other than discrimination on account of race, color, religion, sex or national origin or in violation of section 704(a).

(h) The provisions of the Act entitled "An Act to amend the Judicial Code and to define and limit the jurisdiction of courts sitting in equity, and for other purposes," approved March 23, 1932 (29 U.S.C. 101-115), shall not apply with respect to civil actions brought under this section.

(i) In any case in which an employer, employment agency, or labor organization fails to comply with an order of a court issued in a civil action brought under subsection (e), the Commission may commence proceedings to compel compliance with such order.

(j) Any civil action brought under subsection (e) and any proceedings brought under subsection (i) shall be subject to appeal as provided in sections 1291 and 1292, title 28, United States Code.

(k) In any action or proceeding under this title the court, in its discretion, may allow the prevailing party, other than the Commission or the United States, a reasonable attorney's fee as part of the costs, and the Commission and the United States shall be liable for costs the same as a private person.

SEC. 707

(a) Whenever the Attorney General has reasonable cause to believe that any person or group of persons is engaged in a pattern or practice of resistance to the full enjoyment of any of the rights secured by this title, and that the pattern or practice is of such a nature and is intended to deny the full exercise of the rights herein described, the Attorney General may bring a civil action in the appropriate district court of the United

States by filing with it a complaint (1) signed by him (or in his absence the Acting Attorney General), (2) setting forth facts pertaining to such pattern or practice, and (3) requesting such relief, including an application for a permanent or temporary injunction, restraining order or other order against the person or persons responsible for such pattern or practice, as he deems necessary to insure the full enjoyment of the rights herein described.

(b) The district courts of the United States shall have and shall exercise jurisdiction of proceedings instituted pursuant to this section, and in any such proceeding the Attorney General may file with the clerk of such court a request that a court of three judges be convened to hear and determine the case. Such request by the Attorney General shall be accompanied by a certificate that, in his opinion, the case is of general public importance. A copy of the certificate and request for a three-judge court shall be immediately furnished by such clerk to the chief judge of the circuit (or in his absence, the presiding circuit judge of the circuit) in which the case is pending. Upon receipt of such request it shall be the duty of the chief judge of the circuit or the presiding circuit judge, as the case may be, to designate immediately three judges in such circuit, of whom at least one shall be a circuit judge and another of whom shall be a district judge of the court in which the proceeding was instituted, to hear and determine such case, and it shall be the duty of the judges so designated to assign the case for hearing at the earliest practicable date, to participate in the hearing and determination thereof, and to cause the case to be in every way expedited. An appeal from the final judgment of such court will lie to the Supreme Court.

In the event the Attorney General fails to file such a request in any such proceeding, it shall be the duty of the chief judge of the district (or in his absence, the acting chief judge) in which the case is pending immediately to designate a judge in such district to hear and determine the case. In the event that no judge in the district is available to hear and determine the case, the chief judge of the district, or the acting judge, as the case may be, shall certify this fact to the chief judge of the circuit (or in his absence, the acting chief judge) who shall then designate a district or circuit judge of the circuit to hear and determine the case.

It shall be the duty of the judge designated pursuant to this section to assign the case for hearing at the earliest practicable date and to cause the case to be in every way expedited.

SEC. 708. EFFECT ON STATE LAWS

Nothing in this title shall be deemed to exempt or relieve any person from any liability, duty, penalty, or punishment provided by any present or future law of any State or political subdivision of a State, other than any such law which purports to require or permit the doing of any act which would be an unlawful employment practice under this title.

SEC. 709. INVESTIGATIONS, INSPECTIONS, RECORDS, STATE AGENCIES

(a) In connection with any investigation of a charge filed under section 706, the Commission or its designated representatives shall at all reasonable times have access to, for the purposes of examination, and the right to copy any evidence of any person being investigated or proceeded against that relates to unlawful employment practices covered by this title and is relevant to the charge under investigation.

(b) The Commission may cooperate with State and local agencies charged with the administration of State fair employment practices laws and, with the consent of such agencies, may for the purpose of carrying out its functions and duties under this title and within the limitation of funds appropriated specifically for such purpose, utilize the services of such agencies and their employees and, notwithstanding any other provision of law, may reimburse such agencies and their employees for services rendered to assist the Commission in carrying out this title. In furtherance of such cooperative efforts, the Commission may enter into written agreements with such State or local agencies and such agreements may include provisions under which the Commission shall refain from processing a charge in any cases or class of cases specified in such agreements and under which no person may bring a civil action under section 706 in any cases or class of cases so specified, or under which the Commission shall relieve any person or class of persons in such State or locality from requirements imposed under this section. The Commission shall rescind any such agreement whenever it determines that the agreement no longer serves the interest of effective enforcement of this title.

(c) Except as provided in subsection (d), every employer, employment agency, and labor organization subject to this title shall (1) make and keep such records relevant to the determinations of whether unlawful employment practices have been or are being committed, (2) preserve such records for such periods, and (3) make such reports therefrom, as the Commission shall prescribe by regulation or order, after public hearing, as reasonable, necessary, or appropriate for the enforcement of this title or the regulations or orders thereunder. The Commission shall, by regulation, require each employer, labor organization, and joint labor-management committee subject to this title which controls an apprenticeship or other training program to maintain such records as are reasonably necessary to carry out the purpose of this title, including, but not limited to, a list of applicants who wish to participate in such program, including the chronological order in which such applications were received, and shall furnish to the Commission, upon request, a detailed description of the manner in which persons are selected to participate in the apprenticeship or other training program. Any employer, employment agency, labor organization, or joint labor-management committee which believes that the application to it of any regulation or order issued under this section would result in undue hardship may (1) apply to the Commission for an exemption from the application of such regulation or order, or (2) bring a civil action in the United States district court for the district where such records are kept. If the Commission or the court, as the case may be, finds that the application of the regulation or order to the employer, employment agency, or labor organization in question would impose an undue hardship, the Commission or the court, as the case may be, may grant appropriate relief.

(d) The provision of subsection (c) shall not apply to any employer, employment agency, labor organization, or joint labor-management committee with respect to matters occurring in any State or political subdivision thereof which has a fair employment practice law during any period in which such employer, employment agency, labor organization, or joint labor-management committee is subject to such law, except that the Commission may require such notations on records which such employer, employment agency, labor organization, or joint labor-management committee keeps or is required to keep as are necessary because of differences in coverage or methods of enforcement between the State or local law and the provisions of this title. Where an employer is required by Executive Order 10925, issued March 6, 1961, or by any other Executive order prescribing fair employment practices for Government contractors and subcontractors, or by rules or regulations issued thereunder, to file reports relating to his employment practices with any Federal agency or committee, and he is substantially in compliance with such requirements, the Committee shall not require him to file additional reports pursuant to subsection (c) of this section.

(e) It shall be unlawful for any officer or employee of the Commission to make public in any manner whatever any information obtained by the Commission pursuant to its authority under this section prior to the institution of any proceeding under this title involving such information. Any officer or employee of the Commission who shall make public in any manner whatever any information in violation of this subsection shall be guilty of a misdemeanor and upon conviction thereof, shall be fined not more than $1,000, or imprisoned not more than one year.

SEC. 710. INVESTIGATORY POWERS

(a) For the purpose of any investigation of a charge filed under the authority contained in section 706, the Commission shall have authority to examine witnesses under oath and to require the production of documentary evidence relevant or material to the charge under investigation.

(b) If the respondent named in a charge filed under section 706 fails or refuses to comply with a demand of the Commission for permission to examine or to copy evidence in conformity with the provisions of section 709(a), or if any person required to comply with the provisions of section 709(c) or (d) fails or refuses to do so, or if any person fails or refuses to comply with a demand by the Commission to give testimony under oath, the United States district court for the district in which such person is found, resides, or transacts business, shall, upon application of the Commission, have jurisdiction to issue to such person an order requiring him to comply with the provisions of section 709(c) or (d) or to comply with the demand of the Commission, but the attendance of a witness may not be required outside the State where he is found, resides, or transacts business and the production of evidence may not be required outside the State where such evidence is kept.

(c) Within twenty days after the service upon any person charged under section 706 of a demand by the Commission for the production of documentary evidence or for permission to examine or to copy evidence in conformity with the provisions of section 709(a), such person may file in the district court of the United States for the judicial district in which he resides, is found, or transacts business, and serve upon the Commission a petition for an order of such court modifying or setting aside such demand. The time allowed for compliance with the demand in whole or in part as deemed proper and ordered by the court shall not run during the pendency of such petition in the court.

Such petition shall specify each ground upon which the petitioner relies in seeking such relief, and may be based upon any failure of such demand to comply with the position of this title or with the limitations generally applicable to compulsory process or upon any constitutional or other legal right or privilege of such person. No objection which is not raised by such a petition may be urged in the defense to a proceeding initiated by the Commission under subsection (b) for enforcement of such a demand unless such proceeding is commenced by the Commission prior to the expiration of the twenty-day period, or unless the court determines that the defendant could not reasonably have been aware of the availability of such ground of objection.

(d) In any proceeding brought by the Commission under subsection (b), except as provided in subsection (c) of this section, the defendant may petition the court for an order modifying or setting aside the demand of the Commission.

SEC. 711. NOTICES TO BE POSTED

(a) Every employer, employment agency, and labor organization, as the case may be, shall post and keep posted in conspicuous places upon its premises where notices to employees, applicants for employment, and members are customarily posted a notice to be prepared or approved by the Commission setting forth excerpts from or, summaries of, the pertinent provisions of this title and information pertinent to the filing of a complaint.

(b) A willful violation of this section shall be punishable by a fine of not more than $100 for each separate offense.

SEC. 712. VETERANS' PREFERENCE

Nothing contained in this title shall be construed to repeal or modify any Federal, State, territorial, or local law creating special rights or preference for veterans.

SEC. 713. RULES AND REGULATIONS

(a) The Commission shall have authority from time to time to issue, amend, or rescind suitable procedural regulations to carry out the provisions of this title. Regulations issued under this section shall be in conformity with the standards and limitations of the Administrative Procedure Act.

(b) In any action or proceeding based on any alleged unlawful employment practice, no person shall be subject to any liability or punishment for or on account of (1) the commission by such person of an unlawful employment practice if he pleads and proves that the act or omission complained of was in good faith, in conformity with, and in reliance on any written interpretation or opinion of the Commission, or (2) the failure of such person to publish and file any information required by any provision of this title if he pleads and proves that he failed to publish and file such information in good faith, in conformity with the instructions of the Commission issued under the title regarding the filing of such information. Such a defense, if established, shall be a bar to the action or proceeding, notwithstanding that (A) after such act or omission, such interpretation or opinion is modified or rescinded or is determined by judicial authority to be invalid or of no legal effect, or (B) after publishing or filing the description and annual reports, such publication or filing is determined by judicial authority not to be in conformity with the requirements of this title.

SEC. 714. FORCIBLY RESISTING THE COMMISSION OR ITS REPRESENTATIVES

The provisions of section 111, title 18, United States Code, shall apply to officers, agents, and employees of the Commission in the performance of their official duties.

SEC. 715. SPECIAL STUDY BY THE SECRETARY OF LABOR

The Secretary of Labor shall make a full and complete study of the factors which might tend to result in discrimination in employment because of age and of the consequences of such discrimination in employment on the economy and individuals affected. The Secretary of Labor shall make a report to the Congress not later than June 30, 1965, containing the results of such study and shall include in such report such recommendations for legislation to prevent arbitrary discrimination in employment because of age as he determines advisable.

SEC. 716. EFFECTIVE DATE

(a) This title shall become effective one year after the date of its enactment.

(b) Notwithstanding subsection (a), sections of this title other than sections 703, 704, 706, and 707 shall become effective immediately.

(c) The President shall, as soon as feasible after the enactment of this title, convene one or more conferences for the purpose of enabling the leaders of groups whose members will be affected by this title to become familiar with the rights afforded and obligations imposed by its provisions, and for the purpose of making plans which will result in the fair and effective administration of this title when all of its provisions become effective. The President shall invite the participation in such conference or conferences of (1) the members of the President's Committee on Equal Employment Opportunity, (2) the members of the Commission on Civil Rights, (3) representatives of State and local agencies engaged in furthering equal employment opportunity, (4) representatives of private agencies in furthering equal employment opportunity, and (5) representatives of employers, labor organizations, and employment agencies who will be subject to this title.

Appendix II

CONSTITUTION OF THE UNITED STATES

We the people of the United States, in order to form a more perfect union, establish justice, insure domestic tranquility, provide for the common defense, promote the general welfare, and secure the blessings of liberty to ourselves and our posterity, do ordain and establish this Constitution for the United States of America.

ARTICLE I

Section 1. All legislative powers herein granted shall be vested in a Congress of the United States, which shall consist of a Senate and House of Representatives.

Section 2. (1). The House of Representatives shall be composed of members chosen every second year by the people of the several States, and the electors in each State shall have the qualifications requisite for electors of the most numerous branch of the State legislature.

(2). No person shall be a Representative who shall not have attained to the age of twenty-five years, and been seven years a citizen of the United States, and who shall not, when elected, be an inhabitant of that State in which he shall be chosen.

(3). Representatives and direct taxes[1] shall be apportioned among the several States which may be included within this Union, according to their respective numbers, which shall be determined by adding to the whole number of free persons, including those bound to service for a term of years, and excluding Indians not taxed, three fifths of all other persons.[2] The actual enumeration shall be made within three years after the first meeting of

---

[1]Modified as to income taxes by the 16th Amendment.

[2]Replaced by the 14th Amendment.

the Congress of the United States, and within every subsequent term of ten years, in such manner as they shall by law direct. The number of Representatives shall not exceed one for every thirty thousand, but each State shall have at least one Representative; and until such enumeration shall be made, the State of New Hampshire shall be entitled to choose three, Massachusetts eight, Rhode Island and Providence Plantations one, Connecticut five, New York six, New Jersey four, Pennsylvania eight, Delaware one, Maryland six, Virginia ten, North Carolina five, South Carolina five, and Georgia three.

(4). When vacancies happen in the representation from any State, the executive authority thereof shall issue writs of election to fill such vacancies.

(5). The House of Representatives shall choose their Speaker and other officers; and shall have the sole power of impeachment.

SECTION 3. (1). The Senate of the United States shall be composed of two Senators from each State, chosen by the legislature thereof,[3] for six years; and each Senator shall have one vote.

(2). Immediately after they shall be assembled in consequence of the first election, they shall be divided as equally as may be into three classes. The seats of the Senators of the first class shall be vacated at the expiration of the second year, of the second class at the expiration of the fourth year, and of the third class at the expiration of the sixth year, so that one third may be chosen every second year; and if vacancies happen by resignation, or otherwise, during the recess of the legislature of any State, the executive thereof may make temporary appointments until the next meeting of the legislature, which[3] shall then fill such vacancies.

(3). No person shall be a Senator who shall not have attained to the age of thirty years, and been nine years a citizen of the United States, and who shall not, when elected, be an inhabitant of that State for which he shall be chosen.

(4). The Vice President of the United States shall be president of the Senate but shall have no vote, unless they be equally divided.

---

[3]Modified by the 17th Amendment.

(5). The Senate shall choose their other officers, and also a president pro tempore, in the absence of the Vice President, or when he shall exercise the office of President of the United States.

(6). The Senate shall have the sole power to try all impeachments. When sitting for that purpose, they shall be on oath or affirmation. When the President of the United States is tried, the Chief Justice shall preside: and no person shall be convicted without the concurrence of two thirds of the members present.

(7). Judgment in cases of impeachment shall not exceed further than to removal from office, and disqualification to hold and enjoy any office of honor, trust or profit under the United States: but the party convicted shall nevertheless be liable and subject to indictment, trial, judgment and punishment, according to law.

SECTION 4. (1). The times, places and manner of holding elections for Senators and Representatives, shall be prescribed in each State by the legislature thereof; but the Congress may at any time by law make or alter such regulations, except as to the places of choosing Senators.

(2). The Congress shall assemble at least once in every year, and such meeting shall be on the first Monday in December, unless they shall by law appoint a different day.

SECTION 5. (1). Each House shall be the judge of the elections, returns and qualifications of its own members, and a majority of each shall constitute a quorum to do business; but a smaller number may adjourn from day to day, and may be authorized to compel the attendance of absent members, in such manner, and under such penalties as each House may provide.

(2). Each House may determine the rules of its proceedings, punish its members for disorderly behavior, and, with the concurrence of two thirds, expel a member.

(3). Each House shall keep a journal of its proceedings, and from time to time publish the same, excepting such parts as may in their judgment require secrecy; and the yeas and nays of the members of either House on any question shall, at the desire of one fifth of those present, be entered on the journal.

(4). Neither House, during the session of Congress, shall, without the consent of the other, adjourn for more than three days, nor to any other place than that in which the two Houses shall be sitting.

SECTION 6. (1). The Senators and Representatives shall receive a compensation for their services, to be ascertained by law, and paid out of the Treasury of the United States. They shall in all cases, except treason, felony and breach of the peace, be privileged from arrest during their attendance at the session of their respective Houses, and in going to and returning from the same; and for any speech or debate in either House, they shall not be questioned in any other place.

(2). No Senator or Representative shall, during the time for which he was elected, be appointed to any civil office under the authority of the United States, which shall have been created, or the emoluments whereof shall have been increased during such time; and no person holding any office under the United States, shall be a member of either House during his continuance in office.

SECTION 7. (1). All bills for raising revenue shall originate in the House of Representatives; but the Senate may propose or concur with amendments as on other bills.

(2). Every bill which shall have passed the House of Representatives and the Senate, shall, before it become a law, be presented to the President of the United States; if he approve he shall sign it, but if not he shall return it, with his objections to that House in which it shall have originated, who shall enter the objections at large on their journal, and proceed to reconsider it. If after such reconsideration two thirds of that House shall agree to pass the bill, it shall be sent, together with the objections, to the other House, by which it shall likewise be reconsidered, and if approved by two thirds of that House, it shall become a law. But in all such cases the votes of both Houses shall be determined by yeas and nays, and the names of the persons voting for and against the bill shall be entered on the journal of each House respectively. If any bill shall not be returned by the President within ten days (Sundays excepted) after it shall have been presented to him, the same shall be a law, in like manner as if he had signed it, unless the Congress by their adjournment prevent its return, in which case it shall not be a law.

(3). Every order, resolution, or vote to which the concurrence of the Senate and House of Representatives may be necessary (except on a question of adjournment) shall be presented to the President of the United States; and before the same shall take effect, shall be approved by him, or being disapproved by him, shall be repassed by two thirds of the Senate and House of Representatives, according to the rules and limitations prescribed in the case of a bill.

SECTION 8. (1). The Congress shall have power to lay and collect taxes, duties, imposts and excises, to pay the debts and provide for the common defense and general welfare of the United States; but all duties, imposts and excises shall be uniform throughout the United States;

(2). To borrow money on the credit of the United States;

(3). To regulate commerce with foreign nations, and among the several States, and with the Indian tribes;

(4). To establish an uniform rule of naturalization, and uniform laws on the subject of bankruptcies throughout the United States;

(5). To coin money, regulate the value thereof, and of foreign coin, and fix the standard of weights and measures;

(6). To provide for the punishment of counterfeiting the securities and current coin of the United States;

(7). To establish post offices and post roads;

(8). To promote the progress of science and useful arts, by securing for limited times to authors and inventors the exclusive right to their respective writings and discoveries;

(9). To constitute tribunals inferior to the Supreme Court;

(10). To define and punish piracies and felonies committed on the high seas, and offenses against the law of nations;

(11). To declare war, grant letters of marque and reprisal, and make rules concerning captures on land and water;

(12). To raise and support armies, but no appropriation of money to that use shall be for a longer term than two years;

(13). To provide and maintain a navy;

(14). To make rules for the government and regulation of the land and naval forces;

(15). To provide for calling forth the militia to execute the laws of the Union, suppress insurrections and repel invasions;

(16). To provide for organizing, arming, and disciplining the militia, and for governing such part of them as may be employed in the service of the United States, reserving to the States respectively, the appointment of the officers, and the authority of training the militia according to the discipline prescribed by Congress;

(17). To exercise exclusive legislation in all cases whatsoever, over such district (not exceeding ten miles square) as may, by cession of particular States, and the acceptance of Congress, become the seat of the government of the United States, and to exercise like authority over all places purchased by the consent of the legislature of the State in which the same shall be, for the erection of forts, magazines, arsenals, dockyards, and other needful buildings; and

(18). To make all laws which shall be necessary and proper for carrying into execution the foregoing powers, and all other powers vested by this Constitution in the government of the United States, or in any department or officer thereof.

SECTION 9. (1). The migration or importation of such persons as any of the States now existing shall think proper to admit, shall not be prohibited by the Congress prior to the year one thousand eight hundred and eight, but a tax or duty may be imposed on such importation, not exceeding ten dollars for each person.

(2). The privilege of the writ of habeas corpus shall not be suspended, unless when in cases of rebellion or invasion the public safety may require it.

(3). No bill of attainder or ex post facto law shall be passed.

(4). No capitation, or other direct tax, shall be paid, unless in proportion to the census or enumeration herein before directed to be taken.[4]

(5). No tax or duty shall be laid on articles exported from any State.

(6). No preference shall be given by any regulation of com-

---

[4]Modified by the 16th Amendment.

merce or revenue to the ports of one State over those of another: nor shall vessels bound to, or from, one State, be obliged to enter, clear, or pay duties in another.

(7). No money shall be drawn from the Treasury, but in consequence of appropriations made by law; and a regular statement and account of the receipts and expenditures of all public money shall be published from time to time.

(8). No title of nobility shall be granted by the United States: and no person holding any office of profit or trust under them, shall, without the consent of the Congress, accept of any present, emolument, office, or title, of any kind whatever, from any king, prince, or foreign State.

SECTION 10. (1). No State shall enter into any treaty, alliance, or confederation; grant letters of marque and reprisal; coin money; emit bills of credit; make anything but gold and silver coin a tender in payment of debts; pass any bill of attainder, ex post facto law, or law impairing the obligation of contracts, or grant any title of nobility.

(2). No State shall, without the consent of the Congress, lay any imposts or duties on imports or exports, except what may be absolutely necessary for executing its inspection laws; and the net produce of all duties and imposts, laid by any State on imports or exports, shall be for the use of the Treasury of the United States; and all such laws shall be subject to the revision and control of the Congress.

(3). No State shall, without the consent of Congress, lay any duty of tonnage, keep troops, or ships of war in time of peace, enter into any agreement or compact with another State, or with a foreign power, or engage in war, unless actually invaded, or in such imminent danger as will not admit of delay.

ARTICLE II

SECTION 1. (1). The executive power shall be vested in a President of the United States of America. He shall hold his office during the term of four years, and, together with the Vice President, chosen for the same term, be elected, as follows:

(2). Each State shall appoint, in such manner as the legislature thereof may direct, a number of electors, equal to the whole number of Senators and Representatives to which the State may be entitled in the Congress: but no Senator or Representative, or person holding an office of trust or profit under the United States, shall be appointed an elector.

The electors[5] shall meet in their respective States, and vote by ballot for two persons, of whom one at least shall not be an inhabitant of the same State with themselves. And they shall make a list of all the persons voted for, and of the number of votes for each; which list they shall sign and certify, and transmit sealed to the seat of the government of the United States, directed to the president of the Senate. The president of the Senate shall, in the presence of the Senate and House of Representatives, open all the certificates, and the votes shall then be counted. The person having the greatest number of votes shall be the President, if such number be a majority of the whole number of electors appointed; and if there be more than one who have such majority, and have an equal number of votes, then the House of Representatives shall immediately choose by ballot one of them for President; and if no person have a majority, then from the five highest on the list the said House shall in like manner choose the President. But in choosing the President, the votes shall be taken by States, the representation from each State having one vote; a quorum for this purpose shall consist of a member or members from two thirds of the States, and a majority of all the States shall be necessary to a choice. In every case, after the choice of the President, the person having the greatest number of votes of the electors shall be the Vice President. But if there should remain two or more who have equal votes, the Senate shall choose from them by ballot the Vice President.

(3). The Congress may determine the time of choosing the electors, and the day on which they shall give their votes; which day shall be the same throughout the United States.

(4). No person except a natural born citizen, or a citizen of the United States, at the time of the adoption of this Constitution, shall be eligible to the office of President; neither shall any person

[5]This paragraph was replaced in 1804 by the 12th Amendment.

be eligible to that office who shall not have attained to the age of thirty five years, and been fourteen years a resident within the United States.

(5). In the case of the removal of the President from office, or of his death, resignation, or inability to discharge the powers and duties of the said office, the same shall devolve on the Vice President, and the Congress may by law provide for the case of removal, death, resignation, or inability, both of the President and Vice President, declaring what officer shall then act as President, and such officer shall act accordingly, until the disability be removed, or a President shall be elected.

(6). The President shall, at stated times, receive for his services, a compensation, which shall neither be increased nor diminished during the period for which he shall have been elected, and he shall not receive within that period any other emolument from the United States, or any of them.

(7). Before he enter on the execution of his office, he shall take the following oath or affirmation:—"I do solemnly swear (or affirm) that I will faithfully execute the office of President of the United States, and will to the best of my ability, preserve, protect and defend the Constitution of the United States."

SECTION 2. (1). The President shall be commander in chief of the army and navy of the United States, and of the militia of the several States, when called into the actual service of the United States; he may require the opinion, in writing, of the principal officer in each of the executive departments, upon any subject relating to the duties of their respective offices, and he shall have power to grant reprieves and pardons for offenses against the United States, except in cases of impeachment.

(2). He shall have power, by and with the advice and consent of the Senate, to make treaties, provided two thirds of the Senators present concur; and he shall nominate, and by and with the advice and consent of the Senate, shall appoint ambassadors, other public ministers and consuls, judges of the Supreme Court, and all other officers of the United States, whose appointments are not herein otherwise provided for, and which shall be established by law: but the Congress may by law vest the appointment of such inferior officers, as they think proper, in the President alone, in the courts of law, or in the heads of departments.

(3). The President shall have power to fill up all vacancies that may happen during the recess of the Senate, by granting commissions which shall expire at the end of their next session.

SECTION 3. He shall from time to time give to the Congress information of the state of the Union, and recommend to their consideration such measures as he shall judge necessary and expedient; he may, on extraordinary occasions, convene both Houses, or either of them, and in case of disagreement between them, with respect to the time of adjournment, he may adjourn them to such time as he shall think proper; he shall receive ambassadors and other public ministers; he shall take care that the laws be faithfully executed, and shall commission all the officers of the United States.

SECTION 4. The President, Vice President and all civil officers of the United States, shall be removed from office on impeachment for, and conviction of, treason, bribery, or other high crimes and misdemeanors.

ARTICLE III

SECTION 1. The judicial power of the United States, shall be vested in one Supreme Court, and in such inferior courts as the Congress may from time to time ordain and establish. The judges, both of the Supreme and inferior courts, shall hold their offices during good behavior, and shall, at stated times, receive for their services, a compensation, which shall not be diminished during their continuance in office.

SECTION 2. (1). The judicial power shall extend to all cases, in law and equity, arising under this Constitution, the laws of the United States, and treaties made, or which shall be made, under their authority;—to all cases affecting ambassadors, other public ministers and consuls;—to all cases of admiralty and maritime jurisdiction;—to controversies to which the United States shall be a party;—to controversies between two or more States;—between a State and citizens of another State;[6]—between citizens

[6]Restricted by the 11th Amendment.

of different States,—between citizens of the same State claiming lands under grants of different States, and between a State, or the citizens thereof, and foreign States, citizens or subjects.

(2). In all cases affecting ambassadors, other public ministers and consuls, and those in which a State shall be party, the Supreme Court shall have original jurisdiction. In all the other cases before mentioned, the Supreme Court shall have appellate jurisdiction, both as to law and fact, with such exceptions, and under such regulations as the Congress shall make.

(3). The trial of all crimes, except in cases of impeachment, shall be by jury; and such trial shall be held in the State where the said crimes shall have been committed; but when not committed within any State, the trial shall be at such place or places as the Congress may by law have directed.

SECTION 3. (1). Treason against the United States, shall consist only in levying war against them, or in adhering to their enemies, giving them aid and comfort. No person shall be convicted of treason unless on the testimony of two witnesses to the same overt act, or on confession in open court.

(2). The Congress shall have power to declare the punishment of treason, but no attainder of treason shall work corruption of blood, or forfeiture except during the life of the person attainted.

ARTICLE IV

SECTION 1. Full faith and credit shall be given in each State to the public acts, records, and judicial proceedings of every other State. And the Congress may by general laws prescribe the manner in which such acts, records and proceedings shall be proved, and the effect thereof.

SECTION 2. (1). The citizens of each State shall be entitled to all privileges and immunities of citizens in the several States.

(2). A person charged in any State with treason, felony, or other crime, who shall flee from justice, and be found in another State, shall on demand of the executive authority of the State from which he fled, be delivered up, to be removed to the State having jurisdiction of the crime.

(3). No person held to service or labor in one State, under

the laws thereof, escaping into another, shall, in consequence of any law or regulation therein, be discharged from such service or labor, but shall be delivered up on claim of the party to whom such service or labor may be due.

SECTION 3. (1). New States may be admitted by the Congress into this Union; but no new State shall be formed or erected within the jurisdiction of any other State; nor any State be formed by the junction of two or more States, or parts of States, without the consent of the legislatures of the States concerned as well as of the Congress.

(2). The Congress shall have power to dispose of and make all needful rules and regulations respecting the territory or other property belonging to the United States; and nothing in this Constitution shall be so construed as to prejudice any claims of the United States, or of any particular State.

SECTION 4. The United States shall guarantee to every State in the Union a republican form of government, and shall protect each of them against invasion; and on application of the legislature, or of the executive (when the legislature cannot be convened) against domestic violence.

ARTICLE V

The Congress, whenever two thirds of both Houses shall deem it necessary, shall propose amendments to this Constitution, or, on the application of the legislatures of two thirds of the several States, shall call a convention for proposing amendments, which, in either case, shall be valid to all intents and purposes, as part of this Constitution, when ratified by the legislatures of three fourths of the several States, or by conventions in three fourths thereof, as the one or the other mode of ratification may be proposed by the Congress; Provided that no amendment which may be made prior to the year one thousand eight hundred and eight shall in any manner affect the first and fourth classes in the ninth section of the first article, and that no State, without its consent, shall be deprived of its equal suffrage in the Senate.

ARTICLE VI

SECTION 1. All debts contracted and engagements entered

into, before the adoption of this Constitution, shall be as valid against the United States under this Constitution, as under the Confederation.

SECTION 2. This Constitution, and the laws of the United States which shall be made in pursuance thereof; and all treaties made, or which shall be made, under the authority of the United States, shall be the supreme law of the land; and the judges in every State shall be bound thereby, anything in the constitution or laws of any State to the contrary notwithstanding.

SECTION 3. The Senators and Representatives before mentioned, and the members of the several State legislatures, and all executive and judicial officers, both of the United States and of the several States, shall be bound by oath or affirmation to support this Constitution; but no religious test shall ever be required as a qualification to any office or public trust under the United States.

ARTICLE VII

The ratification of the conventions of nine States shall be sufficient for the establishment of this Constitution between the States so ratifying the same.

Done in Convention by the unanimous consent of the States present the seventeenth day of September in the year of our Lord one thousand seven hundred and eighty-seven, and of the independence of the United States of America the twelfth. In witness whereof we have hereunto subscribed our names.

GO WASHINGTON—
Presidt. and Deputy from Virginia

Articles in addition to and amendment of the Constitution of the United States of America, proposed by Congress, and ratified by the legislatures of the several States, pursuant to the fifth article of the original Constitution.

ARTICLE I[7]

Congress shall make no law respecting an establishment of

[7]The first ten Amendments were adopted in 1791.

religion, or prohibiting the free exercise thereof; or abridging the freedom of speech, or of the press; or the right of the people peacefully to assemble, and to petition the government for a redress of grievances.

ARTICLE II

A well regulated militia, being necessary to the security of a free State, the right of the people to keep and bear arms, shall not be infringed.

ARTICLE III

No soldier shall, in time of peace be quartered in any house, without the consent of the owner, nor in time of war, but in a manner to be prescribed by law.

ARTICLE IV

The right of the people to be secure in their persons, houses, papers, and effects, against unreasonable searches and seizures, shall not be violated, and no warrants shall issue, but upon probable cause, supported by oath or affirmation, and particularly describing the place to be searched, and the persons or things to be seized.

ARTICLE V

No person shall be held to answer for a capital, or otherwise infamous crime, unless on a presentment or indictment of a grand jury, except in cases arising in the land or naval forces, or in the militia, when in actual service in time of war or public danger; nor shall any person be subject for the same offense to be twice put in jeopardy of life or limb; nor shall be compelled in any criminal case to be a witness against himself, nor be deprived of life, liberty, or property, without due process of law; nor shall private property be taken for public use, without just compensation.

ARTICLE VI

In all criminal prosecutions the accused shall enjoy the right to a speedy and public trial, by an impartial jury of the State and district wherein the crime shall have been committed, which district shall have been previously ascertained by law, and to be informed of the nature and cause of the accusation; to be confronted with the witnesses against him; to have compulsory process for obtaining witnesses in his favor, and to have the assistance of counsel for his defense.

ARTICLE VII

In suits at common law, where the value in controversy shall exceed twenty dollars, the right of trial by jury shall be preserved, and no fact tried by a jury shall be otherwise reexamined in any court of the United States, than according to the rules of the common law.

ARTICLE VIII

Excessive bail shall not be required, nor excessive fines imposed, nor cruel and unusual punishments inflicted.

ARTICLE IX

The enumeration in the Constitution, of certain rights, shall not be construed to deny or disparage others retained by the people.

ARTICLE X

The powers not delegated to the United States by the Constitution, nor prohibited by it to the States, are reserved to the States respectively, or to the people.

ARTICLE XI[8]

The judicial power of the United States shall not be construed to extend to any suit in law or equity, commenced or prosecuted against one of the United States by citizens of another State, or by citizens or subjects of any foreign State.

ARTICLE XII[9]

The electors shall meet in their respective States and vote by ballot for President and Vice President, one of whom, at least, shall not be an inhabitant of the same State with themselves; they shall name in their ballots the person voted for as President, and in distinct ballots the person voted for as Vice President, and they shall make distinct lists of all persons voted for as President, and of all persons voted for as Vice President, and of the number of votes for each, which lists they shall sign and certify, and transmit sealed to the seat of the government of the United States, directed to the president of the Senate;—The president of the Senate shall, in the presence of the Senate and House of Representatives, open all the certificates and the votes shall then be counted;—The person having the greatest number of votes for President, shall be the President, if such number be a majority of the whole number of electors appointed; and if no person have such majority, then from the persons having the highest numbers not exceeding three on the list of those voted for as President, the House of Representatives shall choose immediately, by ballot, the President. But in choosing the President, the votes shall be taken by States, the representation from each State having one vote; a quorum for this purpose shall consist of a member or members from two thirds of the States, and a majority of all the States shall be necessary to a choice. And if the House of Representatives shall not choose a President whenever the right of choice shall devolve upon them, before the fourth day of March next following, then the Vice President shall act as President, as in the case of the death or other constitutional disability of the President.—The person having the greatest number of votes as Vice President, shall be the Vice President, if such number be a majority of the whole number of electors appointed, and if no person have a majority, then from the two highest numbers on the list, the Senate shall choose the Vice President; a quorum for the purpose shall consist of two thirds of the whole number of Senators, and a majority of the whole number shall be necessary to a choice. But no person constitutionally ineligible to the office of President shall be eligible to that of Vice President of the United States.

---

[8]Adopted in 1798.
[9]Adopted in 1804.

ARTICLE XIII[10]

SECTION 1. Neither slavery nor involuntary servitude, except as a punishment for crime whereof the party shall have been duly convicted, shall exist within the United States, or any place subject to their jurisdiction.

SECTION 2. Congress shall have power to enforce this article by appropriate legislation.

ARTICLE XIV[11]

SECTION 1. All persons born or naturalized in the United States, and subject to the jurisdiction thereof, are citizens of the United States and of the State wherein they reside. No State shall make or enforce any law which shall abridge the privileges or immunities of citizens of the United States; nor shall any State deprive any person of life, liberty, or property, without due process of law; nor deny to any person within its jurisdiction the equal protection of the laws.

SECTION 2. Representatives shall be appointed among the several States according to their respective numbers, counting the whole number of persons in each State, excluding Indians not taxed. But when the right to vote at any election for the choice of electors for President and Vice President of the United States, Representatives in Congress, the executive and judicial offices of a State, or the members of the legislature thereof, is denied to any of the male inhabitants of such State, being twenty-one years of age, and citizens of the United States, or in any way abridged, except for participation in rebellion, or other crime, the basis of representation therein shall be reduced in the proportion which the number of such male citizens shall bear to the whole number of male citizens twenty-one years of age in such State.

SECTION 3. No person shall be a Senator or Representative in Congress, or elector of President and Vice President, or hold any office, civil or military, under the United States, or under any state, who, having previously taken an oath, as a member

---

[10]Adopted in 1865.

[11]Adopted in 1868.

of Congress, or as an officer of the United States, or a member of any State legislature, or as an executive or judicial officer of any State, to support the Constitution of the United States, shall have engaged in insurrection or rebellion against the same, or given aid or comfort to the enemies thereof. But Congress may by a vote of two thirds of each House, remove such disability.

SECTION 4. The validity of the public debt of the United States, authorized by law, including debts incurred for payment of pensions and boundaries for services in suppressing insurrection or rebellion, shall not be questioned. But neither the United States nor any State shall assume or pay any debt or obligation incurred in aid of insurrection or rebellion against the United States, or any claim for the loss or emancipation of any slave; but all such debts, obligations and claims shall be held illegal and void.

SECTION 5. The Congress shall have power to enforce, by appropriate legislation, the provisions of this article.

ARTICLE XV[12]

SECTION 1. The right of citizens of the United States to vote shall not be denied or abridged by the United States or by any State on account of race, color, or previous condition of servitude.

SECTION 2. The Congress shall have power to enforce this article by appropriate legislation.

ARTICLE XVI[13]

The Congress shall have power to lay and collect taxes on incomes, from whatever source derived, without apportionment among the several States, and without regard to any census or enumeration.

ARTICLE XVII[13]

The Senate of the United States shall be composed of two

[12]Adopted in 1870.
[13]Adopted in 1913.

Senators from each State, elected by the people thereof, for six years, and each Senator shall have one vote. The electors in each State shall have the qualifications requisite for electors of the most numerous branch of the State legislatures.

When vacancies happen in the representation of any State in the Senate, the executive authority of such State shall issue writs of election to fill such vacancies: *Provided,* That the legislature of any State may empower the executive thereof to make temporary appointments until the people fill the vacancies by election as the legislature may direct.

This amendment shall not be so construed as to affect the election or term of any Senator chosen before it becomes valid as part of the Constitution.

ARTICLE XVIII[14]

SECTION 1. After one year from the ratification of this article the manufacture, sale, or transportation of intoxicating liquors within, the importation thereof into, or the exportation thereof from the United States and all territory subject to the jurisdiction thereof for beverage purposes is hereby prohibited.

SECTION 2. The Congress and the several States shall have concurrent power to enforce this article by appropriate legislation.

SECTION 3. This article shall be inoperative unless it shall have been ratified as an amendment to the Constitution by the legislatures of the several States, as provided in the Constitution, within seven years from the date of submission hereof to the States by the Congress.

ARTICLE XIX[15]

The right of citizens of the United States to vote shall not be denied or abridged by the United States or by any State on account of sex.

The Congress shall have power to enforce this article by appropriate legislation.

ARTICLE XX[16]

SECTION 1. The terms of the President and Vice President

shall end at noon on the 20th day of January, and the terms of Senators and Representatives at noon on the 3rd day of January, of the years in which such terms would have ended if this article had not been ratified; and the terms of their successors shall then begin.

SECTION 2. The Congress shall assemble at least once in every year, and such meeting shall begin at noon on the 3rd day of January, unless they shall by law appoint a different day.

SECTION 3. If, at the time fixed for the beginning of the term of the President, the President elect shall have died, the Vice President elect shall become President. If a President shall not have been chosen before the time fixed for the beginning of his term, or if the President elect shall have failed to qualify, then the Vice President elect shall act as President until a President shall have qualified; and the Congress may by law provide for the case wherein neither a President elect nor a Vice President elect shall have qualified, declaring who shall then act as President, or the manner in which one who is to act shall be selected, and such person shall act accordingly until a President or Vice President shall have qualified.

SECTION 4. The Congress may by law provide for the case of the death of any of the persons from whom the House of Representatives may choose a President whenever the right of choice shall have devolved upon them, and for the case of the death of any of the persons from whom the Senate may choose a Vice President whenever the right of choice shall have developed upon them.

SECTION 5. Sections 1 and 2 shall take effect on the 15th day of October following the ratification of this article.

SECTION 6. This article shall be inoperative unless it shall have been ratified as an amendment to the Constitution by the legislatures of three fourths of the several States within seven years from the date of its submission.

---

[14]Adopted in 1919. Repealed by Article XXI.

[15]Adopted in 1920.

[16]Adopted in 1933.

ARTICLE XXI[17]

SECTION 1. The Eighteenth Article of Amendment to the Constitution of the United States is hereby repealed.

SECTION 2. The transportation or importation into any State, Territory or Possession of the United States for delivery or use therein of intoxicating liquors in violation of the laws thereof is hereby prohibited.

SECTION 3. This article shall be inoperative unless it shall have been ratified as an amendment to the Constitution, within seven years from the date of submission hereof to the States by the Congress.

ARTICLE XXII[18]

SECTION 1. No person shall be elected to the office of the President more than twice, and no person who has held the office of President, or acted as President, for more than two years of a term to which some other person was elected President shall be elected to the office of the President more than once. But this Article shall not apply to any person holding the office of President when this Article was proposed by the Congress, and shall not prevent any person who may be holding the office of President, or acting as President, during the term within which this Article becomes operative from holding the office of President or acting President during the remainder of such term.

SECTION 2. This article shall be inoperative unless it shall have been ratified as an amendment to the Constitution by the legislatures of three-fourths of the several States within seven years from the date of its submission to the States by the Congress.

ARTICLE XXIII[19]

SECTION 1. The District constituting the seat of Government of the United States shall appoint in such manner as the Congress may direct:

---

[17]Adopted in 1933.
[18]Adopted in 1951.
[19]Adopted in 1961.

A number of electors of President and Vice President equal to the whole number of Senators and Representatives in Congress to which the District would be entitled if it were a State, but in no event more than the least populous State; they shall be in addition to those appointed by the States, but they shall be considered, for the purposes of the election of President and Vice President, to be electors appointed by a State; and they shall meet in the District and perform such duties as provided by the twelfth article of amendment.

SECTION 2. The Congress shall have power to enforce this article by appropriate legislation.

ARTICLE XXIV[20]

SECTION 1. The right of citizens of the United States to vote in any primary or other election for President or Vice President, for electors for President or Vice President, or for Senator or Representative in Congress, shall not be denied or abridged by the United States or any State by reason of failure to pay any poll tax or other tax.

SECTION 2. The Congress shall have power to enforce this article by appropriate legislation.

ARTICLE XXV[21]

SECTION 1. In case of the removal of the President from office or of his death or resignation, the Vice President shall become President.

SECTION 2. Whenever there is a vacancy in the office of the Vice President, the President shall nominate a Vice President who shall take office upon confirmation by a majority vote of both Houses of Congress.

SECTION 3. Whenever the President transmits to the President pro tempore of the Senate and the Speaker of the House of Representatives his written declaration that he is unable to discharge the powers and duties of his office, and until he transmits to them a written declaration to the contrary, such powers

[20]Adopted in 1964.

and duties shall be discharged by the Vice President as Acting President.

SECTION 4. Whenever the Vice President and a majority of either the principal officers of the executive departments or of such other body as Congress may by law provide, transmit to the President pro tempore of the Senate and the Speaker of the House of Representatives their written declaration that the President is unable to discharge the powers and duties of his office, the Vice President shall immediately assume the powers and duties of the office as Acting President.

Thereafter, when the President transmits to the President pro tempore of the Senate and the Speaker of the House of Representatives his written declaration that no inability exists, he shall resume the powers and duties of his office unless the Vice President and a majority of either the principal officers of the executive department or of such other body as Congress may by law provide, transmit within four days to the President pro tempore of the Senate and the Speaker of the House of Representatives their written declaration that the President is unable to discharge the powers and duties of his office. Thereupon Congress shall decide the issue, assembling within forty-eight hours for that purpose if not in session. If the Congress, within twenty-one days after receipt of the latter written declaration, or, if Congress is not in session, within twenty-one days after Congress is required to assemble, determines by two-thirds vote of both Houses that the President is unable to discharge the powers and duties of his office, the Vice President shall continue to discharge the same as Acting President; otherwise, the President shall resume the powers and duties of his office.

---

[21]Adopted in 1967.

INDEX

C

D

E

H

I

J

K

L

O

P

Q

R

S

T

U

V

W

Y